TRAUMA & RESILIENCE

A Handbook

TRAUMA & RESILIENCE

A Handbook

Effectively Supporting Those Who Serve God

Frauke C. Schaefer, MD and Charles A. Schaefer, PhD
Editors and Contributors

TRAUMA & RESILIENCE © 2012 Frauke C. Schaefer, MD and Charles A. Schaefer, PhD. All rights reserved.

ISBN PRINT: 978-0-692-64831-5

All Scripture quotations, unless otherwise indicated, are taken from HOLY BIBLE, NEW INTERNATIONAL VERSION containing the Old Testament and The New Testament Zondervan Publishing House, Grand Rapids, Michigan.

Cover Design and Interior Book Design by Sarah O'Neal | eve custom artwork
Cover Image Courtesy of iStockphoto/Amanda Rohde

CONTENTS

PREFACE	i
Frauke and Charlie Schaefer	
I REFLECTIONS ON A THEOLOGY OF SUFFERING	1
Scott E. Shaum	
II STORIES OF TRAUMA IN MINISTRY	26
1. Civil War and Evacuation - *Karen Carr, Ghana*	26
2. Brush with Renal Cancer - *Allan and Betsy Poole, U.S.A.*	28
3. A Devastating Accident in Africa - *Ann Hamel, Rwanda*	32
4. Losing Loved Ones - *Jerry Sittser, U.S.A.*	35
5. Robbery and Betrayal - *Dan Crum, Kenya*	38
III RESOURCES FOR EFFECTIVE SUPPORT	43
1. Normal Reactions After Trauma - *Karen Carr*	43
2. Effective Community Support - *Karen Carr*	73
3. Personal Resilience - *Karen Carr*	93
4. Healthy Stress Management - *Frauke Schaefer*	105
5. Managing Severe Traumatic Stress - *Frauke Schaefer*	118
6. Spiritual Resources in Dealing With Trauma - *Charlie and Frauke Schaefer*	134
7. Prayer That Heals - *Ann Hamel*	177
SUMMARY OF MAIN POINTS	193
Frauke and Charlie Schaefer	
APPENDICES	195
A. Worksheet: Toward a Theology of Risk and Suffering - *Scott E. Shaum*	197
B. Common Reactions to Trauma - *Karen Carr*	201
a. Adults	201
b. Children	205
c. Adolescents	207
d. Cross-Cultural Worker Stress Inventory	209

C. Books, Online Resources, Counseling Centers, Conferences, and Training - *Charlie Schaefer*	213
BIBLIOGRAPHY	221
ABOUT THE AUTHORS	227

ACKNOWLEDGEMENTS

The inspiration to write a book about this topic originally came from Dr. Dan G. Blazer. We are grateful for his vision, tireless support, and the footprints he left in our lives as a mentor in research and Christian life. He and Dr. Tom Hale, Jr., have gladly imparted their wisdom as consulting editors.

This book could not have been written without the networking possibilities and professional development provided by our annual Mental Health and Missions Conference (MHM Conference) in Angola, Indiana, where the authors met and developed the concept of the book.

A special thank-you goes to Rev. Elizabeth Stout, professional editor and spiritual director, who not only provided highly skilled editorial services, but also enhanced our resilience with her unique kind of humor.

Sarah O'Neal lent her creativity to the design, while Dr. Brent Lindquist guided us in the publication of this book.

We are indebted to Dr. Christine Rost for her valuable input on the treatment of severe traumatic stress, Dr. Richard Gorsuch on intrinsic religiosity, and Dr. Rebekah Eklund on lament.

A profound thank-you to all storytellers who opened up vulnerable parts of their lives for our benefit; Dr. Jerry Sittser shared his experience of tragic loss (previously published in *A Grace Disguised*) "in a nutshell" for the purpose of this book.

We are indebted to our counselees, clients and patients, who have generously shared their experiences with us, and by so doing have allowed us to read the book of their lives and hearts, which has taught us a lot.

We thank our families and friends for bearing with us while this project took more time than envisioned.

Frauke and Charlie Schaefer
Chapel Hill, North Carolina, U.S.A.
August 2012

PREFACE
Frauke and Charlie Schaefer

Serving God in ministry is one of the most exciting and satisfying ways of life. At the same time it is challenging, risky, and often exhausting.

As missionaries in international settings, we each sensed a closeness to God unlike anything we had experienced before. Charlie directed a computer center in Togo, with a mission involved in Bible translation. Frauke served as director of a leprosy hospital in Nepal, with a mission focused on health and community development. These assignments were life changing for us. What a privilege to take part in building the kingdom of God in these special places by reaching out to the poor and relating across cultural boundaries! Sure, there were added risks compared to back home. But, most important, God's presence seemed so obvious, pervasive, and personal when taking risks in his name.

What also struck both of us was the high quality of missionaries we came to know. They were amazing people: bold, hardy, sacrificial, and dedicated to their calling. But ongoing high stress, frequent overwork, relational struggles, and effects of traumatic events took their toll on many. Some just survived rather than thrived in their ministry; some returned home prematurely. Back in our home countries, we felt God nudging us to support those who serve. Could giving appropriate support help mission personnel continue their important work without burning out or leaving their ministries prematurely? Could distress and impairment after severe trauma be reduced? We dedicated ourselves to the study of mental health in psychology and psychiatry, looking for ways to benefit missionaries and pastors with our expertise. Studying the Bible and our professional textbooks side-by-side to integrate faith and knowledge became our most important undertaking.

After Frauke's emigration from Germany to the U.S.A. and our marriage in 2000, she did a residency in psychiatry at Duke University in North Carolina. Dr. Dan G. Blazer, a seasoned researcher at Duke, who worked in medical mission in Central and West Africa early in his career, was willing to mentor an epidemiological research project about trauma, traumatic stress, and resilience among missionaries (Schaefer et al., 2007). One of the key findings of this research was that the missionaries studied were remarkably resilient, even though they had higher rates of exposure to severe trauma than people in their home countries, and lived in challenging environments. Of course, those who were involved in multiple traumatic events abroad, had known interpersonal violence, or lived in very unstable conditions (such as frequent fighting, civil war, and crime) were quite likely to suffer posttraumatic distress. Nevertheless, missionary resilience also increased as the number of traumatic experiences increased. Is it possible to strengthen missionaries' resilience even though they are going through trauma and the resulting damage? This was fascinating! A similar observation was described in the Bible long ago:

> Blessed are those whose strength is in you, who have set their hearts on pilgrimage. As they pass through the Valley of Baca, they make it a place of springs (Ps 84:5-6a, NIV).

The "Valley of Baca" is a place of misery, adversity, pain, and tears. As God seeking pilgrims pass through this valley and shed their tears, it becomes fertile, well watered ground for new growth. This phenomenon of growth after trauma and misery had already attracted research attention for about a decade, and was described as "posttraumatic growth." Reading research papers and the Bible side-by-side provided even more detail. Trauma not only affects our brains, our relationships, and our perceptions, but severe trauma can also shatter our assumptions about God, the world, others, and ourselves.

For people of faith, particularly those in ministry and mission, this means that the very foundation of our lives, our connection to God, can be affected or even broken by catastrophic circumstances. In a period of struggle after a traumatic event, one's spiritual foundation is often reshaped or reconstructed. When a person's immediate experience does not fit with previous beliefs and expectations, a grappling process starts. This struggle can lead to various outcomes. An individual can recover but remain profoundly affected; some can be fully restored; others can be restored to a place even stronger than before; a few can lose strength as well as their faith. This process of living through the aftermath of severe trauma is a divide upon which the very foundations of life can be deepened or lost. The recovery process holds the potential to refine us in terms of what really matters, and contains a creative and generative element with the signature of the Most High.

Research on posttraumatic growth led to intriguing questions: What conditions, if in place, could bring about the best possible reconstruction process? What factors may lead to long-term strengthening of resilience and deepening of faith? To understand more about these conditions, we looked at spiritual factors in relation to the consequences of trauma, including both posttraumatic stress and growth (Schaefer, et al., 2008). A model emerged that describes how these factors may play a role in affecting outcomes. There are probably more spiritual factors that affect this outcome than those already researched and described in scientific journals. It is therefore important to complement our understanding with the real stories of people in ministry, and the stories of those coming alongside when "life hits hard," as well as with relevant passages from the Bible.

Scripture is eloquent about the normality of suffering in a fallen world, and the uniqueness of the triune God entering into human suffering in the person of Jesus Christ. Reconnection and reshaping of our relationships with God are described in various ways. The concepts of training and refining are mentioned:

> Consider it pure joy, my brothers, whenever you face trials of many kinds, because you know that the testing of your faith develops perseverance. Perseverance must finish its work so that you may be mature and complete, not lacking anything (James 1:2-4, NIV).

> In this you greatly rejoice, though now for a little while you may have had to suffer grief in all kinds of trials. These have come so that your faith—of greater worth than gold, which perishes even though refined by fire—may be proved genuine and may result in praise, glory and honor when Jesus Christ is revealed (1 Pet 1:6-7, NIV).

Human struggles, confusion, and darkness after major life events are described in many sections of the Bible such as the Psalms, the book of Job, and in post-resurrection appearances of Jesus. For the believer, more often than not these struggles do not end in despair, but in finding "springs" in the midst of the "valley of Baca" (Ps 84: 5-6). It has been an exciting journey to discover more about the conditions that are helpful in these struggles after trauma. There is a sense of hope and expectancy in the dark night of most tragic and destructive events. However, merely committing these observations to ink in a research journal did not seem to do them justice.

In 2009, the annual Mental Health and Mission conference in Indiana, U.S.A. selected the theme "Assessing and Fostering Resilience in Missionaries." It was inspiring to hear excellent speakers with important thoughts and research to contribute. Scott Shaum spoke about "Resilience Gained through Life's Hardships." He had spoken previously at the same conference about a "Theology of Suffering." Dr. Ann Hamel discussed the role of prayer in trauma healing. Dr. Karen Carr from the Mobile Member Care Team in West Africa elaborated about the importance of community for trauma resilience. We (Charlie and Frauke) held a workshop about "Biological and Spiritual Tools for Resilience." At this conference the idea was born to make these important insights available to the broader community of people supporting missionaries and pastors. This book was to be a resource for caring peers gifted in listening, encouragement, and practical support. These peers could be trained crisis responders, member care personnel, local administrators, and organizational leaders. Peers are the ones most immediately available, and as such, a part of the natural support system. This book will also resource and inspire Christian mental health professionals supporting people in ministry. The vision was born! To our delight and excitement, all of the potential authors immediately agreed that the book was worth writing.

Our Own Story of Trauma

We went through our own crisis and reconstruction process. The first five years of our married life went smoothly. After moving from Germany, Frauke deepened friendships with women who would go through the thick of life with her. As a couple, we worked together, and at times traveled to care for missionaries in crisis. One morning, Frauke was leaving for a conference and Charlie was finishing preparations for a church retreat that would begin the next day. Charlie, a dedicated long-distance runner, went out for an easy morning run, and didn't return.

Frauke became alarmed, began searching for him in likely places, but he wasn't in any of them. Upon calling the police, she learned that Charlie had been taken to the hospital and was disoriented after collapsing during his run. There was bleeding of unknown cause inside his skull. Frauke's medical mind started racing. Why did this happen? What will become of Charlie? Will his brain be affected long-term? Will he be disabled? Will we be able to continue working with missionaries? Frauke's heartbeat quickened, her muscles tensed, and she felt nauseated. She was experiencing that caffeinated charge that unmistakably signals high stress. She became focused and alert and any tender feelings were a million miles away. Frauke had reached crisis management mode, a state of mind she was very familiar with as a physician.

Fortunately, Frauke had the immediate impulse to call for help from her family and church community, initiated practical arrangements for Charlie's client appointments for the day, and for a replacement at the next day's retreat where Charlie was to have been the main speaker. Shortly, our pastor, Charlie's relatives, and his closest colleague were at Frauke's side.

Being enveloped in a community of practical, emotional, and spiritual support for several weeks, Charlie went through neurological intensive care and later recovery at home. A wise woman advised Frauke: "Sometimes, the greatest help you can provide to others is to allow them to help you." She took that to heart and welcomed a loving, caring team of people who brought food and provided company. They came to pray and linger for a time. Their care was God's presence and love in the midst of shattered plans and dreams.

After Charlie's collapse, Frauke felt distant from God and was evading his presence. Although communication between her and God was good, she had gnawing questions when she slowed down. Why did this happen when we were doing what we believed God wanted us to do? How could Charlie's collapse fit into God's plan? Why were we unable to lead the retreat that was so diligently prepared and prayed for? After a while, Frauke gained courage to direct these questions to God. An immediate response came through the peace of realizing God was assuring her, "I am with you and I know." God also seemed to be saying that deepening our love and trust in him was more important than ministering to others at the moment.

Understanding of Trauma in this Book

Our general understanding of *trauma* in this book is any serious event that threatens or affects the life or physical integrity of a person, or a loved one. Experiencing, witnessing, or becoming aware of such an event creates intense fear, helplessness, or horror in the affected person. Our various authors may have a slightly different understanding of trauma and indicate this in their respective sections.

This Book's Outline and Use

Our book provides practical, theological, psychological, stress management, and spiritual resources for those who support people in ministry during crisis. There are also many sections likely to benefit those who have gone through crises themselves.

Though you may start with any section that appears most relevant to your situation, concepts in "Reflections on a Theology of Suffering" in Chapter I are foundational.

The "Stories of Trauma in Ministry" in Chapter II take us into the community of those who have gone through crisis. Each story and traumatic situation is unique. Narrators invite the reader into their own painful struggles, and reflect on what helped them along. They also account for any deepening or strengthening that came as a result of the crisis and struggle thereafter. As you read these examples, notice both the breadth of situations and reactions, and what has been of help as people came alongside. We trust that these personal accounts of vulnerability, pain, and strength will resonate and inspire.

Chapter III, "Resources for Effective Support" will broaden understanding of reactions, stress management, and types of effective support. Included are a variety of practical tools. Special emphasis is given to resources that address the spiritual struggle after trauma. Those spiritual factors important for a positive outcome, such as community support, intrinsic religiosity, and forgiveness, receive particular attention. The role of healing prayer in restoration and strengthening of our bond with God conclude this comprehensive resource section.

The Appendices include helpful worksheets, a collection of additional resources such as books, websites, training opportunities, and contact information for missionary counseling centers worldwide.

Limitations

Though our main concepts are research based, this book intends to be a practical resource for people accompanying those in the crucible of trauma. It strives to clarify concepts and processes without an expectation of being complete. We are presenting tools we found helpful in our extensive experience of accompanying traumatized Christians as professional counselors. The tools we selected can easily be taught, and used by concerned fellow Christians and missionaries without professional crisis training. Though this book equips Christian nonprofessional supporters, professional care will usually need to dovetail with peer-to-peer support. The "Reflections on a Theology of Suffering" chapter is a thoughtful approach to the topic of a pastor, spiritual director, and trainer, who frequently supports missionaries. Other pastors and theologians will have different emphases or understandings of this topic. May this rendering challenge all of us to develop our own Bible-based theology of suffering. Over time we hope to dialogue with those who read and work with this book, to later update and complement the content.

We are glad that *Trauma and Resilience: Effectively Supporting Those Who Serve God* caught your attention! May God's Spirit accompany you on your journey through it, and as you come alongside those who suffer as they serve God.

CHAPTER 1
REFLECTIONS ON A THEOLOGY OF SUFFERING

Scott E. Shaum

I am easily confused by life. At times the mysteries of God's ways are simply that, mysteries that I will never be able to sort out. For example, when I read about Hannah, a simple woman who was loved by her husband, a woman made barren by God (and the ridicule she endured because of it), I am reminded that I do not understand God's ways (1 Sam 1:5-6). I know God is good and loving, yet he also does things I don't like! These dual dynamics of a world filled with both beauty and pain, and a God who is a personally pursuant Father and a Holy, Mysterious Other, can leave me confounded. And the times I am most perplexed are the very times I do not have energy to ponder them. When I am at my lowest, weakest, darkest, most confused point along this winding journey, my longing is to be encouraged, to be known, and to be tended to.

I have learned that God is always there. He is always tending to me. I may not feel it or sense it, yet it is true. How do I know? I have gleaned this truth from the many stories of broken lives in the Bible, from the hundreds of amazing people my wife and I have been privileged to journey with around the world, and from our own pain-filled, beauty-filled lives. Paradox is the reality of the Kingdom of Christ. We are offered love, grace, forgiveness and life. And we are taken down a path that leads to Calvary. Ours is a lifelong process of relinquishing control so that we may in ever increasing levels, know God's love for us and be shaped into Christ's image, that we may show that love to others. As we will see in this chapter, personal suffering is one of the ways and means God takes us where he knows we must go to experience the fullest of his love and redemption.

This chapter will take a glimpse into what I hope will lead the reader to develop a personal theology of suffering. There are volumes on the subject of suffering, yet there is room for more reflection upon it. When I am immersed in a very personal time of adversity and loss, perspective is critical. Perspective does not deliver me from my pain or solve my problems but it can provide the gift of truth. The truth is that God is love, that pain is a norm of human experience and also a grace, yes, a grace, from God. His wisdom so exceeds mine that he knows how best to take me where he knows I need to go on my pilgrimage. With that perspective I can take a deep breath and rest just a little.

Allow me to explore this paradox from just one passage. In 2 Corinthians 1, Paul tells us that we "have a God of comfort." Again and again the words *comfort* or mercies are used in verses 3 through 7. And yet, alongside these words of comfort are equally frequent words of suffering and adversity. Paul is saying that these two realities can and do coexist. The comfort I so often seek in my own life is resolution. I cry out to God to solve my problems and heal my pains. Sometimes God resolves, but not always. Though God might not resolve our problems, he does promise to be present with us in the midst of them. The Greek root of the word *comfort* in 2 Corinthians 1 is the same word Jesus uses in the upper room to tell that God will send "the Comforter." The comfort God promises, no matter how dark our path, no matter how profound our loss, no matter how great our pain, is himself. He is with us in all things and through all things. My first reaction is to resent the hurts I have experienced in this life. But there is a grace I have enjoyed in these hurts that would not have happened if all went well: the reality of the True God with me. This is a great encouragement indeed.

A. A Personal Brush with Suffering

Soon after the tragic events of September 11, 2001, in the U.S., I was at the annual Pastors to Missionary (PTM) conference.[1] There God stirred in me through the thematic call from the speakers that we must develop a healthy theology of suffering. During the next year I chipped away at central texts to discover a more realistic and biblical theology of suffering. Since that time, two major shifts have happened. One is that I have been asked to speak on this subject in international settings. Responding to these invitations has continued to shape my journey. Even more shaping has been my experience of two brushes with death from tropical diseases, the last one leaving me with a moderate case of Chronic Fatigue Syndrome. God has taught me that I cannot merely teach on suffering; I must also suffer. I am not only going through adversity myself, but also entering into life's difficulties as a result of caring for others. Adversity is part of my calling, and suffering has taken on a different shade. There is much pain and suffering around us and in this world. For anyone called to tend to others, the ability to journey well in the midst of challenges and personal darkness is very important.

B. Toward a Biblical Theology of Suffering

Volumes have been written over centuries on suffering. This is a brief consideration of the subject based on some central New Testament texts. These are enough to provide a new set of glasses through which to see life events.[2] I will not deal with the "why" of suffering, which is cloaked in mystery. Yet we continue to anguish over this question. I will deal with how God uses suffering in our lives, to take painful realities and make beauty. In my health struggles I wrestled for a year with the question of what God was up to. Why was I left in pain and loss? I went to serve others and got sick myself. Is this how it works?

All of us experience hardships. As I made my way through darkness, certain truths aided me in regaining perspective. These same truths can guide us in journeying with others through their darkness.

Importance of Theology of Suffering

As people caring for others, we need to think carefully about suffering. Pastors and global servants live under high duress. The Word of God indicates that our volatile world will become increasingly violent as Christ's Second Advent approaches. The remaining unreached regions and modern subcultures of the world will be won for Christ at high personal cost. The Western church has drifted toward a consumer culture and commitment to self-comfort. This reality has eaten away at our understanding of suffering and the cross, a central theme in God's Word. Hardship is the norm, and God does not gloss over that reality. It is imperative to think biblically.

Our Transformation

Holistic transformation leads to growth and maturation. Our need for growth encompasses emotional, spiritual and relational areas of our lives. Thus, when God transforms my character, I grow in my ability to love both him and others. I even learn to love myself, with a healthy, wizened self-concept. I have a certain set of relational beliefs and skills that I use in relating both to others and to God. If others experience me as an aloof, secretive, rather distant person, I will not suddenly blossom into a close, warm, transparency in my prayer life. I am likely to be distant and protective of myself with God, too. Who I am on an interpersonal level will reveal a great deal about my relationship with God. As I endure hardship and grow in patience, I become more patient in my circumstances, in waiting on God and others. Holistic transformation is what God is after. As I become more like Christ, I will act more and more like him in all of my spiritual, emotional, and relational dealings. I am becoming more like *all* of Christ. Suffering is one of the ways God causes us to grow and become mature adults, shaped into the image of our Lord.

Redemptive Purpose of Suffering

In studying central biblical passages, I conclude that God has designed the redemptive process so we move toward holistic maturity, in part, through various afflictions. We need more than just hardship to mature; we need love, truth, grace, time, and relationships. Yet God has orchestrated hardship, affliction, external trials, mixed with internal temptations, that we may emerge strengthened. In trials I learn truths that I would otherwise not be open to. More important than mere learning, the human soul can be deepened, strengthened, and matured. Trials are part of the path for all who desire to be transformed into the image of Christ. The human soul needs difficulty to reach maturity, just as physical growth often involves stress, challenge, or pain. In summary, suffering is necessary for maturity to take place. We may not like this nor fully understand it, but it is biblical reality.

To avoid all suffering, to arrange a life of unending comfort, to eradicate all hardship from our lives, is sabotaging a vital part of the maturation process. In our affluent Western culture (with heated leather car seats, climate-controlled homes, and "mega stuff-marts"), we not only believe in a life of comfort, we think we deserve it. This prevailing sentiment has infiltrated the church and impacts our own view of suffering. Media have affected both secular and Christian strata of society in our own and other parts of the world. We must never lose sight of the reality that the centerpiece of God's redeeming work is the cross, a place of intense physical, emotional, and spiritual suffering.

Definition of "Suffering"

The Greek New Testament uses several words for *suffering* in English. These Greek words give breadth to English translations, such as *affliction, trial, testing, temptation, persecution, rebuke, insult, grief, reproach,* and more. Two Greek words are central in many of the passages I will refer to, and their meanings convey the idea that all hardships can be labeled as suffering. Any experience of difficulty falls into the broad category of suffering. The Bible does not compare nor minimize any form of human hardship, as is wise for us to do. If it is difficult for you, then it is indeed a difficulty. The first word to consider is *parasmos (πειρασμος)*. Used in key passages such as James 1 and 1 Peter 1, this term has a dual connotation, referring to both outward trials and inward temptations. For example, James states, "My brethren, count it all joy when you fall into various trials" (Jas 1:2, NKJV). Then in verse 12 he adds, "Blessed is the man who endures temptation." The "trials" in verse 2 are external and the "temptation(s)" of verse 12 are internal. Both words are from the same Greek word. James names neither the specific trials nor the specific temptations. Seldom do the New Testament authors define them. This is deliberate. What is of supreme concern are not the circumstances at hand, but how they are impacting us and how we are responding. What may be a trial for me may be no big deal to you. The concern is the totality of the impact that an ordeal has on our person. This word *parasmos* encompasses the breadth of human experience in the context of a fallen world. Any physical, emotional, spiritual, relational, or circumstantial hardship we experience (cancer, earthquake, or interpersonal conflict) fall under this word's meaning.

A second Greek word is *thlipsis* (θλιπσις). This word is used 45 times in the New Testament, 24 times by Paul alone. It is also generic, including any physical, emotional, or spiritual hardship known to humankind. I prefer the word *affliction* as an English rendition of *thlipsis*. Western thinking tends to have two dishonoring responses to suffering. One reaction is to over-spiritualize. We might think that if we have not been maligned or persecuted for our faith, then we have not truly suffered. This makes suffering a spiritual medal of honor or, maybe, in an extreme case, intentionally sought out. The other extreme response is Westerners who lean toward minimization or outright dismissal of hurts. We think we ought not to be taking it so hard. "It's no big deal" or "I shouldn't struggle so much" are common trains of thought. In The United States, we are permeated with a can-do spirit. If we just try harder and do better, we can figure life out and get on top of everything. These are humanistic, unbiblical and dishonoring responses to life's hardships. The Word of God never spiritualizes, dismisses, or minimizes our pain. We should do the same by fully honoring what we are encountering and living well through it.

The biblical words *parasmos* and *thlipsis* entail *any* difficulty whether physical, emotional, relational, spiritual, or circumstantial. They encompass suffering that is self-inflicted and inflicted upon us. They allow for natural disasters, disease, accidents, abuse, and oppression. They do not allow simplistic responses, over-spiritualization or minimization. Once I began to reassess some of my personal experiences, I realized that God has allowed me to have afflictions of various kinds, and used them in redemptive ways in my formation. However, this discovery did not remove my pain.

Suffering, a Working Definition

Here is a working definition for suffering: Suffering is *any* experience that causes internal or external duress physically, emotionally, spiritually, or relationally. In this fallen world all humankind suffers. Key biblical passages indicate that God's goodness uses suffering to bring us both temporary and eternal benefit. God's redemptive work can be powerfully known in the context of suffering.

Various biblical passages show how God uses personal hardships to shape and mature us. Pain can be caused by others, deliberately or accidentally, by external circumstance (natural disaster or an auto accident), or even self-inflicted by foolish choices. There are larger issues at stake from a spiritual perspective, not only observable circumstances. For example, if I make the foolish choice of embezzling because of personal debt, I will suffer the consequences. Yes, this suffering is self-inflicted, and I deserve the consequences. But God is gracious.

> Suffering is *any* experience that causes internal or external duress physically, emotionally, spiritually, or relationally.

He will forgive as I confess and repent, and wisely use circumstances to shape me. If I am sexually abused, there will be layers of physical and emotional pain, not to mention legal dynamics. All of these layers are deeply painful. God can use any aspect of suffering for his good purposes with us, to bring out truths in us that might otherwise never be learned. I will go on to examine not specific pains, nor causes, nor even ramifications, but rather how God uses pain to shape us into the image of Christ. Suffering and trials are common to a Christ-follower or a non-follower. What is different for a Christian? For those who belong to Christ, there is another dimension of suffering: We can share in the sufferings of Christ.

Often sharing in the sufferings of Christ is understood as persecution. As I gain deeper insight into the Word, I am learning about a great mystery. All of us have dry or wilderness times in our pilgrimage with God. St. John of the Cross wrote extensively about the "dark night of the soul." There are hardships that the Spirit of Christ will lead us into. These too are sufferings that God uses to shape us.

- The word *suffering* includes all human experiences of pain. The Bible has references to very specific sufferings (e.g. persecution), but also many generic references to sufferings that are normative to the breadth of human experience.
- God never dismisses nor minimizes human experience of pain. We must not do so either.
- The circumstance causing pain is of lesser concern than how it is impacting us and how we are responding to it.
- All humans suffer. For the believer, there is the additional dynamic of suffering for our faith and in our walk with God.

C. God's Purposes for a Believer's Suffering

Purpose 1: Affliction and Transformation

James 1 and Romans 5 and 8 are central to the issue of personal affliction and can be compared to draw out essential truths.

> My brethren, count it all joy when you fall into various trials, knowing that the testing of your faith produces patience. But let patience have its perfect work, that you may be perfect and complete, lacking nothing (Jas 1:2–4, NKJV).

> Through whom [Jesus Christ] also we have access by faith into this grace in which we stand, and rejoice in hope of the glory of God. And not only that, but we also glory in tribulations, knowing that tribulation produces perseverance; and perseverance, character; and character, hope (Rom 5:2-4, NKJV).

Both passages describe a process of personal and spiritual growth that is stimulated by affliction:

> Count it all joy ... **knowing that:**
> Various Trials >> Patience >> Mature, Entire, Lacking Nothing
> (Jas 1:2-4)

> Glory in tribulation ... **knowing that:**
> Tribulation >> Endurance >> Character >> Hope
> (Rom 5:2-4)

God's Purpose: God's goal is our maturity, reflected in Christlike character (See Rom 8:29). God intends for us to grow holistically. This truth is stated in the phrases "perfect [mature] and complete, lacking nothing" and "produces ... character." A trial can be as mild as being patient with a house full of loud active kids, or as traumatic as the death of a child. Trauma is not a prerequisite for growth. However, the text simply states that God uses all hardships redemptively. Both Paul and James state that patience (some texts use the words *endurance* or *perseverance*) can be a fruit of hardship. God has designed us so that affliction is required to take us to certain places in our growth. If I never have a setback, if I always get what I want when I want it, I will *never* grow in patience. There is no other way to develop patience than through adversity, and patience begets further character shaping in terms of love, kindness, and godliness. All these traits are gathered in this one word, *character*.

> **God has designed us so that affliction is required to take us to certain places in our growth.**

Jerry Sittser shares the traumatic loss of his mother, wife, and daughter in a car accident. He observed "though I experienced death, I also experienced life in ways I never thought possible before – not after the darkness as we might suppose, but *in* the darkness. I did not go through pain and come out the other side; instead, I lived in it and found within the pain the grace to survive and eventually grow.... Sorrow took residence in my soul and enlarged it." (Sittser, 1995, 37) In the midst of the darkness Sittser was transformed. He experienced life in ways he never thought possible; he grew; his soul was enlarged. This is a wonderful description of holistic maturation. Although I would not wish such pain and loss on anyone, God can use the mildest inconveniences and the most horrid losses to shape us. He is a good, wise, powerful, and kind God who takes the awful experiences in our lives and brings beauty from them.

Paul, James, and other New Testament authors make the clear statement that trials produce "character." Without trials, some level of character growth would not happen. Although suffering is not the only thing needed to mature (we need grace, love, truth, others, and time to grow), it is a part of it.

The believer's perspective: The phrase "knowing that" is key in both passages. There is a truth that will give us perspective in the midst of difficulty. This perspective is essential, transcendent, and eternal. God's purposes for hardships are good and not random. "Perspective is everything" rings true when we find ourselves in the midst of trials. God will use these terrible experiences for good ends. In essence, the process will stink but we will like the fruit.

The Believer's Response: James says "joy!" Paul exclaims "glory!" These are terms I find strange while I am groping in darkness. James and Paul can speak of joy in the midst of trials because of their awareness of God's good, redemptive activity through them. It is not pain that produces joy for them; it is in knowing that God is at work. James and Paul learned to desire the Christlikeness that God wants for his people. If suffering is a means to Christlikeness, then so be it. They saw beyond the present painful circumstance to the long-term benefit. The Bible does not encourage us to feel joyful about pain, but rather joy about God's caring presence with us as we go through suffering and anticipate transformation. How can we have such a response? By seeking what God desires in us, namely mature, Christlike character. When God's desire becomes ours, then we increase our capacity for acceptance, and perhaps even thankfulness and joy through adversity.

All of this is easy to write about and difficult to live. In the midst of hardship, I wrestle with God. I may be very angry, sad, or hurt. I hate the pain. I want problems resolved. I do not want to have to endure. Yet, sometimes

God allows me to remain in my pain to lovingly move me toward holistic maturity. As I remember this truth, I gain perspective. The tension and the hardship are not changed, but I journey better in this paradoxical hard time. I want out of the pain, but I am learning to endure well in it. In wrestling with my own illnesses, a day came when I prayed, "Father, I do not like this, I still want you to take it away, but teach me to steward this well. Teach me whatever I need to learn." Such prayers involve honesty and seeking God, without minimization or spiritualization. He has answered that prayer and has not completely removed the effects of the illness. I am a changed person.

One commentator on the letter of James reminds us that "God is in the business of building up strong men and women who can persevere in hard times without fainting... Too often we are so eager to escape our difficulties that we seek mere relief from the trial, rather than gain every possible spiritual benefit from it" (Hodges, 1994, 19).The first purpose we are considering is that God uses affliction as an essential element in the holistic maturation process. God desires from his children the response of joyful perseverance in the anticipation of his work in the midst of the suffering, rather than begrudging acquiescence. Essential to such a response is perspective, a keen and transcendent awareness that God is pursuing our maturity in Christ with love.

Purpose 2: Affliction Tests and Strengthens Faith

Peter affirms that: "In this you greatly rejoice, though now for a little while, if need be, you have been grieved by various trials, that the genuineness of your faith, being much more precious than gold that perishes, though it is tested by fire, may be found to praise, honor, and glory at the revelation of Jesus Christ" (1 Pet 1:6–7, NKJV). Crucial to the strengthening effect is our response to difficulties. Many opt to doubt God's goodness, become self-consumed, and seek comfort above all. Such choices will jeopardize the benefits that could come through enduring. Thus, the second purpose is that God uses adversity to test and strengthen our faith.

> God has a wisdom I will not always understand.

This "faith testing" can be lost in our Christian jargon. We know it, but our eyes glaze over from familiarity. Ours is a journey of faith. Without faith, it is impossible to please God (Heb 11:6). Faith is such a crucial quality of a Christ-follower that God is always working to increase our capacity to trust. We learn to trust that God is good and wise even if our life does not go as we would like. I have learned that God has a wisdom I will not always understand. In suffering we learn that his ways are not ours. If I had my way, I would sign up for a mature faith workshop and be done with it. But God's way is to use trials to refine my faith as fire refines gold. Though I do not understand that, I am asked to trust that his intent is good and loving. As my faith has been tried, I have been learning to trust.

Purpose 3: Affliction Can Foster Obedience over Pain Avoidance

Later in Peter's first letter he states, "Therefore, since Christ suffered for us in the flesh, arm yourselves also with the same mind, for he who has suffered in the flesh has ceased from sin, that he no longer should live the rest of his time in the flesh for the [evil desires] of men, but for the will of God" (1 Pet 4:1–2, NKJV). The type of suffering Peter refers to here is defined in 1 Peter 3:17 as suffering for doing right. The recipients of Peter's letter were being persecuted on account of their faith. Peter repeatedly holds Jesus up as the model for how to respond in a hostile environment.

Peter makes an amazing claim regarding our spiritual growth *if* we submit to such difficulties. He uses the attention-grabbing phrase, "who has suffered in the flesh has ceased from sin." Peter asserts that whoever chooses to endure hardship demonstrates that obeying God, not avoiding hardship, is the most important motivation. Choosing to obey God even when this involves suffering has a morally strengthening effect. Commitment to a pattern of action that prioritizes obedience over seeking self-comfort results in transformation and growth in my capacity to seek God's way over mine. This is a lifelong process. Suffering is one means of this growth.

How do we respond to unrelenting pain in life? Do we self-medicate through excessive shopping, eating, alcohol, play, rage, or work? Or do we keep in step with the Spirit and walk in obedience and joyful endurance? God's desire for us is to walk in his ways regardless of temporary hardship. God is committed to building that determination in us. Are we as determined to learn it? The Father is seeking sons and daughters who endure well.

Purpose 4: God Uses Difficulties to Transform Character

Hebrews 12:5–11 is key to understanding our Heavenly Father's motives in allowing his children to endure tough times. Since this is a longer passage, we will look at it in sections.

> And you have forgotten the exhortation which speaks to you as to sons: "My son, do not despise the chastening of the LORD, nor be discouraged when you are rebuked by Him; for whom the LORD loves He chastens, and scourges every son whom He receives" (Heb 12:5–6, NKJV).

Suffering can have the purpose of instruction. When we are in hard times, God has our attention like no other time. We ask different questions about God, life, and ourselves. These are all ways the Spirit is seeking to form us. The most helpful posture is one of asking, "God, what would you like me to learn from you in this? Teach me."

> If you endure chastening, God deals with you as with sons; for what son is there whom a father does not chasten? But if you are without chastening, of which all have become partakers, then you are illegitimate and not sons. Furthermore, we have had human fathers who corrected us, and we paid them respect. Shall we not much more readily be in subjection to the Father of spirits and live? (Heb 12:7–9, NKJV).

Another principle is that suffering is an indicator of divine parental care. Freedom from discipline is not to be desired. If a parent does not correct us, she or he is neglectful. God always teaches us from a posture of healthy, pure Fatherly love. This is an important truth to remember when life feels dark and God feels distant: the Father is present and loving us.

> For they indeed for a few days chastened us as seemed best to them, but He for our profit, that we may be partakers of His holiness. Now no chastening seems to be joyful for the present, but painful; nevertheless, afterward it yields the peaceable fruit of righteousness to those who have been trained by it (Heb 12:9–11, NKJV).

A final key truth is that yielding to God's shaping process leads to life. This life that God graces us with has a "peaceable fruit of righteousness." By discipline we are shaped into the image of Christ. God's goal is that we share in "His holiness," that we grow in Christlike character.

Therefore, a fruitful response to suffering is to seek understanding of which character trait God is addressing and to respond in trusting acceptance and submission, from 1 Peter 4:1–2. My own illness exposed my tendency toward self-centeredness. When most ill, I was very angry that I could not do what I wanted, when I wanted. As months passed, things that used to be important to me, such as my exercise routine, began to fade because I did not have the energy. Over time I gained a different perspective. God was training me to embrace a different set of priorities. To learn my lesson, I needed to see the specific area God was addressing. Otherwise, once out of the hardship I might settle back into the old way of living. With my energy level restored, I can live out the lessons he taught me. I can resolve to obey him rather than comfort myself.

We all have character flaws, and God will address them in his timing. As we stumble along this path of hardship, we can ask God to teach us. He is eager to do this for his children. The Spirit will help us to see. Ours is a loving Father who trains his children to live godly, Christlike lives. That is true life, not an illusion.

A common response to prolonged hardship is to assume God is punishing us. What did we do wrong? What restitution could we make? This is an unhealthy and non-biblical train of thought. God does not base his acceptance of us on our performance. Neither does he reject or punish us on that basis. His movement toward us is always based on the work of Christ on the cross. God's response to us is always rooted in love. No exceptions. If I sin, does God still love me? My response is, yes. He always delights in me. He will not be pleased with my actions, but God does not value me based on performance. Intimacy with God can be hindered by my hurtful and sinful actions. The way of confession and forgiveness is always open through the power of the self-sacrifice of Jesus. God can be grieved by my actions, but his love abides. He is still for me. He still pursues me. Relationship is restored when I confess and seek his forgiveness. John wrote, "There is no fear in love. But perfect love drives out fear, because fear has to do with punishment. The one who fears is not yet made perfect in love" (1 Jn 4:18, NIV). God loves us deeply. We fear that we are being found out and punished. "Being made perfect in love" allows us to step into the light whenever we have wandered.

There we have forgiveness and restoration. But there are consequences for my actions. If I rob a bank, God will forgive me, but I still have to go to prison. An example that is simplistic but true. God will use our failures and the pain they cause to shape us. Our human assumption is that pain is "bad" and to be avoided at all costs. But what if God has allowed pain as a grace to take us where we would otherwise never go?

> But what if God has allowed pain as a grace to take us where we would otherwise never go?

Both the righteous and the wicked suffer. A trusting, submissive, and teachable spirit allows us to gain from a tough experience. There is nothing worse than going through a hard time and getting nothing positive out of it! Affliction can become an opportunity for those who turn to God.

Purpose 5: Spiritual Heritage and Eternal Reward

Jesus' entire life was marked by suffering and trials, from his childhood flight to Egypt, to the Nazareth rejection, to the cross. In the Sermon on the Mount, Jesus taught about suffering caused by human resistance to believers living for God's purposes.

> Blessed are those who are persecuted for righteousness' sake, for theirs is the kingdom of heaven. Blessed are you when they revile and persecute you, and say all kinds of evil against you falsely for My sake. Rejoice and be exceedingly glad, for great is your reward in heaven, for so they persecuted the prophets who were before you (Mt 5:10–12, NKJV).

The word *glad* appears contradictory in this context. The Greek term rendered *glad* in English is derived from two words that mean to "leap exceedingly." A vivid picture indeed! Jesus puts two realities together in this teaching: Eternal reward ("for great is your reward in heaven") and spiritual heritage ("for so they persecuted the prophets who were before you") and ties them to personal suffering. To suffer persecution for one's faith is to show loyalty to Jesus Christ. To suffer persecution is to walk the same road as the prophets, saints, and martyrs. According to Jesus, to share in persecution is not a penalty, but rather a glory. "Rejoice at such moments," Jesus said, "and be glad." Count it a privilege to join the community of sufferers in Christ.

This line of thinking is Kingdom-oriented and there is little in our

Western culture to encourage it. In the United States, there is a deeply imbedded assumption that I have a right to the "pursuit of happiness," and nothing and no one ought to get in the way. Following this assumption, even God should not impede the pursuit of happiness. But this is not biblical! Reality is glory *through* the cross. Reality is the downward trajectory of Christ as described in Philippians 2:5–8 by Paul. Christ emptied himself of his deified state, to become a man. He sought no human pedestals, but rather became a servant. Even more, he died a criminal's death. This is the path we are called to emulate, not one of comfort, fulfillment, ease, and plenty. Christ's call to follow him supersedes all cultural and societal beckoning. An important cross-reference for this teaching is in the book of Philippians. Paul writes: "For to you it has been granted on behalf of Christ, not only to believe in Him, but also to suffer for His sake" (Phil 1:29, NKJV). God was extending two graces to the Philippians. First was salvation in Christ; second was suffering for Christ. This statement has profound implications for how we respond to this type of suffering. From God's perspective, suffering for the sake of Christ is a gift on par with personal salvation. It is a grace, a gift. How can this be? "For theirs is the kingdom of heaven," Jesus would reply.

According to Matthew 5 and Philippians 1, suffering for Christ's sake is a gift. Polycarp (70 –155 A.D.), a pupil of the Apostle John, understood this truth when he declared at his death by persecution, "I thank thee that thou hast graciously thought me worthy of this day and of this hour." He was echoing Peter and John from Acts 5:41: "The apostles left the Sanhedrin, rejoicing because they had been counted worthy of suffering for the Name [of Jesus]" (NIV).

Purpose 6: Suffering Increases Capacity for Mystery

Pat Russell writes, "Suffering is not a question that demands an answer. It is not a problem that demands a solution. Suffering is a mystery that demands a presence" (Russell, 2011, 29). The "presence" Russell is calling for is my being awake, aware and attentive to God in the context I find myself in. It is too easy to numb myself and thus miss the opportunity to know God in new ways. There is so much to suffering that we cannot understand. God's ways are truly not our ways, and his wisdom is incomprehensible. I know God is good and wise. All painful circumstances are within range of God's goodness and wisdom. Joseph, Daniel, Ruth, Hannah and Samuel experienced deep pain and loss, some of which was extremely unjust. They all experienced redemption in the midst of hardships. Joseph never grew up in his own culture. Daniel was denied the right to worship in his own land. Ruth was a widowed foreigner. Hannah was abused by her rival even when she bore a son to keep her promise. Samuel spent his early childhood and teen years far from home living and working in the Tabernacle (1 Sam 2–3).

These stories inform me as I seek to understand mine. There are greater purposes that I cannot see. Hannah was a "mere" housewife *and* she bore a great prophet who brought the nation together (1 Sam 1). Ruth was a widowed foreigner who became the great-great-grandmother of King David (Ruth 1 and 4:1-22). These women could never see the national gain that would come out of their personal loss. How does my loss benefit others? Paul boldly states that his sufferings fill up those still lacking for the church (Col 1:24). Somehow in our sufferings for God, we join in Christ's suffering (2 Tim 1:8; Phil 1:29, 3:10). What's more, we also join in the sufferings of the church around the world. Not only persecution, but also addressing poverty; social, political, and religious oppression; and the lack of many other resources are ways of joining in his suffering. Hardships that occur while following Christ join in the universal hurts of all those who name the Name.

I continue to be confused by many of the hurts my friends and I have experienced. I don't understand my mother-in-law's death in a car accident or my friend Kirk's death to ALS in his forties. Nor do I understand my fellow Christ-followers' sufferings in other countries. Even though I claim the biblical truths by faith, I still hurt. I will still grieve past and future losses. To honor both biblical revelation (truth) and life experiences, we simultaneously grieve and walk by faith in a God who is able to see us through any and all of life's hardships. My suffering demands that I walk in the presence of God and together with my fellow pilgrims in this harsh world. Adversity has slowed me down and taken me deeper that I might abide with God better. As I get further into this journey, God's guidance continues to be there, but it requires longer times of stillness and waiting to discern what he is saying. Suffering is teaching me to be present.

> Adversity has slowed me down and taken me deeper that I might abide with God better.

Summary: Those Born into Christ Are Born into Adversity

We have looked at six fundamental truths found in New Testament passages on suffering, which is nowhere near an exhaustive list of God's many purposes and uses. *Some* of God's purposes for our affliction are:

1. To mature us in Christlike character;
2. To strengthen our faith and develop us into persevering sons and daughters;
3. To develop a resolve to obey God over any form of pain avoidance;
4. To train us from unChristlike ways toward greater godliness;
5. To accrue eternal reward and partake in a rich spiritual heritage of God's servants who have endured affliction in the midst of service;
6. To increase our capacity for mystery.

God has created the human soul so it requires some element of suffering to reach its full depth of maturity. This is the path that he has marked out for all who desire to be transformed into the image of Christ. The diagram on the following page illustrates the flow of the truths in this section.

D. Application: Caregiving

Those called into caregiving are called to enter into the adversity of others and to journey with them through it. This book provides specific, practical means of caring in the event of trauma. I would like to reflect on how these truths impact the way we provide care. We are reminded of the challenge in Proverbs 17:17 that "a brother is born for adversity." I invite you to wrestle with this as you care for others.

Not Undermining God's Redemptive Work

God has designed the redemptive process so that we reach our full depth of maturity, in part, through suffering and afflictions. This has huge implications for how we respond to others in their suffering. If I were to help the person find a solution to his or her pain as quickly as possible, I *might* be undermining the redemptive work God wants to do through a prolonged period of endurance. In the presence of difficulties of any severity, a care

18 TRAUMA & RESILIENCE

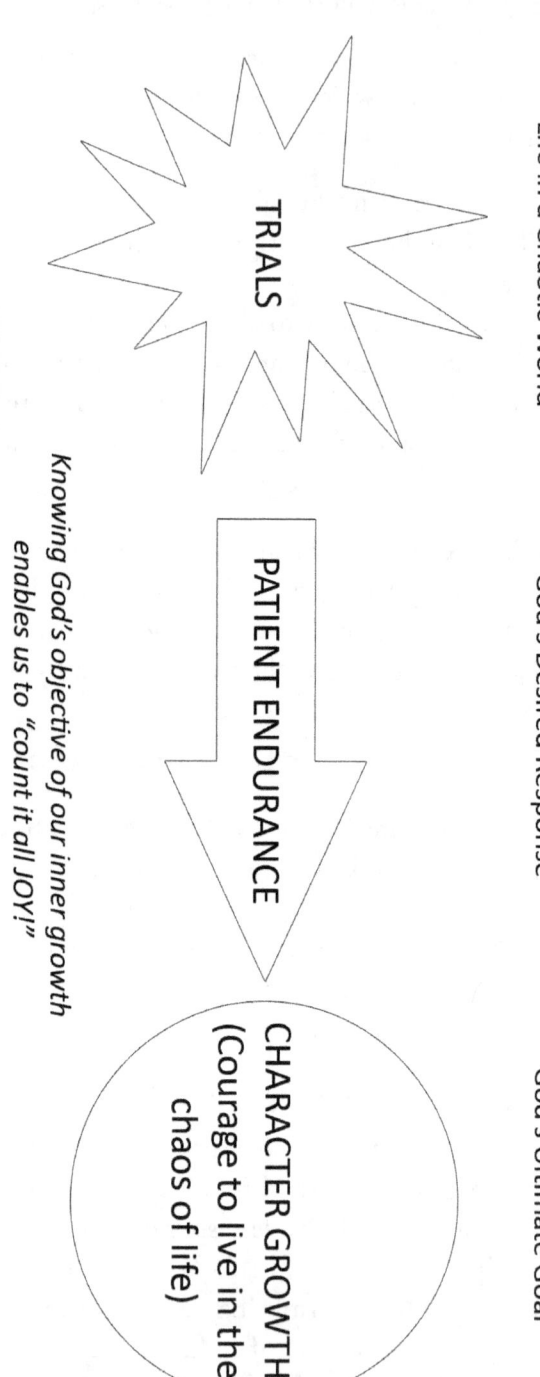

provider's *primary* response is not finding a remedy, but being a journey mate through hardship as God's purposes are explored.

I emphasize the word *primary* because there are many other responses we can have. Often we need to refer suffering people to mental health or medical professionals for adequate care. As a shepherd, however, one comes alongside those serving God in this troubled world. Even after referring people for therapy, I still want to be *with them* in their process. All of us need to be shepherded, especially through the valleys of darkness.

In seeking to fulfill this calling, we must be mindful of two temptations. First, we like to be needed. However, what people really need is Christ. Our goal needs to be bringing Christ to the person, and the person to Christ. Secondly, we like to fix stuff. Please, do not try to fix people or their problems. Whatever may need to be "fixed," it will be helped by love and accompaniment. God will deliver them when the time is right. My primary role is to be a companion in this process. There is no greater gift we can give someone suffering than our simple, abiding, enduring presence.

Four Postures for Being with Those in Affliction

Four postures are essential for being with someone in a season of affliction. These postures increase our ability *to discern* God's transcendent work, and our capacity *to be with* others in this process. Questions for reflection are suggested for each of the postures that will aid proper alignment in times of intense ministry.

Posture 1: Posture of God-Awareness

The Apostle Paul instructs us that God has destined us to "be conformed to the likeness of his Son" (Rom 8:29, NIV). Jesus constantly sought to discern his Father's will. Thus, our first response in the presence of one in affliction must be the question "What is God up to here?" We are not primarily seeking solutions; but insight. Proverbs 18:13 states, "He who answers before listening—that is his folly and his shame" (NIV). Our first and foremost posture is one of *watchful listening*. How is Christ already at work here? How can I join in God's sovereign purposes? Am I willing to seek after God and listen on behalf of the one who is struggling?

When I sit with another person through deep anguish and tears, I seek to discern God's activity and the level of awareness of the individual.

Caution must be exercised here. Often in trauma, the wounds are so raw that objectivity is almost unattainable. Insight into what God is up to may not be the immediate, but rather the long-term need. Simply be present in the name of Christ. The degree to which I journey with another is the degree to which I discern. As in spiritual formation, we assume that God is present and forming the person. I am not the shaper; I am observing the Shaper at work. Watchful listening is one posture of caring for a person who is suffering.

> ### POSTURE 1: PROCESSING QUESTIONS
>
> 1. How can I grow in God-awareness and listening to this person?
> 2. How can I remind myself that I am not the primary caregiver, but that God is?
> 3. How can I grow in bringing Christ to people and people to Christ?

Posture 2: Posture of Being With

The greatest need in a time of trauma is accompaniment. A companion can gently take the arm and slowly, wisely guide the one in pain through gradual restoration. My heart posture is not that of a superior or problem-solver, but of a companion. Often there is professional protocol. Though I am mindful of that, I offer myself as present, attentive, available and gently caring.

This simple, yet profound, act of presence is a great gift. In 2 Corinthians the God of comfort or mercies is praised. The word for comfort in Greek is actually *paraklete*. This is the same word Jesus used of the Spirit as comforter and helper. This Greek word means "come alongside." God's comfort to us in pain is his Presence. He may not solve our problems as we would like, but he will be present with us in the midst of them.

> One of the greatest honors in this life is to be a companion of others in trauma, loss, grief and redemption.

As Paul wrote in 2 Corinthians 1:3–7, we are also to be *parakletes*. One of the greatest honors in this life is to be a companion of others in trauma, loss, grief and redemption.

> **POSTURE 2: PROCESSING QUESTIONS**
>
> 1. How am I at simply being with another?
> 2. How can I grow in this heart posture of presence for others?
> 3. What spiritual practices might aid me in being present to others?

Posture 3: Posture of Giving Ourselves

"The good shepherd lays down his life for the sheep" (Jn 10:11, NIV). As an ongoing act; we are called to be people laying down their lives for their brothers (1 Jn 3:16) and sisters. Epaphroditus is a biblical example of this posture. Paul tells us that Epaphroditus came close to death (Phil 2:27) for Paul's betterment. The church at Philippi sent one of their own, this unsung hero named Epaphroditus, to Paul to provide care. He most likely encouraged the apostle by bringing a letter, some sort of monetary gift, and some items to keep him warm. Paul thanked the Philippian church for these gifts. However, what really ministered to Paul was Epaphroditus, the person. What did he do to minister to Paul, who, like many contemporary pastors and missionaries, was never far from hardship? "Because for the work of Christ he [Epaphroditus] came close to death, not regarding his life, to supply what was lacking in your service toward me" (Phil 2:30, NKJV).

The phrase "came close" is a fascinating word picture. The Greek word translated "came close" is a single word *paraboloni* (παραβλονι), a gambling term referring to one who exposes himself to danger for the sake of another. In the First Century it was an advocate, who, in the interest of friendship, exposed himself to dangers. In legal strife, he took up the client's cause even as far as the emperor. In the post-apostolic church, a group risked their lives in a ministry of nursing the contagiously ill and burying the dead. They called themselves the *paraboloni*.

Epaphroditus was that kind of "gambling" man. His work was self-sacrifice. He was sent out to serve Paul, and the stakes were high. He held nothing back. He risked his life for Paul's betterment. The imprisoned Paul was ministered to by the personal presence and sacrifice of another. This is the role of a shepherd. Shepherds are called to live sacrificially and be willing to lay their lives down.

Tending to others in trauma can lead to secondary or vicarious trauma. Coming alongside empathically, and hearing tragic stories exposes caregivers to pain of their own. All that pain accumulates and impacts us. Tending to those in pain will mean that to some degree I will enter pain. I will weep. I will be reminded of how cruel this world can be. My heart will be deeply troubled. As I benefit others, I might also suffer harm. As I continue to come alongside others in deep pain and trauma, I am, literally, laying my life down for another. Jesus tells us there is no greater love than this (Jn 15:13).

> **POSTURE 3: PROCESSING QUESTIONS**
>
> 1. How prepared am I to be poured out for others?
> 2. Am I willing to repeatedly go into difficult relationships and volatile countries to serve his servants? Am I willing to lay my life down for others? Why or why not?
> 3. How am I caring for myself as a caregiver?

Posture 4: Posture of Enduring

God is urgent, but not in a rush. It is urgent that our hearts be shaped into the image of Christ, even if it takes decades for that work to take place. How pretentious to think that I can bring healing and closure with a brief visit or simple advice. Learning to endure well my own hardships, together with a practice of solitude (sitting still, silent, and alone with God) has helped me to linger well with others. I am learning to be quiet, wait, wonder, abide, and be with another. All these abilities are essential to the shepherd of sufferers.

Frequently, traumatized people will struggle for an extended time. My patience with another's pain may wear out long before their pain does. God has me endure my own pain in order to learn to endure well with others in theirs.

> **POSTURE 4: PROCESSING QUESTIONS**
>
> 1. Am I willing to endure with the one who is being called by God to endure pain?
> 2. Have I fostered in my heart both space and the capacity to linger in difficult caregiving scenarios?
> 3. Does the pace of my life allow for periods of unhurried time to wait on God and sit with others as they endure affliction?

E. Conclusion

This world is a violent, volatile place. We all experience afflictions *and* God is always present with us in dark times. God has designed the human soul with hardship as an ingredient for the process of holistic maturation. Hardship is not all we need to grow, but we do need it. The care provider's primary responsibility is to work with God while journeying with others through their hardships. We serve well when we increase our understanding of God's use of affliction in shaping our lives, and develop the capacity to journey with others in hard times. Are we willing to lay our lives down for others? Have we created space in our hearts to *be* with others in their troubles? Those called into such ministry are "born for adversity" (Prov 17:17, NIV).

Notes for Chapter I

1. See barnabas.org for information on the annual PTM (Pastors to Missionary) Conference.
2. Portions of this chapter were previously published in Tender Care (Rockford, IL: Barnabas Books, 2008). Permission has been granted by Barnabas International for republishing in this volume.

CHAPTER II
STORIES OF TRAUMA IN MINISTRY

Story 1
Civil War and Evacuation
Karen Carr, Ghana

It is one thing to know about risks intellectually, and another to live them in daily reality. The Mobile Member Care Team (MMCT) is an interdisciplinary, intermission group with skills in training, counseling, and administration. Our purpose is to increase resilience and promote caring, supportive relationships among missionaries. We are governed by a Board of mission leaders and work in partnership with mission organizations responding to requests for workshops, crisis intervention, and counseling. Most of us had already lived in Africa, and knew we would be exposed to trauma along with the challenge of maintaining our own mental health while caring for others. The team of three came to Abidjan, Côte d'Ivoire (Ivory Coast), in 2000 to work with mission communities in 14 West African countries.

The first two years were especially intense for us. In addition to the normal challenging components of ministry start-up and cross-cultural living, we were in a very volatile country with increasing violence and civil unrest. As a psychologist trained to avoid "dual relationships," I was impacted by grief and pain because the missionaries I counseled were part of my extended missionary family. I already knew some of them from training and social events, and they were now suffering serious crises such as the death of loved ones, armed robbery, kidnapping, beating, and rape. These missionaries were part of my personal life, part of the fabric of my own social support system. I was in their world, they were in mine, and our worlds had been permanently changed.

These experiences, and my internal reaction to them, set the stage for how I would experience and respond to the large-scale crisis in store for me. I woke up on September 19, 2002, in Bouaké, a city in central Ivory Coast, to the sound of machine guns. We had just begun leading a workshop for 14 cross-cultural workers, training them to facilitate interpersonal skills workshops. My first thought as I lay in bed and listened to the exchange of gunfire in the distance was that a known gang of robbers had finally been trapped and were having a shoot-out with the police. As gunfire intensified, I suspected another attempted coup in the country. Radio news at 6 a. m. confirmed that rebels were attacking government troops in three strategic locations, including Bouaké. This began an eight-day siege that kept us in a building, trapped in crossfire between government and rebel troops.

There were times when rocket fire was very loud and close. We put mattresses against the windows as protection from shattering glass. We lay face down on the floor, pressing against the side of the wall. I remember holding the ankle of the person lying ahead of me and praying that the Lord would give us peace of heart. He did give us peace and comfort. At times we sang (quietly, so the rebels wouldn't know we were there) hymns in harmony to highlight our oneness in Christ. No one panicked, cried, or argued. We naturally found our roles as we endured the crisis together. Four of us led in decision making; others carried buckets from the well (our water had been cut), prepared food, worked on our security, or stayed on their knees in prayer.

Phone calls from family, friends, mission leadership, and the U.S. embassy, came in continuously. Daily, sometimes hourly, assuring calls from our mission leaders gave us comfort as they assured us of their efforts to help secure our evacuation. We were told to stay put and wait for safe evacuation. We worried that plans organized by the U.S. embassy might not include Nigerians who were part of our group, so we agreed that some of us would stay behind with them if it came to that.

Then a group of 40 Liberians came to the gate, threatened, frightened, seeking refuge. One was known to us, and the rest were his extended family. We allowed them in but were torn about letting them stay. That would increase our own risk, and yet if we turned them away, they might be blamed for trouble-making and killed. When we prayerfully decided to hide them on our compound, I struggled with guilt that I had even considered turning them out.

Two times were hardest for me in those eight days. One, when we heard a mob coming closer and closer. The Liberians were completely silent and I could see the look of shock and fear in their faces. Even the youngest children were completely silent. I had been to Rwanda and heard stories of the genocide there. I imagined this mob breaking in and slaughtering the Liberians right before our eyes. I felt afraid and helpless. We all prayed for safety and gradually the sound of the mob died down, heading in a different direction.

Two, when suddenly an intense battle involving heavy artillery began right outside our courtyard walls. We ran for the building, crouched down, and hit the ground with each burst of gunfire. Running behind a dear friend, I tried to imagine what we would do if one of us were shot. We had no way to get to a clinic and knew only elementary first aid. We all got in safely, but the thought of what might have happened impacted me emotionally even more than what actually happened.

After eight days of waiting, we were evacuated out of Bouaké with the supervision of French soldiers. And yes, all of us came out together as one unified group. Before scattering to our different countries of residence, we had time together to acknowledge and celebrate what each of us had done to contribute to our joint survival. We laughed, cried, and hugged, knowing that this experience would bond us for life.

In subsequent days, we were exhausted, numb, and disoriented. It was hard to be productive. The future of Côte d'Ivoire was so uncertain. Shortly after we were evacuated, we were blessed to receive care from counselors from the States who came to us in Abidjan, our home base. They devoted hours to us individually and as a team.

Aided by the counselors' good listening and safe presence, I talked about the culmination of stressful events of the past year and began working through fear, anger, and grief. I cried, I asked questions that didn't have answers like, "Why did God allow this to happen?" I went back to the roots of why I was there (God gave me a love for missionaries and called me to this work). Those roots were deep and enduring and assured me that God would equip me to do the work he had called me to do. It wasn't about my strength or energy or will, really. It was about knowing that this was exactly what I was supposed to do. Motivated by love for the people I was helping and joy in doing so, I could keep on going.

Being reminded of the Lord's call in my life was a key in my recovery and ability to return to the intensity and demands of ministry. I also worked on my theology of suffering. Some of what I heard and witnessed went beyond my sense of justice, fairness, and even my concept of God's character and will. Wrestling and crying through this, coming to peace about God's sovereignty in the midst of confusion and uncertainty, was an important part of processing the trauma. Getting away to a beautiful beach just outside the city with my beloved teammates, watching birds, praying, and studying the psalms all brought me back to a place of reflection, truth, and perspective. Most significant was Job 19:25, "But as for me, I know that my Redeemer lives, and he will stand upon the earth at last." It helped me to consider that the many injustices might not be redeemed in my lifetime, but they would indeed be redeemed.

After rest and vacation for some days, restoring us to a place of renewed energy and vision, our team entered a new season of work. War and violence continued, so we chose to relocate together in Ghana, still centrally located in our 14-country service area. This move opened up new doors of opportunity to be more deeply involved with Africans. Some time later the Lord led me to do more work in the area of forgiving those who had hurt people I cared about. This gave me a greater freedom and release to continue walking with others in the midst of intense pain and suffering, bear their burdens, and then release them at the Cross.

Story 2
Brush with Renal Cancer
Allan and Betsy Poole, U.S.A.

Allan had known the Lord since his college years and felt a strong call to serve God as a pastor, a vocation as exciting as it was daunting. It was a true gift when he met Betsy, who took the call of being a pastor's wife seriously and agreed to join hands with him, for better or for worse. They enjoyed a loving and solid marriage and had two children who they dearly loved. Their ministry was rewarding and fruitful, and Allan's relationship with his senior pastor was deep and trusting. They both had strong friendships in and around church life. Allan was often awed by what he discovered about God during theological studies. Both were open to experience God in direct, personal, and unique ways.

During a retreat with seminary friends, Allan sensed that the following year would be a "big year" for him. However, he was not expecting to be surprised by a "flood of blood and junk" when he used the bathroom one day. He was very alarmed, but after examination, his physician assured him that this was nothing to be concerned about. Allan and Betsy thoroughly enjoyed the following months, which included a time of theological study. Allan especially enjoyed learning more about the Trinity. Betsy studied *The Pilgrim's Progress*, which enlarged her interior spiritual landscape. They were about as "shored up" as they could be for something unexpected. Unexpected things so far had not occurred to Betsy.

A few months later Allan suffered a more serious attack. This time he immediately was referred to a specialist. After examination, he heard troubling news from the physician: "We have a problem." There was a tennis-ball-size cancerous tumor in one of Allan's kidneys. When he called Betsy with the news, she was with close friends painting the nursery for their third child, due soon. The news was a shock and having friends close by was a huge advantage. Throughout the challenges of the weeks ahead, good friends helped in a myriad of thoughtful ways. Additional tests for Allan were ordered immediately and revealed lesions in his liver. This was hard to digest. It was heart-wrenching to think that he might not be alive to see his children grow up, including one not yet born; and he might be leaving his wife alone with all of these responsibilities.

Shortly after this diagnosis, Allan sat at his desk and his eyes fell on the icon of the Trinity from the recent course. At that moment he experienced God in a special way. It felt like God was talking to Allan as he gazed at the icon depicting the Old Testament Trinity by Rublev sitting at a table: "Your place at the table is secure." At this moment he became able "to relinquish his own uncertainty into the certainty of God's welcome. He was his."

Allan and Betsy had let Ed, their senior pastor, know from the moment they became aware there was a health problem. Among other traits of a wonderful pastor, Ed had an amazing ability to be there and listen, and then put the concerns before God in prayer. At the same time he was very practical and immediately released Allan from pastoral duties. A congregational prayer meeting was called for Allan and Betsy that night, and friends in the congregation made plans to help with child care and meals, so that Allan and Betsy could focus on what they had to deal with emotionally. Allan was to have an operation in just four days. There was an overwhelming response to the call to prayer that night. Prayers were urgent and expectant, including an earnest request that the Lord would "shrink the tumor." Everyone gathered around them and lifted their concerns up before God. This prayer meeting made God's presence even more real to Allan and Betsy, as though they had entered another sphere.

The surgery was an eight-hour ordeal. Early reports were hopeful, with no indication of lymph node involvement. Allan entered the slow process of recovery. It was hard to live through months of getting strength back after this "violent surgery."

By God's mercy, Betsy went into labor two weeks late, a full six weeks out from Allan's surgery. Gratefully, Allan then was able to stand upright and be a part of this awesome event. Together Betsy and Allan welcomed their daughter into this life. Allan felt like his life was starting again. He was able to reenter church activity a few months after surgery. There were periods of darkness during those months, where Allan felt like his supporters "forgot to pray that day," and then periods of enough strength to meet the day's challenges.

Early in the illness, Allan and Betsy held on to each other in many ways, and at the same time felt quite separate. Betsy could only follow Allan so far in facing his illness, and she had fears about her own and the children's future that could not be shared at that time. Allan was focusing on getting well with all the strength available.

Allan continued to follow up with doctors for his renal cancer. Each visit and scan would bring up fears about unwelcome findings, but they would press on with regular appointments. Following Allan's surgery, random aches and pains would raise anxiety, causing his mind to speed ahead to possible catastrophic diagnoses. For example, when he had visual disturbances due to a migraine, fears of brain metastases seized him. He had never before known physical fears.

Betsy's experience as wife, mother, and caregiver was different. Soon after Allan's severe diagnosis, both sets of parents traveled from out of town. Close friends sat Betsy down insisting, "You need to let people help you. This is a community life event. Just tell us what you need and we will organize it. "Eventually convinced, Betsy was willing to list her practical needs, such as bathing her children, washing hand-me-down baby clothes in anticipation of the delivery, yard work, and clearing the gutters. A care team was set up with friends and members of the congregation to address practical needs. Allan's father, who had much more hospital experience than Betsy, immediately offered to spend nights with his son in the hospital. Betsy's parents settled in a local hotel and took the lion's share of child care.

At least two incidents touched Betsy's heart in a special way: A friend had washed all the baby clothes and added new blankets, sleepers, and clothing for the new baby under the meticulously folded clothes. For Betsy, this was a very tangible experience that "God loves you." A man, whose son had found Christ through Allan's ministry, sent a generous check for "incidentals." This care reached deep into Betsy's soul, as it was both concrete and supernatural.

Betsy felt emotionally buoyed and carried in the early days, and met practical challenges with great strength. When Allan returned to more normal life again, about four months after surgery, she "crashed" for a short time, feeling unusually frightened. Friends, who could accept her in that state without trying to fix her, were precious and incredibly helpful.

As Allan and Betsy look back, they both are sure they never would want to live through this ordeal again. However, they bear witness that in the midst of this their faith grew much deeper. They now know without a doubt that "what they put their trust in, is true." Prepared well in their biblical understanding of suffering, there was never a negative correlation between their faith and this illness.

Allan and Betsy have felt much more equipped in pastoral ministry as a result of their experience. They are not afraid to walk into a room where someone just received bad news. Observers testify that Allan is a calm and reliable presence in these situations. For Betsy, the physical manifestations of God's presence and closeness were life changing and an almost tangible reality. It created in her a "peace that surpasses understanding." God's tangible presence through others in many small and loving acts assured her that there do not have to be words when entering pain and crisis with another. These situations are less about us and more about giving way for God to enter in.

Allan and Betsy are intensely grateful for the loving, prayerful, and practical support they received from their senior pastor, congregation, family, and friends. Members of the congregation would repeatedly thank them for accepting care. Truly, allowing others to support them in their time of need was critical. Living through this became a communal experience.

Allan reflects: "Most of us would like to have a life that is all joy and no suffering. I know I would. But the world is a broken place, and I am glad that doesn't take God by surprise. In fact, in Jesus Christ God enters the world in all its hurt and rebellion and suffers right along with us, not as some idealized human being, but as one who knows—really knows—our plight. The very good news is that God gets the last word, not our broken world. He lives; trusting in him, we will as well. I am grateful for that very real comfort."

Story 3
A Devastating Accident in Africa
Ann Hamel, Rwanda

On July 27, 1990, my husband Adrian, our three sons (ages 8, 6, and 3), and I were on our way home to Rwanda after having spent two weeks in Zimbabwe, Zambia, and Tanzania. Rwanda had been our home since 1982 when we moved there from Burundi to help with the building and development of the Adventist University of Central Africa. The university was built to serve French-speaking students from Africa and the Indian Ocean. Rwanda had been chosen as the country in which to build the university because, at that time, Rwanda was considered the most peaceful and stable country in French-speaking Africa. We moved there a short time after the president of Rwanda had donated land for the university.

As pioneers, there were challenges living the way we had to live, especially with a baby. Our oldest son was just eight months old when we moved there. We went to Africa when I was 21, right after I graduated from college. My husband had graduated the year before me. We were in our mid-20s at this time and we both had a passion for serving God. We loved the fact that we were a part of something bigger than us, that we were helping to build a university to educate men and women to carry the gospel of Jesus Christ to the far corners of Africa. We enjoyed being the first missionaries to actually live at the university site, with all the challenges that came with it.

We made the trip to Zimbabwe in 1990 with friends, both physicians, who also had three young children about the ages of our sons. On the last day of the trip we traveled much longer than we had the other days because we wanted to make it across the Rwanda-Tanzania border before it closed at sundown. When we stopped for our picnic lunch that day we could see the mountains of Rwanda ahead of us and we thanked God for our safe and enjoyable trip. As we crossed the Rwanda-Tanzania border that evening we looked forward to a shower and a comfortable bed to sleep in that night.

My next memory is awakening in a hospital bed in Brussels, Belgium, not knowing where I was or how I'd gotten there. As I gazed at the huge, jagged wounds on my legs I didn't realize they were my legs. I learned from the friend who had traveled with us that our family had had a head-on collision with a truck shortly after crossing the border. My husband had been killed instantly and had already been buried in Rwanda. My three-year old son was four floors above me in the pediatric unit. His skull was fractured, his leg was crushed, and two toes were missing. My six-year old and eight-year old sons were still in Rwanda. They had been the only family members at their father's funeral.

As the reality of what happened sank in I was overwhelmed. All of my life I had seen God as my heavenly Father. I willingly left the comfort and security of life in America to serve God in Africa but I trusted him to take care of me and my family. As I grappled with what had happened, I regretted that any of us had survived this horrible accident. Death seemed preferable to the life that I had before me. My pain was so intense that I only thought of how to escape it. I looked at the IV drip and asked our physician friend to put something in there that would end my life. I didn't want to face a future without my husband and without God.

Prior to this I did not believe that a Christian would ever become suicidal. I believed that trust in Christ would be adequate protection against that level of despair. What I didn't realize was the potential for pain to block one's awareness of the presence of God. In my mind I imagined God looking down from heaven with love and care all of my life, then turning his face from me as our car went around that corner to face an oncoming truck. The conditions of my life, at this time, screamed that God was not there. Or if he was he didn't care. What I realize now is that my theology of suffering was inadequate for the crisis I was facing. The two weeks that I spent in Belgium were the two most difficult weeks of my life. Yet God had not abandoned me. He was there and he came to me in many ways through many people.

This accident has had a defining impact on my life. While it challenged my relationship with God more than anything ever has, it has also deepened my relationship with him in a way that nothing else could have. The spiritual crisis I was in was every bit as serious and debilitating as the emotional crisis. There was so much to grieve. Multiple losses complicate the grieving process. The greatest loss was definitely the death of my husband and best friend, the father of my children. In losing him I also lost my identity as a missionary, my home and the life we'd built together in Rwanda. Being a missionary was the only life I'd known since graduating from college. It was a life that I believed God had created me for. I lost the social support system in the community of fellow missionaries that we had there. I lost the sense of worth that comes with being a part of something bigger than we were. I also lost the childlike trust that I had in God as my heavenly Father. I was now faced with the task of developing a trust that could sustain me as I faced new challenges.

The challenges ahead of me were huge but there were many things that helped as I faced them. The support structure within our church provided the practical support that I needed both medically in the aftermath of the accident, and financially as I began the process of rebuilding my life. Equally important, however, was the emotional support I received by being a part of the family of God. While the circumstances of my life screamed that God was not there, God became visible and revealed Himself to me through many people. Over and over again in the weeks and months after our accident people, often strangers, revealed the love of Jesus to me through their acts of kindness and support. I also began to see a Christian counselor to help me work through the pain of the multiple losses I had to face.

Recovery physically, emotionally, and spiritually was slow. By the time I had recovered enough physically to go back to Rwanda to see my husband's grave for the first time, war had broken out there. It was a whole year after our accident before the country was stable enough for us to return. Going back and saying good-bye to our life there and to the people that we loved so dearly was an essential step in enabling me to begin the long and often painful process of rebuilding my life. When we returned to the United States after our pilgrimage back to Rwanda I enrolled in the PhD program in Counseling Psychology at Andrews University in Berrien Springs, Michigan. Grieving the losses I'd sustained and finding new meaning for my life were both crucial aspects of healing.

Over the next three years the war in Rwanda continued. Then on April 6, 1994, the news came that President Juneval Habyarimana's plane had been shot down. The news of his death sparked a violent reaction and the people of Rwanda reacted in a way that most never imagined possible. I grieved for the people of Rwanda. They were my people, both tribes. I had known them as a kind and gentle people and my heart was linked to theirs. What was happening in Rwanda affected me deeply. As the genocide spread to our campus the missionaries were evacuated and our school was lost. We had been the first missionaries to move onto that campus. Our youngest son had been the only missionary child born there and my husband the only missionary buried there. The pain and suffering I had experienced was not only mirrored but multiplied in the genocide that swept through the country. Many in Rwanda also felt that God had abandoned them.

Fortunately we serve a God who heals. While I pursued my studies and sought healing and wholeness in my life, God brought a wonderful man to me and my sons. Five years after our accident Loren asked me to marry him and we blended our seven children into one family. Recently we went back to Rwanda as a family, the first time we'd been back since we were there a year after the accident. God is also bringing healing to Rwanda. As missionaries, we are often asked to participate in the suffering of the people we are serving. Part of the good news that we are privileged to share is that we serve a God who heals.

Story 4
Losing Loved Ones
Jerry Sittser, U.S.A.

My story of loss is simple enough, but the consequences are not. In 1991 our family was driving home from a powwow at the Coeur d'Alene Indian reservation in rural Idaho. In our minivan were my wife Lynda, my mother Grace, who was visiting us for the weekend, our four children (Catherine, 8, David, 7, Diana Jane, 4, and John, 2), and I. A speeding car, driven, we found out later, by a man who was too inebriated to drive responsibly, jumped his lane on a lonely stretch of highway in rural Idaho and crashed head-on into our minivan. My mother, my wife, and Diana Jane died almost immediately (as did the driver's wife and unborn child). My youngest, John, was seriously injured but has since recovered; Catherine, David, and I sustained only minor injuries. The line between living and dead was frighteningly straight and sharp and clear, like the cut of a scalpel.

That was twenty years ago. Still, two memories remain vivid, as if I am still at the scene. I doubt whether they will ever fade. The first is the gruesome sights and sounds and smells of the accident. I still see broken glass and broken bodies; I still hear the sound of crunching metal and blaring sirens; I still smell the violence of it all. My instinctual response was to get the kids out of the driver's seat door, the only one that would open. I quickly surveyed the damage, took pulses, did mouth-to-mouth, and cried out for help. I still feel these memories as blows. I shudder and shiver when they come to mind, which is often. My choice over the years was between staring the memories down or going insane.

The other memory is the silence of the emergency vehicle. A witness must have called the police, for eventually many police cars and emergency vehicles arrived on the scene. About an hour after the accident my three surviving children and I were loaded into an ambulance and driven to the nearest large hospital, which was some 45 miles away. During that hour all was silent, silent like an empty cathedral, silent with the gravity of the tragedy, silent though my children whimpered softly. The silence allowed me to think, my brain becoming a bastion of rationality. I looked into the jaws of the crash, baring its teeth at me, and saw that I had only two options. Either I could allow it to set a trajectory of pain for us that would probably never end, or I could face it squarely and say, in effect, "Enough! The bleeding stops right here and right now." Between fight and flight, I chose the former. It is the closest I have ever come, I think, to the kind of ferocious love and determination that must sweep over a woman when she gives birth.

How can I explain this strange juxtaposition of emotion and calm rationality? It has never left me, not entirely. The accident transformed me into an intensively emotional and an intensively rational person. I am emotional because it cut so deep and inflicted so much pain, rational because it cleared my mind of clutter, forced me to think about what I believe is true, and challenged me to give myself to the things that matter most in life. These two capacities of the soul—emotion and rationality—can work in harmony. Here is what I mean.

First, emotion. Surprisingly, what tormented my soul the most was bewilderment. I felt like a person who hears a familiar language but for some reason can't understand a word of it, as if letters, words, and accents are all scrambled. The accident didn't make any sense to me. I cocked my head, furrowed my brow, and looked with puzzlement, thinking, "What just happened here? I don't get it." Other emotions surfaced, too, but none quite as powerful as bewilderment.

My friends were wise enough to listen to my feelings without needing to mollify them or push them aside, though I am sure they were tempted to. They realized that emotions like anger, sorrow, fear, and confusion are simply there, as natural to the human condition as hunger, thirst, or fatigue. I was not the first person in history to feel such strong emotion, nor was I going to be the last. The Bible itself acknowledges emotions as valid; the psalms give voice—in prayer, no less—not only to wonder and joy but also to grief, frustration, anger, and helplessness. The Bible does not avoid feelings. Emotion is channeled toward God, assuming that God is great enough to absorb it.

My emotions demanded my attention; they could not—and would not—be denied. I had to face them squarely, plunge into the darkness, and work them through. Friends helped; time helped. Time doesn't and can't heal all things, but time provides a space in which healing can happen. It took a long time and a lot of time to absorb these strong emotions into my life as they became a more familiar and natural part of the landscape. They have never left me entirely. But emotions certainly feel different now, less intrusive, invasive, and brutal. They have become my friends more than my enemies.

Second, rationality. Loss is not simply an emotional experience. It is also intellectual; forcing us to think about what is true, right, and real. Everyone believes something in the face of loss. One might decide to deny the existence of God and conclude that life is utterly meaningless and random. But that, too, is a rational response to the problem of suffering. I did not turn away from or blame God after the accident. Instead, I questioned everything. What makes the best sense out of life? That God exists, or that God doesn't exist? That there is a universal morality, or that there is none? That God is in control, or that life itself is random? It strikes me as dishonest and irresponsible to put only God on trial after an experience of suffering. We should entertain and examine all the big questions of life. Over time I returned to the Christian faith with renewed appreciation and confidence, because it provided the best answers to the deepest questions imposed on me.

There is danger in the extremes of heartless head or headless heart. What happened touched the raw nerve of my emotions, and also put my beliefs into question. Neither capacity of the soul, emotions or rational inquiry, can exist without the other if we wish to remain human. In the years following the trauma, I became a more emotional person as well as a more thoughtful person.

My perspective now is to see the accident not as an isolated event but as a chapter in a larger story. Much has happened since then. Three years ago Catherine married and moved to Bogotá, Columbia, serving as a missionary with her husband. She now lives in Portland, where she teaches. Last year I was remarried to an old friend, Patricia. This spring David graduated from Duke Divinity School and John from Seattle Pacific University. They are all thriving, and so am I. The accident is now part of a larger landscape of memory and meaning that is rich beyond measure. The scar, however deep and severe, has become a mark of grace. Why it occurred still eludes my understanding, and probably always will. But what has come as a result is palpably clear, and for that I thank God every day.

Story 5
Robbery and Betrayal
Dan Crum, Kenya

Connie and I served as career missionaries in Kenya, working with the Maasai people since 1988. In August, 1997, we and our three young children had just returned from a home assignment. We anticipated a full term in the bush, ministry growth, and close family connection.

Our world was turned upside down one dark night in September, when a gang of three to five men armed with machetes and clubs broke into our home in the bush and spent ten minutes robbing us of $1500 before they ran off. I was hit on my arm with a club, causing a deep gash, which later required stitches. Connie screamed when I was hit. I was marched around the house to lead the thieves to our money. I kept my eyes down because if I could recognize any of them, and if they knew it, they might kill me. Connie was threatened with a machete in the hall on her way to get all the kids in one place. The kids heard and saw everything. It was a horrible experience.

We left at daybreak to get medical attention. After ten days in Nairobi, where we received medical attention and bought new locks, we returned to the village. I wanted to talk to church leaders to let them know we were OK.

By now, people were also talking about the robbery and wondering how to catch the thieves.

When we pulled up to the house, there were a handful of people there to give their sympathies and see how we were doing. I sat and visited with a few church leaders and our neighbor about the robbery. The church leaders were understanding, sympathetic, and very upset for us. They were obviously concerned for our welfare and were there to show love and support. None of them seemed to know who might have done this.

Our neighbor was convinced he knew whom to blame: a jealous leader from another clan. Rather than being concerned about our welfare, this neighbor began to focus on how we could continue to meet his own needs and contribute to his status. I was shocked that someone we had known and trusted was using me to compete with another clan. As long as this jealousy and competition existed, our lives would be in continual danger. I was angry, deeply upset, and suddenly felt unprotected at the obvious lack of care for my family, and knew I would have to make a move immediately. My wife's anguish was intense over losing her home and the community she had come to know and love in deep Maasailand. She screamed in frustration and shouted, "Don't these men know how awful they make it for everybody here?" We left shortly thereafter in total uncertainty, from double crisis of robbery and betrayal.

We spent the next few days at a teammate's house, numb and in shock trying to comprehend what all this meant. We had lost our home (the only one we ever built for ourselves), our ministry, our innocence, our Maasai friends, and more.

Over the next two months our lives became topsy-turvy. We didn't know where home was anymore. We wanted justice, but none was coming. This was the darkest time for us on the field. We moved into Nairobi and changed ministry focus. We couldn't just "get over it." Our temporary housing was close to a counseling center where we processed our trauma. Our team was inexperienced at helping anyone through a crisis like this. They were helpful the first month, but we were mostly left to ourselves after that. They gave us time to pray and ponder our future. Many expected us to "get over it" quickly and move on. All of us were fragile, each dealing with our own issues in our own time frame. Later, as we processed this more, we realized we felt hurt and angry that our team had not cared for us more. Trust in nationals (not one another, thankfully) took a while to rebuild, and we finally chose who seemed most likely to be worthy of our trust and started there.

Several factors helped us initially through this sudden shift. One was finding a house in Nairobi available for three months. We had regular beds again, and a kitchen for cooking. The second was keeping up a routine for homeschool. Connie and a volunteer continued the kids' education. The third was ongoing counseling that walked us through our feelings and processing. Fourth, I went a couple of times to meet with the church leaders to encourage them. This provided a sense of normalcy to us.

I never complained to God about this event, as God laid on my heart a few days afterward that he was with us the whole time and saw everything. "I saw them hit your arm, and I cried for you." "I saw them threaten your wife, which penetrated my heart, too." Knowing that God was present and full of compassion for my family was a source of healing.

Still, we struggled. Facing the possibility of being killed during the armed robbery really shook me up. When I realized the neighbor's betrayal, I fully understood the threat our lives had been under that night. It was hard to trust. Who really knew what had happened and who was watching us? Flashlights triggered emotions in us. An electric company repair truck showed up in the driveway in Nairobi at two o'clock in the morning when I was away. Connie and the kids all got into the same room, frightened at dark figures arriving unannounced in the middle of the night.

It was hard to make decisions. We prayed about future ministry options, still not feeling safe to return to the bush. Our healing gradually progressed as we came in contact with other missionaries who had experienced a similar crisis. They knew how we felt, and could practically speak the words we were thinking. Those who expressed concern and empathy were a divine comfort for us. If we had asked to "go home" to the U.S.A., we would have received a lot of sympathy from family and friends. But Connie and I both felt that processing this event on the field was a better way to go, since people there were more likely to understand and to help us through the healing needed. It was hard to do, but God gave us strength to stay.

Another factor in my healing was the process of giving up my desire for justice, and forgiving those who had harmed me and my family. Several months after the event, I realized the thieves still had a hold on me because of my drive for them to be caught. A friend at church told me, "The problem with thieves is that they are always out of money and on the run." I laughed. Somehow, that helped me realize I could move on, free from seeking justice in order to quell my anger, because the thieves were still trapped in their own evil schemes. That was a form of justice to me, and I felt free to stop focusing on them. What a release! Although I felt I needed to end the relationship with the neighbor who betrayed me, I was able to continue to trust the Christian Maasai leaders who never wavered in their support and encouragement.

God also worked on my heart to help me realize that traumatic events are not easily fixed and healing takes time. Before then, I thought that Christians could, and should, be able to overcome their challenges and setbacks through prayer, Bible-reading, and a little bit of time. Having grown up in a safe environment and community at home, and having never experienced a crisis or trauma, this was the simple perspective I had. "Get over it," sums up how I felt. The months of processing taught me to accept and not judge other people who have been through trauma. So now I tell them, "Take your time," instead of "get over it." I've also learned that leaders must have patience as people process trauma because God is in no hurry.

Despite the horror of the robbery, the terrible betrayal of one we trusted, and all our resulting losses, the Lord used this event for good. We were forced into a relocation and new ministry that turned out much to our advantage. The churches we worked with are now 14 with well over 1,000 believers, and still growing. A number of years later, the Lord led us into a ministry of caring for traumatized missionaries. With the compassion we received from him, we are able to give compassion to others.

CHAPTER III
RESOURCES FOR EFFECTIVE SUPPORT

SECTION 1
Normal Reactions After Trauma
Karen Carr

A. Definitions

The terms trauma and crisis are often used interchangeably. An event is defined as traumatic by the scientific community if there was real or threatened loss of life or physical harm, either personally experienced or witnessed (American Psychiatric Association, 2000). The impact of the traumatic event on the person is called psychological trauma. Defining what "qualifies" as a crisis is difficult because of differences in the subjective experience of pain. Crisis has been defined as "a temporary state of upset and disorganization, characterized chiefly by an individual's inability to cope with a particular situation using customary methods of problem solving, and by the potential for a radically positive or negative outcome" (Slaikeu, 1990, 15). So, a trauma is a subset of a crisis.

The word crisis is also used to describe the internal reaction to an event. People will say, "I had a crisis" as well as "I am in crisis." When someone is in crisis, it means that something terrible happened and that the ability to cope with it goes beyond the normal ability to cope and recover. In that sense, what is a crisis to one person may be routine for another. I remember one time sitting with a missionary who described her experience of the beginning of the genocide in Rwanda. She heard the sound of a huge explosion and wrote back to her family in the U.S, "That was no every day, common, ordinary grenade." Her family wrote back, "What do you mean *every day, ordinary, common* grenade?" She had become so accustomed to grenade sounds around her that they did not induce a fear response. But, this louder explosion, which turned out to be the president's plane being shot down, caused her to feel strong reactions of fear.

B. Incidence and Types of Trauma

Crisis and trauma are inevitable for most human beings. As men and women of faith, we are told to expect suffering. "Dear friends, do not be surprised at the painful trial you are suffering, as though something strange were happening to you" (I Peter 4:12, NIV). But, we are surprised when terrible things happen. We don't expect it and our initial reaction is disbelief and denial as if to say, "This isn't possible. It can't be true because it isn't right and it doesn't fit my perception of what is just and good." Some may even feel that people, who dedicate their lives to full-time Christian service, should be more protected by God and miraculously escape experiences of violence. This is exactly the theology of Job's friends. *If you are living a pure and holy life, you will not suffer* is the inherent theology of suffering in Bildad's comment, "...if you are pure and live with integrity, he (God) will surely rise up and restore your happy home" (Job 8:6, NLT).

The results of a 2005 study comparing frequency of trauma among missionaries with that of the U.S. population defy this false belief. The study found that missionaries in West Africa and Europe had encountered more severe trauma than the general U.S. population. Missionaries in West Africa experienced significantly more trauma than missionaries in Europe and those in Europe experienced significantly more trauma than the general U.S. population. In West Africa, 92% of the male and 85% of the female missionaries reported one or more severe traumas in their life. In Europe, 82% of male and 73% of female missionaries reported one or more severe traumas. In comparison, in a sample of the general population of the U.S., 61% of men and 51% of women reported one or more severe traumas. The differences are even greater when comparing these three populations by who had experienced three or more severe traumas (table *Frequency of Trauma*).

FREQUENCY OF TRAUMA AMONG MISSIONARIES AND THE POPULATION OF THE USA		
Population	% men with 3 and more traumas	% women with 3 and more traumas
U.S. General Population*	10%	5%
Missionaries in Europe#	47%	30%
Missionaries in West Africa#	71%	64%

* Data according to National Comorbidity Survey (Kessler, 1995)
\# Missionary study results (Schaefer, 2007), N=250.

The most common traumas for the West Africa missionaries were serious illness (61%); car, train, or plane accidents (56%); unexpected death of family member or close friend (51%); immediate exposure to fighting, civil unrest, or war (48%); burglary (41%); serious threat or harm to family member or close friend (38%); seeing another person seriously injured or dying as a result of accident or violence (34%); and evacuation (31%). For missionaries from Europe, the most common traumas were car, train, or plane accidents (66%); unexpected death of a family member or close friend (54%); and burglary (38%).

C. Context of the Trauma

In order to understand a person's reaction to a trauma, we need to understand the context. Oftentimes if I ask my friend who is fluent in French the meaning of a particular French word, she will answer, "What's the context?" The word has so many possible meanings, that without understanding what came just before and just after it, she may give the wrong interpretation.

Understanding the context related to trauma means:

- **looking** at what was going on in the person's life before the trauma;
- **asking** about specific aspects of the trauma itself;
- **learning** how people have responded to the trauma victim which will

also give us some insights into the adequacy of the person's support system.

Pre-Trauma Factors

There are many events or conditions that might positively or negatively affect the impact of the trauma. These might include:

- Previous experience with personal crisis (can help or hinder)
- Pre-existing psychological disorder (depression, post-traumatic stress, anxiety disorder)
- Certain personality characteristics can be helpful, but can also increase risk of negative impact such as being detail oriented, liking to be noticed, high control needs, action oriented or risk taker, and needing to be needed.
- Tendency to oversimplify problems or underestimate realities
- Shame or guilt tendencies either related to culture or personal background
- Excessively independent (resisting help from others) or dependent (clingy)
- Destructive habits – overeating, smoking, drinking
- Access to support system – quality of relationships
- Medical condition
- Hormonal changes: adolescence, pregnancy, menopause
- Spiritual condition
- Level of energy or exhaustion, level of margin
- Parent-child or family issues
- Relationships to family in home country and supporters
- Recent experiences of loss or major change or transition
- Working theology of suffering
- Cultural and family norms regarding suffering and expression of pain

In my story of civil unrest and evacuation (Story 1), I said, "The first two years of MMCT's ministry was especially intense. In addition to the normal challenging components of ministry start-up and cross-cultural living, we were living in a very volatile country with increasing violence and civil unrest…I found myself increasingly impacted by grief because of the pain of counseling missionaries who had become part of my extended missionary family. In those first years, some of the missionaries I had come to know through trainings as well as social events suffered terrible crises such as the death of loved ones, armed robberies, kidnappings, beatings, and rape..." In this narrative are a number of relevant pre-trauma factors including *prior exposure to trauma, feelings of grief, and increased stress.* Because I know the personal experience of this person quite intimately, I can also reveal other relevant pre-trauma factors which included a *crumbling theology of suffering, a personal desire to control things that cannot be controlled, and an increasing sense of anger and injustice.*

Looking back at the stories told in the beginning of this book, we can draw out relevant pre-trauma factors, both positive and negative, that have an impact on the authors' reaction to the crisis itself. Dan Crum's (Story 5) family had just returned from home assignment so they were in a *time of transition.* Allan and Betsy's (Story 2) marriage had been built on a solid foundation and was a strong source of *emotional support,* as was the close community they had around them. Ann (Story 3) describes pre-trauma experiences of a *coup, travel stresses, and ministry satisfaction.*

As we enter into the role of helping someone who has been traumatized, it will be helpful to listen for pre-trauma factors relevant for that person. We might also draw them out by asking questions such as, "What significant things were going on in your life just prior to this event?" We may be tempted to only listen for the negative and stressful events, but knowing a person's pre-trauma strengths and resources (relational, emotional, and spiritual) will also inform us about what might be most helpful in their healing process.

Nature of the Traumatic Event

There are many aspects of the traumatic event that can influence the severity of the emotional reaction to it as well as the significance of the event. For example:

Was it...
- Nonviolent or violent
- Human induced or natural
- Intentional or accidental
- Preventable or non-preventable

Was there...
- Involvement of child victims
- Lack of warning
- Proximity to the event and some degree of personal danger
- Severity and duration of event

How much...
- Role and responsibility of the person at the event (leader, parent, dorm parent)
- Personal blame/fault
- Personal identification with victim(s)

What is the...
- Meaning of the event
- Long-term effect (e.g., rape results in pregnancy; accident causes limb loss)

What was the...
- Degree of uncertainty during the event
- Frequency of the event
- Behavior of any others involved in the crisis with them
- Response of others during and since the event (e.g., response of neighbors, colleagues, leaders, member care, friends and family back home)

A closer look at Jerry's story (Story 4) helps to understand the severity of the crisis by looking at each of the factors such as:

- **Violent** – people were killed and injured
- **Human induced** – the driver of the other car caused it
- **Accidental**
- **Preventable** – the other driver made a choice to get drunk
- **Involved child victims** – Jerry's own children
- **Lack of warning** – there was no time to react or prepare
- **Proximity to the event and degree of personal danger** – Jerry was in the car and was at risk for severe personal injury
- **Severity and duration of the event** – his mother, wife, and daughter were killed
- **Role and responsibility of person** – son, husband, and father; driver of the victims' car

- **Personal blame or fault** – none
- **Personal identification with victims** – very close
- **Meaning of the event** – questions about what he believed
- **Long-term effect** – permanent loss of loved ones
- **Degree of uncertainty during the event** – uncertainty about who would survive injuries
- **Frequency of event** – one time
- **Behavior of any others involved in crisis** – emergency workers, friends, family all supportive

This long list of critical aspects of Jerry's trauma can help to understand the many layers and levels of grief and loss that Jerry experienced in the days to come. Some of these categories are objective and measurable, such as the presence of child victims. Others are more subjective and can vary from person to person. For example, what level of personal blame is attributed to the event? If Jerry had been the one responsible for the accident, his recovery process may have looked very different as he would have been wrestling with his own guilt and shame as well as the judgment of others. In many cases, even when there is no actual fault on the part of the surviving victim, the person will feel guilt and shame.

Reaction of Others to the Traumatic Event

The response of others during and after the traumatic event is often very important in the victim's reaction. Jerry (Story 4) said, "My friends were wise enough to listen to my emotions without feeling the need to mollify them or push them aside, though I am sure they were tempted to, largely because they were so concerned about me." Dan Crum (Story 5) said, "I was angry, deeply upset, and suddenly felt unprotected at the obvious lack of care for my family." Dan and his wife also said, "Later, as we processed this more, we realized that we felt hurt and angry that our team had not cared for us more." I (Story 1) pointed out that, "One of the greatest comforts for us was daily, and sometimes even hourly, phone calls from our mission leadership assuring us of their efforts on our behalf."

A missionary was driving through an African village when a young person ran out into the road and was killed as the car struck him. Angry villagers began running towards the car and he had to flee to the police station or risk being dragged out of his car and beaten to death. Another missionary expressed his wonder and gratitude for people who came running to help after he had struck and killed a child on a remote African road and then crashed into a nearby ditch after his car flipped in his effort to miss hitting the child. If people feel that they are cared for and protected by those at the scene of the trauma, it can mitigate the harmful impact.

Likewise, the behaviors and words of friends, family, leaders, co-workers, and strangers after the event can serve as salt in the wound or healing balm. As Job pours out the agony of his suffering in the presence of his friends, Bildad replies, "How long will you go on like this? You sound like a blustering wind" (Job 8:2, NLT). This remark has the impact of dragging Job into deeper despair, "Whatever happens, I will be found guilty. So what's the use of trying?" (Job 9:29, NLT). It is abiding presence, loving listening, and timely words that bring the healing presence of Christ to the sufferer. "The Sovereign Lord has given me his words of wisdom, so that I know how to comfort the weary," says Isaiah 50:4 (NLT). Comfort is wisdom incarnate.

D. Our Whole Being Response (BASICS)

Karl Slaikeu (Slaikeu, 1990, 164-165) coined a helpful acronym (BASIC) to help tease out the various aspects of a whole system's response to a trauma. We at MMCT have added an S on the end for a category of Spiritual responses. For each of these areas, we will look at common trauma reactions for both children and adults. Giving victims a list of common reactions can help them to see that what they are experiencing is not unusual nor is it an indication that something is wrong with them (see Appendices 2. A-C). This simple reassurance can provide relief and comfort to those who may be feeling fearful or frustrated that they are not "just getting over it and moving on." Educating trauma victims about these normal reactions gives them opportunity to recognize and discuss the impact of the trauma, and also may help them to be more patient and gentle with themselves in the recovery process. When presenting the *Common Reactions* to an adult victim (Appendix 2. A), one might say something like this:

> Each person is unique in how they respond to a trauma, so your response may not be the same as another person who has gone through the same or a similar experience. Remember that it

takes time to heal. After you work through these reactions, you will come to a new place in your life characterized by deeper understanding, healthy conclusions, resilience, deeper trust, and an expanded worldview. You will be one who has suffered and yet thrived. Even after many of the memories are gone and you are feeling much better, there may still be things which "trigger" these symptoms and painful memories. If these symptoms become very intense and persist over a long period of time, or if you are noticing impairment in your ministry or relationships, you may want to consider talking with a counselor who specializes in trauma. This does not mean that you are crazy, only that you need some help.

The common reactions that children have to a trauma (Appendix 2. B) can be given to parents, teachers, or other caretakers to help them take part in the child's recovery. They can be counseled to normalize the reactions of children. It can also be reassuring for them to realize that their child is responding in a normal way to a traumatic event. Depending on the developmental level of the child, the list of normal reactions might be given directly to them with opportunity to ask questions or discuss their own reactions (Appendix 2. C).

Behavior of Adults

Typical adult post-trauma behaviors might be categorized into those that are avoidance related and those that are related to a state of heightened physiological arousal. The lingering effects of adrenaline and ongoing physiological responses to trauma reminders may lead one to be hyperactive or slowed down, easily startled, less productive, aimlessly wandering, and tearful. People may also find that they are losing or misplacing things. The pain of the trauma may be so great that some search for ways to escape the intensity. This might manifest in behaviors such as use of alcohol or drugs, becoming overly involved in work, trying to leave behind any reminders of the trauma (including a desire to move away), sudden lifestyle changes, and abandonment of fun activities. This drive to avoid pain can contribute to a reluctance to talk about what happened and a refusal of accepting help. The irony of this is that talking with a trusted and trained helper would contribute to healing, whereas avoidance only reinforces the power of the pain.

A leave-taking or avoidance based on a desire to escape pain is not the same as leaving a situation that continues to be dangerous. For example, the Crums' (Story 5) departure from the village and my departure from the city under siege (Story 1) were actions of survival and prudence. Ann's (Story 3) decision to leave her field of service was based on practical elements of her situation and an awareness of the impact that her needs and those of her children would have on the wider community. In contrast, someone may choose to leave behind their ministry and country of service following a traumatic incident because of a desire to escape any reminder of what has happened. Helpers can encourage trauma victims who have gotten to a safe place to work through some of the traumatic reactions before making major decisions such as relocation or termination of ministry.

Behavior of Children

The most common post-trauma behaviors of children are regressive. This includes things such as a return to thumb sucking, bedwetting, clinging, resumption of outgrown habits, and decline in school performance. Children, who have more limited verbal skills than adults, may act out the traumatic experience through repetitive play with violent themes. This is often an attempt to achieve more mastery or competence in the face of helplessness. The child will often act out situations of danger followed by some kind of rescue or reassurance. Because of less developed abilities to verbalize emotions, behaviors reflecting anger might include disobedience, running away, aggression, competition, and antisocial tendencies. Behaviors reflecting sadness can include apathy, withdrawal, interpersonal problems, and self-deprecation. Behaviors representing fear may include a lack of willingness to go to school or to be separated from the parents, sleeping with parents and refusing to sleep alone, asking for the light to be kept on at night, and a breakdown in the child's ability to cope with new stressful events.

Affect of Adults

What a range of emotions are possible after trauma! Some of the most typical emotional reactions to trauma are shock, anxiety, fear of recurrence, irritability, frustration, feeling overwhelmed, anger at oneself, others, and God, rage, sadness, depression, helplessness or inadequacy, guilt, and loss of sense of humor.

It is hard to define a distinct pattern since individuals are influenced by culture, gender, personality, and history. In the stories, the authors make reference to regret, despair, feeling abandoned by God (Ann's Story, 3); devastation, fears, feeling God's presence (Allan and Betsy's Story, 2); fears, anger, deep upset, anguish, feelings of betrayal, hurt (Crum's Story, 5); worry, peace, guilt, fear, helplessness (Karen's Story, 1); bewilderment, anger, sorrow, fear, and confusion (Jerry's Story, 4). The ones that seem to show up the most are fear, anger, and guilt.

In many ways, the emotional response to trauma is similar to the process of grief (Greeson, 1990, 68). This makes sense given that traumatic events always involve some kind of loss. It could be loss of life or friendship or role or sense of safety or trust or ministry.

Many illustrations of the grief process are linear in nature as shown in the *Grief-Loss-Cycle* (page 54). Westerners may be comforted by seeing a clear path that has a beginning and an end. For those from the Global South, an illustration that is less linear such as a path through various towns might feel more relevant. These types of illustrations can also be useful in helping the person to see that they must go through a kind of valley or death before experiencing the new life that comes with healing and recovery. In *The Pilgrim's Progress*, the main character, Christian, has to pass through *the valley of the shadow of death* before being allowed into the celestial city. He speaks of his experience in this way, "Then I entered into the Valley of the Shadow of Death and had no light for almost half the way through it. I thought I should have been killed there, over and over; but at last, day broke, and the sun rose, and I went through that which was behind with far more ease and quiet" (Bunyan, 1968, 73). Those who try to take a shortcut from the **initial impact of denial and shock** and go directly to the **celebration of new life** will eventually find that they are expending mental energy in trying to hold off, escape, or push back the anger, fear, or sadness that is a necessary part of the healing process.

In actual experience, the post-trauma emotional journey is not at all straightforward or linear. Often people will feel as though they are cycling back through and re-experiencing the same emotions. They may feel they are not making progress. One way to understand this is because a traumatic event has multiple losses with varying degrees of intensity and meaning, one may be in multiple places on the grief curve at once. Explaining this to someone and giving them opportunity to identify where they are in the grief process

54   TRAUMA & RESILIENCE

can be a great way of normalizing their emotional reaction. That helps to reduce some of the feelings of being overwhelmed and out of control.

GRIEF/LOSS CYCLE

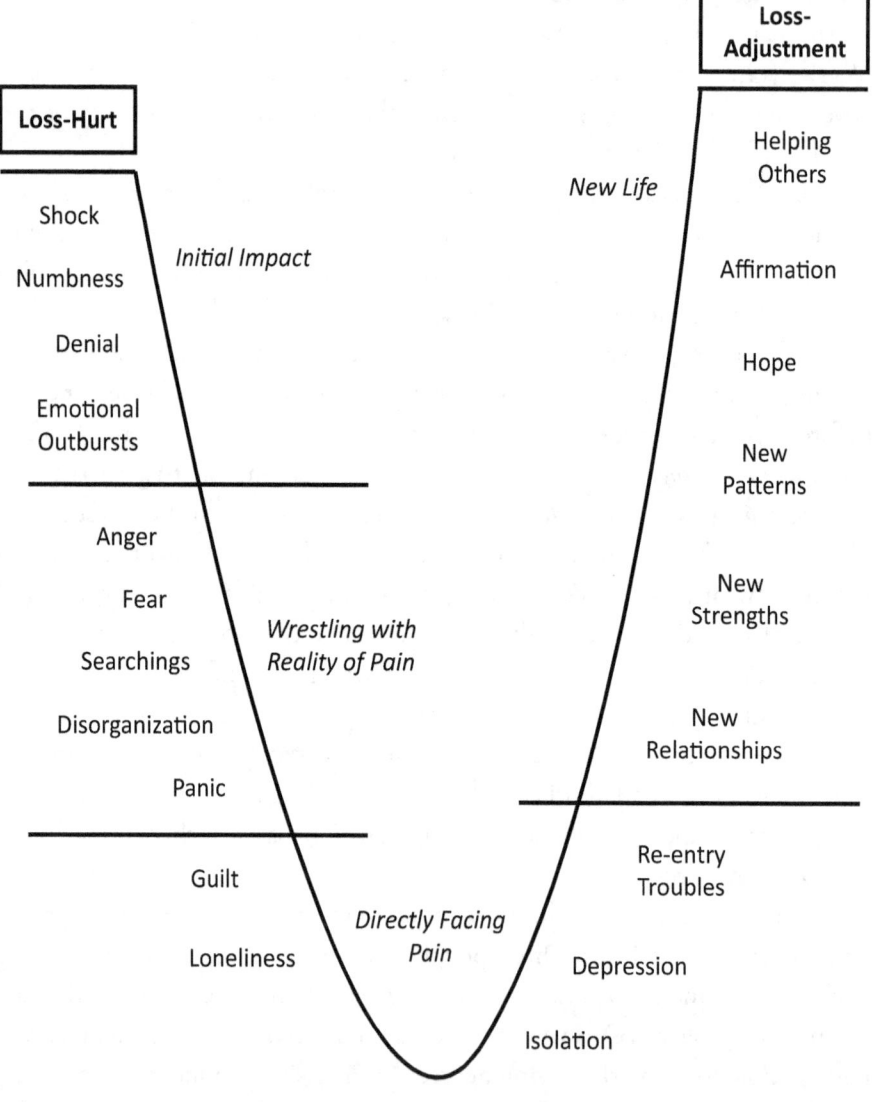

Charlotte Greeson, Mary Hollingsworth, and Michael Washburn
The Grief Adjustment Guide (Sisters, Oregon: Questar Publishers, Inc., 1990).

Affect of Children

Most of the emotions felt by adults are also felt by children, but may be manifested differently. Children do not have as many life experiences to compare the traumatic event with and so the task of processing and understanding the event is unknown, uncharted territory.

When children are feeling shocked and numb, they may act as if nothing has happened. Some children, upon receiving terrible news of the death of a family member, for example, may go outside and begin playing and laughing with their peers. This is the child's way of returning to something familiar, known, and comforting. This may lead adult caregivers to wrongly assume that the child has not been emotionally impacted. In *A World Lost,* Wendell Berry describes the feelings of his child protagonist whose favorite uncle has just been murdered. The child's initial reaction is to spend time playing with his age mates. Later he reflects, "And then the day seemed to collapse around me into what it had become. There was no place, where what had happened had not happened" (Berry, 1996, 18).

A missionary family was traveling to their home village by car when two gunmen drove in front of them and tried to wave them over. As the husband pushed the accelerator to the floor and sped from them, the wife saw one robber point his gun at the car and heard him shout, "I will kill you." Two young children were in the back seat of the car. Neither of them made any sound or said anything during or after the event. After they got to safety, the adults talked amongst themselves but not in earshot of the children. They were relieved that the children seemed to have missed the whole event. A few days later a trauma counselor met with the whole family. At the parents' request she spent some time with the five-year-old child to see if she had been impacted by the event. Was she even aware of what had happened as she had made no reference to it whatsoever? During play with the trauma counselor, using play-doh and toys, the child initiated themes of danger and fear followed by her own verbal reassurances of safety. After about 45 minutes of play and some open-ended questions, the child blurted out, "As we were traveling up here, some bad men pointed guns at us and Daddy drove fast and Mommy prayed." As she talked further, the details of her story made it clear that she was not just repeating something she had heard, but was describing something she had experienced. This gave opportunity for her parents to tell her the facts of what had happened and to reassure her of their care and protection.

Fears and anxieties are often expressed in nightmares, regressive behaviors, clinging, whining, and unwillingness to be separated from loved ones. They may become overly concerned about the safety of parents or develop generalized fears of things that may or may not have an apparent connection to the traumatic event.

Children are also prone to feelings of guilt. These guilt feelings can be caused by a developmental phenomenon of false attribution or an egocentric worldview. In other words, they may believe they did something to cause the event. For this reason, it can be helpful to ask the child, "Why do you think this happened?" in order to draw out any conclusions they have made about their own role. One child was traumatized by the death of her older brother. It came out later that the last thing she had said to him in the heat of sibling argument was, "I hope I never see you again." She therefore felt that she had caused his death, a feeling she concealed for a long time.

The emotions of sadness and depression may be expressed in apathy and withdrawal or sometimes as hostility or belligerence, particularly in teens.

Physical Reactions in Adults

Whenever someone is faced with danger, the brain is designed to respond in certain ways that maximize the person's ability to cope with the crisis. The primary parts of the brain activated during a crisis are the cortex (conscious, thinking part of brain), the limbic system (emotion modulating system which regulates feelings such as fear, pain, and joy), including the hypothalamus (regulates heart rate, body chemistry, immune system, and hormonal systems). Through these systems, there are six primary chemicals (adrenaline, cortisol, norepinephrine, serotonin, endorphins, and ACTH) released into the body and each has adaptive functions. While these chemicals help us to adapt, they can also have negative consequences, particularly if the situation is protracted or is not sufficiently resolved.

Adrenaline (epinephrine) raises physical and mental alertness. The results of higher adrenaline flow are increased heart rate, rapid breathing, tightening muscles, blood sugar increase, dilated pupils, blood flow increase to muscles and brain, decreased digestion, and increased elimination. These physical symptoms create a temporary imbalance that allows us to cope with an emergency. Long term elevated levels of adrenaline can result in anxiety, frustration, impatience, difficulty sleeping, irritability, fatigue, and body aches.

Higher levels of **cortisol** release more sugar into the blood which increases energy but over time decreases the immune response and can produce symptoms of burnout and depression.

Norepinephrine induces hyper-vigilance and enhances problem solving skills of the cortex. Attention increases.

Serotonin creates a calm, relaxed state. It helps to modulate the mood. Interestingly, many antidepressant medications are designed to increase or prolong the presence of serotonin in the brain.

Endorphins are nature's painkillers. They induce a short-term state of calm, relaxation, and feelings of well-being. This is why some people experience a sense of calm and well-being in the initial stages of a crisis. When the Lord gives us "peace that passes understanding" it may be that he is increasing the endorphins in our system!

ACTH reduces the immune system responses for short-term survival by increasing cortisol levels. Over the long term, this makes a person more susceptible to illness and disease.

In addition to the physical symptoms already mentioned, trauma victims may also have shortness of breath, chest pains, nausea or vomiting, muffled hearing, loss of coordination, grinding of teeth, weight change, insomnia, change in sexual functioning or desire, and missed menstrual cycles.

Physical Reactions in Children

Much of what has been said about somatic reactions in adults also applies to children, but it is worth noting that children may be more likely to feel their emotional pain in their body, since their verbal skills for releasing and expressing pain are less developed. Children who complain of chronic stomach aches, headaches, vague pain, or malaise may have unprocessed traumatic feelings. Other common somatic reactions in children would be loss of appetite, pale appearance, bowel or bladder problems, complaints about vision, sleep disturbance, and itching or skin rashes.

Interpersonal Reactions in Adults

A significant part of emotional reactions to trauma in adults can be feeling angry at oneself and others. Feeling vulnerable and sad can cause people to withdraw, affecting relationships at many levels. There are many negative interpersonal reactions typical for the post-traumatic response.

They certainly test the strength and capacity of a person's support system!

Some common reactions include irritability, insensitivity, loss of interest in others, isolating or distancing, insecurity, avoidance of intimacy, suspiciousness, discord or arguments, being critical of others, scapegoating, hypersensitivity, and compulsive talking. While some may engage in behaviors that create distance and isolation, others may become more clingy, dependent, or have fears of being alone. This can also create strain on existing relationships. For this reason, the stronger one's emotional support system prior to trauma, the better one's ability to navigate the tensions that can come from post-trauma relational challenges.

Interpersonal Reactions in Children

Likewise for children, one common interpersonal reaction to trauma is to become more withdrawn and isolated socially. Attachments to family members or primary caretakers may be marked by anxiety or hostility. Some children will become clingy and overly attached to adults. In the confusion of post traumatic reactions, a child needs help to engage constructively with caretakers and peers.

Teenagers often prefer to spend time with their peers because they will naturally gravitate to relationships where they feel most understood and able to process the event. Some adolescents who have been through severe trauma may be tempted to act "too old, too soon," which can lead to taking on responsibilities beyond their developmental abilities or potentially to sexual acting out.

Cognitive Reactions in Adults

Giving someone the opportunity to articulate trauma-related thoughts provides a crucial aspect of understanding the traumatic experience. What a person is thinking during and after a trauma can impact their response on every other level (behavioral, emotional, physical, interpersonal, and spiritual). What a person thinks *might* happen during a trauma can be even more traumatic than what actually happens. For example, in my story (Story 1) I described my thoughts when a mob was coming closer and closer. I imagined this mob breaking into our compound and murdering the Liberian refugees we were hiding. These thoughts created a strong fear reaction and became one of the worst experiences of the entire crisis.

It's important to understand a person's thoughts after trauma. Ann (Story 3) described having suicidal thoughts as the reality of her husband's death sank in and she felt completely overwhelmed. Thankfully she expressed these thoughts to a close friend who was able to give her perspective and support during this devastating time.

Victims of trauma often experience disbelief, horror, confusion, poor concentration, poor decision making abilities, trouble prioritizing, disorientation, poor memory, poor attention, and preoccupation with trauma memories. It is as if all the resources of the brain have been marshaled to try to categorize and make sense of what has happened. This explains why people may not remember things said to them in the hours and days following a trauma.

Thoughts may also be rigid and closed, leading the person to make certain judgments or assumptions not based on reality or total truth. People who have experienced traumatic loss may become cynical or negative in their thinking. They may make negative or critical judgments against themselves (e.g., "I am such a failure").

One of the most common forms of cognition after trauma is hindsight thinking. This is usually prefaced by words such as, "If only," "What if," "Why didn't," and "I should have." One way to understand this is that the brain is trying to work out how to undo what has happened. The traumatic event cannot be accepted as part of the person's understanding of what is right and acceptable. Therefore, the mind tries to figure out what might have been done to prevent the trauma. In some cases, there might have been human error involved, and an analysis of the event can lead the person to rightly judge himself or another as at fault. In this case, the very difficult and ongoing challenge will be to give grace when the fault was unintended and to give forgiveness even if the wrong was intentional.

But, in many cases the person may be fixated on a certain thing they or another did that didn't actually cause the event. As choices are reviewed, one may conclude that if he had not driven down that particular road or he had not had lunch before leaving or he had not left late that the accident would never have happened. In this case, it was not an error of judgment or a mistake that caused the trauma. Rather, the person is attributing the cause and blame to an action or a choice that would not have resulted in a traumatic event in most other circumstances. If the helper tries to convince the person that he is

Cognitive Reactions in Children

Children will also struggle with a shorter attention span and difficulties concentrating after a trauma. Teachers and caregivers may need to give allowances with school assignments and expectations.

As the child remembers and recounts the traumatic event, he or she may have confusion concerning the details, sequencing, and locations of events. If a death has been part of the trauma, younger children may not have the experience or understanding of the permanence of death and may misperceive that the person has just gone away but will return later. This is why it is very helpful for adults to give children a clear age appropriate narrative of what has happened and to answer any questions the child may have about the facts and meaning.

Spiritual Impact in Adults

What do we believe about suffering? What do we believe about God's role in preventing it or in protecting us or those we love? What do we believe about the world and what human beings are capable of? What do we believe about ourselves, our destiny, our future? What hopes and expectations do we have? Any of these beliefs can completely shatter in the moment of a crisis.

When Ann (Story 3) woke up from her coma, she reflected, "All of my life I had seen God as my heavenly Father. I willingly left the comfort and security of life in America to serve him in Africa but I trusted him to take care of me and my family...In my mind I imagined God looking down from heaven with love and care all my life then turning his face from me as our car went around that corner to face an oncoming truck. The conditions of my life, at this time, screamed that God was not there. Or if he was he didn't care."

Although some will experience miraculous interventions from the Lord, others will experience death, persecution, and tremendous loss. Hebrews 11: 4-35 gives spectacular examples of men and women of faith who "received what God had promised them" and "shut the mouths of lions, quenched the flames of fire, escaped death by the edge of the sword, and became strong in battle and put whole armies to flight." Then, without even a pause for breath, we hear about the other great men and women who "earned a good reputation because of their faith" and yet "none of them received all that God promised." These saints were tortured, jeered at, whipped, chained in prison, stoned, sawed in half, and killed with the sword, destitute, oppressed, and mistreated" (Hebrews 11:35-40).

Even though we know this intellectually, the heart cry of so many remains, "Why, God, did you allow this to happen?" Certain aspects of our beliefs, our faith, and our assumptions are shattered and the process of healing is a process of rebuilding new beliefs that stand on the shoulders of suffering.

The result of this journey of death to old beliefs and life to new ones has the potential to result in a deeper, stronger relationship with the Lord and an ability to let God be God rather than constructing him in our own image. Ann (Story 3) goes on to say, "While the circumstances of my life screamed that God was not there, God became visible and revealed Himself to me through many people. Over and over again in the weeks and months after our accident people, often strangers, revealed the love of Jesus to me through their acts of kindness and support."

After I was evacuated (Story 1) and had opportunity to reflect on my own beliefs about suffering and God's role, I came upon a startling Old Testament passage. Job comes to a statement of gospel belief in the midst of intense and unjust suffering:

> I know that my Redeemer (Defender) lives, and that in the end he will stand upon the earth. And after my skin has been destroyed, yet in my flesh I will see God; I myself will see him with my own eyes – I, and not another. How my heart yearns within me (Job 19:25-27, NIV).

In this moment, as I grappled with the injustice of perpetrators who had killed and raped and beaten innocent victims, I reflected on God as redeemer. There is the redemption he has already completed on the cross. There is present redemption that occurs when we are able to see the good that comes out of a bad situation. But, Job seems to be referring to a future redemption, as does Ann (Story 3). This is the redemption that will mean the end of evil and the doing away of sin. Jesus says,

> On the earth nations will be in anguish and perplexity at the roaring and tossing of the sea. Men will faint from terror, apprehensive of what is coming on the world, for the heavenly bodies will be shaken. At that time they will see the Son of Man coming in a cloud with power and great glory. When these things begin to take place, stand up and lift up your heads, because your redemption is drawing near.... Be careful, or your hearts will be weighed down with dissipation, drunkenness and the anxieties of life, and that day will close on you unexpectedly like a trap. For it will come upon all those who live on the face of the whole earth. Be always on the watch, and pray that you may be able to escape all that is about to happen, and that you may be able to stand before the Son of Man (Luke 21:25-28; 34-36, NIV).

Jerry (Story 4) describes his belief reconstruction as much broader than God's role in the trauma. He puts it this way, "I did not turn away from or blame God after the accident. Instead, I questioned everything. What makes the best sense out of life? That God exists, or that God doesn't exist? That there is a universal morality or that there is none? That God is in control, or that life itself is random? It strikes me as dishonest and irresponsible to put only God on trial after an experience of suffering. We should entertain and examine *all* the big questions of life. Over time I returned to the Christian faith with renewed appreciation and confidence, because it provided the best answers to my deepest questions imposed on me."

Depending on one's context of prior traumatic or belief shaping experiences, one may not suffer a shattering of belief in God. In fact, the person may have sensed the Lord's loving presence throughout the trauma and may feel closer to the Lord as a result. As Dan (Story 5) related, "...God laid on my heart a few days after the event that he was with us the whole time and saw everything. "I saw them hit your arm, and I cried for you" "I saw them threaten your wife, which penetrated my heart too." Knowing that God was present and full of compassion for my family was a source of healing."

Trauma has the capacity to shatter our beliefs. The rebuilding process is ultimately one of redemption and finding meaning and purpose in the suffering.

> *The very fire that blackens my horizons warms my soul.*
> *The darkness that oppresses my mind sharpens my vision.*

The flood that overwhelms my heart quenches my thirst.
The thorns that penetrate my flesh strengthen my spirit.
The grave that buries my desires deepens my devotion.
Man's failure to comprehend this intention of God is one of
   life's true calamities.
                              James Mean, *"A Tearful Celebration"*

Spiritual Impact in Children

Children also have a theology of suffering and a worldview that is deeply impacted by trauma. I was amazed when debriefing an eight year old missionary child whose father had been shot by armed robbers. When I asked her what this experience meant to her, she said, "I think that God is giving me an opportunity to trust him more deeply." Although she was a spiritually precocious child, we should not assume that children are not having deep and spiritually significant reflections about their traumatic events.

As mentioned earlier in the Emotions section, it is important to understand what meaning children are attributing to the event. Younger children may engage in "magical thinking" believing, for example, that their wishes and beliefs have caused something to happen. They may also use their imagination to fill in the blanks of their understanding. Children are often listening to what adults are saying about the event but may only pick up certain pieces of it. They will also make assumptions based on their observations of how adults are feeling and reacting.

Section 2 D will give more insights into how to help children as they wrestle through their understanding of the events and their post-traumatic spiritual reactions.

E. Recovery Process

Normal Progress

Yvonne Dolan (Dolan, 1998, 4-7) masterfully articulates the normal progress for someone who suffers to move from an identity of victim to that of survivor, and finally to a place of celebrating one's ability to thrive and to live an authentic life. She points out that many people assume that the final stage of trauma recovery happens when you move from being a victim to being a survivor. Her research and experience revealed that those who remained in the survivor stage were experiencing a low grade depression and general pessimism about life. But it is possible to move beyond this to something that allows one to experience genuine joy. The *Moving from Victim to Survivor to Celebrant* chart (pages 66-67) shows the flow from left to right of the normal healing process. There is a purpose and a task for each stage:

Victim stage: As you acknowledge that something terrible has happened to you, you begin to fulfill the **purpose** of the victim stage. In order to start the healing process, you must face the fact that a bad thing has happened and acknowledge the feelings related to this. The **task** of this stage is to find the courage to tell someone else what has happened to you, honestly and fairly assess what was your responsibility and what was not, and to let go of shame.

Survivor Stage: The **purpose** of the survivor stage is to understand that you have lived beyond the time at which the traumatic experience occurred. The **tasks** are to acknowledge and appreciate the strengths and resources that have allowed your survival and eventual well-being; and to forgive and be forgiven for any wrongdoing.

Celebrant Stage: What can someone who has been through a terrible trauma celebrate? Moving beyond being a survivor into a place of gratitude and joy opens the door for celebrating and embracing life in its fullness. Being a celebrant does not mean that one celebrates the suffering or the trauma itself although some may come to a place of being able to say they are grateful for the experience because of the character change it has produced. The purpose of the celebrant stage is to live a life characterized by fullness, joy, and authenticity. The **tasks** or challenges are to continue to take risks and choose life despite discomfort and unfamiliar territory; and to devote time and energy to positive, healthy choices.

Note that in many ways the movement from survivor to celebrant parallels the phenomenon of post-traumatic growth which is further explored in Section 6 on Spiritual Resources in Dealing with Trauma.

Marietta Jaeger is a woman whose daughter was kidnapped and murdered when her family was on a camping trip. In an ABC news article on January 6, 2006, she described her journey from victim to survivor to celebrant. At first she felt that she could kill the man who had done this to her daughter. Gradually she began a process of praying for him and forgiving him. Eventually when he called to torment her one year later, she asked him what she could do to help him. This question so disarmed him that he revealed his whereabouts, leading to his capture and arrest. After confessing to the murder he committed suicide. But, this did not give Marietta any joy. Rather, she grieved his death and went to visit the mother of her daughter's murderer in order to console her. Although it was a gradual and painful journey, Marietta seems to exemplify the meaning of the word celebrant.

Posttraumatic Complications: Post-Traumatic Stress Disorder (PTSD)

PTSD can occur in the weeks and months after someone experiences a traumatic event involving actual or threatened death or serious injury to self or others. If the person felt intense fear, helplessness, or horror during the trauma, the risk for PTSD is increased. Most people who experience trauma will recover without developing PTSD. The percentage of individuals that develop PTSD varies depending on the nature of the trauma.

Symptoms of PTSD include re-experiencing of the event, avoidance, and increased physiological arousal. Re-experiencing of the event occurs with vivid memories, flashbacks, intense distress when exposed to reminders or triggers, and physiological reactions to internal or external cues that symbolize the event. A flashback is a very intense and vivid memory of the traumatic event that gives the person the sensation that they are back in the traumatic event.

Those suffering from PTSD may feel numb and will persistently avoid thoughts, feelings, and conversations associated with the trauma as well as activities, places or people that bring back memories. They may be unable to recall aspects of the trauma, have less interest in significant activities, and feel detached. Symptoms of increased arousal include difficulty falling or staying asleep, irritability or outbursts of anger, difficulty concentrating, hypervigilance, and exaggerated startle response. Hypervigilance is a term used to describe a state of mind that is always anticipating and scanning the environment for danger. A person who is hypervigilant is always on high alert and ready to respond. Over time, of course, this would be exhausting and would also interfere with one's ability to focus on interactions with people.

PTSD at its roots is a fear-based disorder. Fear is a natural emotional reaction to dangerous or threatening situations, an adaptive response that alerts us to possible harm and prepares us to protect ourselves, either by

MOVING FROM VICTIM TO SURVIVOR TO CELEBRANT

Victim Behavior	Survivor Behavior	Celebrant Behavior
Self-pity limiting action Passive	Beginning to take control Beginning to thaw out or heal	Achieving mastery Active
Victim Affect (Emotions)	**Survivor Affect (Emotions)**	**Celebrant Affect (Emotions)**
Helpless Feel out of control Angry Numb, avoidance of feelings In pain as remember past Controlled by depression, anxiety, hatred, bitterness Shame, self-dislike	Sense of satisfaction re survival Beginning to feel strong Hope re resources/choices Feeling less intensely about painful memories Influenced by, not controlled by past Shame being resolved	Committed to move forward Planning for the future Sense of humor restored Feeling excitement about present and future Feeling strong Acquiring peace, happiness, renewal, optimism despite scars Free from shame
Victim Somatic	**Survivor Somatic**	**Celebrant Somatic**
Controlled by physical complaints Addictions, self-destructive	Getting stronger physically with few complaints Committed to physical health	Physically healthy and less focused on health problems Ordinary life interesting without "adrenaline fix"

MOVING FROM VICTIM TO SURVIVOR TO CELEBRANT
Continued

Victim Interpersonal	Survivor Interpersonal	Celebrant Interpersonal
Hoping to be rescued Secondary gains convince to remain in victim role	Recognition of one's potential to change and grow Relationships are returning to mutual and satisfying	Self-determined in context of healthy relationship Reaching out to others; feeling compassion Connecting with others in pain without a need to hide Feel a sense of wonder and awe with new relationships
Victim Cognitive	**Survivor Cognitive**	**Celebrant Cognitive**
Perception of lacking choices Thoughts focused on past Controlled by memories Sense of no future	Coping skills are working well Thoughts focused on present Beginning to integrate memories Mind open to new possibilities	Increase in creative coping Future and present more vivid than past
Victim Spiritual	**Survivor Spiritual**	**Celebrant Spiritual**
Identity as a victim Still living as if in the trauma Has not yet learned from experience; likely to repeat trauma	Triumph and victory over trauma Confronting the trauma Committed to healing and to trusting God	Finding meaning and delight in life Has grown from the trauma Committed to loving again Resilient

fleeing or fighting. Overwhelming stress or prolonged, intense, generalized, and maladaptive fears can lead to other anxiety disorders.

Posttraumatic Complications: Other Anxiety Reactions

It is interesting that "Be anxious for nothing" or "Fear not" are the most frequent commands in the Bible. This seems to reflect the Lord's understanding that many things in life can cause us to be anxious, that anxiety can cause us considerable harm, and that he has a way to free us from our distress. *Common Symptoms of Anxiety* are listed in a chart.

COMMON SYMPTOMS OF ANXIETY

- Feelings of apprehension
- Difficulties with concentration
- Feeling tense, jumpy
- Anticipating the worst
- Irritability
- Restlessness
- Feeling like one's mind has gone blank
- Watching for signs of danger
- Sweating
- Frequent urination or diarrhea
- Shortness of breath
- Tremors
- Muscle tension
- Headache
- Fatigue
- Insomnia
- Pounding heart

There are several types of *anxiety disorders* that can develop after overwhelming traumatic events. These include:

1. **Generalized Anxiety** is characterized by at least six months of persistent and excessive anxiety and worry. The symptoms are restlessness, fatigue, concentration problems, irritability, muscle tension, and sleep disturbance. It can occur in adults or children.

2. **Panic Attacks** are characterized by short periods of intense fear or discomfort during which the person experiences things such as rapid heartbeat, sweating, trembling, shortness of breath, feeling of choking, chest pain, nausea, dizziness, feelings of unreality, fear of losing control or going crazy, and fear of dying. This is infrequently seen in children.

3. **Separation Anxiety.** The child has excessive anxiety for at least four weeks concerning separation from the home or from parents or

caregivers. The child has persistent and excessive worry about losing attachment figures, reluctance or refusal to go to school, spend a night at friends, or do things that involve separation; it may have nightmares with themes of separation, or repeated complaints of physical symptoms such as stomach aches, headaches, nausea when separation is actual or anticipated.
4. **Specific Phobias**: Marked and persistent fear that is excessive or unreasonable, cued by the presence or anticipation of a specific object or situation (e.g., snakes, flying, seeing blood).

Posttraumatic Complications: Depression

Depressed feelings are a normal part of the traumatic response as well as the grieving process. But, if these feelings persist and intensify and cause one's world to become hopeless and small, it may have developed into a clinical depression that needs professional treatment. A person might become clinically depressed following trauma for a number of reasons. They may be vulnerable to depression because of family history or previous experience of depression. The nature of the trauma may have caused them to have unremitting chronic stress leading to a breakdown of normal coping mechanisms. A person can be struggling with ongoing unforgiveness and bitterness that can lead to depressive symptoms.

SYMPTOMS OF CLINICAL DEPRESSION

- Feeling depressed, sad, or empty
- Less interest or pleasure in activities
- Increase or decrease in weight and/or appetite
- Not able to sleep or sleeping a lot
- Feeling agitated and restless or very slowed down
- Fatigued or very low energy
- Feeling worthless or excessively guilty
- Inability to concentrate or make a decision
- Thinking about death or having suicidal thoughts with or without a plan

Depressed feelings after trauma are normal, but clinical depression is a mood disorder characterized by depressed mood or irritability most of the day for at least two weeks causing impairment in functioning. Typical *Symptoms of Clinical Depression* are compiled in the previous chart.

Depression in men sometimes goes undiagnosed because it can look more like anger than sadness. *Frequent Characteristics of Depression in Men* are summarized in a table below (Hart, 2001, 29).

FREQUENT CHARACTERISTICS OF DEPRESSION IN MEN

- Irritability
- Hostility/rage
- Short tempered
- Moodiness
- Venting of anger
- Acting out feelings more than verbally expressing them
- Refusing to talk
- Overreacting to life stresses (i.e., noise made by kids)
- Withdrawal from loved ones
- Avoidance of intimacy
- Silent treatment
- Escapist behavior (watching TV, alcohol abuse)
- Violence towards spouse
- Sexual addictions
- Workaholism
- Frequent job changes
- High risk activities (driving too fast, exposing self to danger)
- Physical symptoms – headaches, chronic pain, digestive problems

---

Depression in children often manifests differently than adult depression. Children do not have the same capacity as adults to articulate what they are feeling. Their depression may go unnoticed or attributed to misbehavior, unless parents, teachers, and counselors are aware of the frequent *Characteristics and Indicators of Childhood Depression* (refer to chart on the next page).

CHARACTERISTICS AND INDICATORS OF CHILDHOOD DEPRESSION

CHARACTERISTICS

- Feels sad or irritable
- Feels bored or uninterested in things
- Has trouble sleeping
- Is fatigued or has very low energy
- Feels no one loves him/her
- Thinks about death or wishes he/she were dead
- Feels like crying or cries more than usual
- Thinks that bad things happen because of him/her (guilt)
- Talks about facing problems and having no solutions (hopelessness)

INDICATORS

- Has behavior problems at school or home
- Has been diagnosed with Attention Deficit Disorder
- Has anxieties and fears
- Feels lonely
- Feels stupid or bad
- Has a drop in school grades
- Has problems with friendships

The good news is that depression is very treatable! It is important to get a thorough medical evaluation as well as psychological assessment when depressive symptoms are present for longer than two weeks. Depression is most effectively treated with a combination of medication and short-term psychotherapy. There are also spiritual strategies that can reduce depressive symptoms: prayer, scripture memorization, praise, and worship. Depression that strongly affects a person's functioning or is associated with suicidal thinking needs immediate professional attention including medication evaluation.

Posttraumatic Complications: Addictions

When the emotional pain of trauma is buried or suppressed, the natural healing process is prevented. Some will try to numb the intensity of the pain through behaviors that give temporary relief and a compelling sense of well-being. Once the momentary fix wears off and the pain re-emerges with increasing intensity, the drive to return to that solution can become addictive. This creates a new set of issues and often leads to decay of health, compromised spiritual and emotional well-being, and the deterioration of relationships. Trauma victims are vulnerable to substance addictions such as alcohol or drugs. Typically we think of drugs as illegal substances but addictive substances also include prescription drugs (e.g., anti-anxiety medications such as Valium, Ativan or painkillers such as Oxycodon or Percocet). Another type of addiction which may be precipitated by unresolved trauma or grief is internet pornography. This is becoming increasingly common among Christians including the missions population and is characterized by secrecy and shame. Self-mutilation or cutting can arise out of an inability to give verbal expression to pain and has an addictive component difficult to overcome without help.

Finally, eating disorders such as anorexia (self-starvation) or bulimia (binge eating and purging) are also connected to unresolved emotional pain. It is important for caregivers to be aware that addictions can develop months or years after trauma, and to approach symptoms with compassion as well as a firm resolve. Willpower alone is not sufficient for recovery from addictions. Layers of support are needed for the addict as well as the loved ones to help establish boundaries and a safe environment for working through the pain causing and stemming from the addiction.

SECTION 2
Effective Community Support
Karen Carr

The deep communal dynamic of the Trinity bears witness to how much God cares about relationship. We were not designed to cope with trauma alone. Rather, in and through relationships with God and each other, we are restored, refined, and shaped into God's image. Scripture verses appeal to the body of believers to love, bear with, support, and carry each other's burdens. Through loving, resilient community we sustain our witness, longevity in service, and well-being.

The author of Hebrews describes the suffering and faith of Christians who have gone before us, and then applies it to our own lives: "Therefore, since we are surrounded by such a huge cloud of witnesses to the life of faith..." The words that follow make a key connection. They tie the power of community to perseverance in this life of trials and suffering. "...let us strip off every weight that slows us down, especially the sin that so easily trips us up. And let us run with endurance the race God has set before us" (Hebrews 12:1-2, NLT).

The image that comes to mind is a marathon runner feeling the cramps of dehydration, muscle fatigue, and exhaustion from battling thoughts that beg him to lie down and quit. I remember seeing a video of Derek Redmond, a 1992 Olympic runner who was devastated by a severe hamstring injury during his final race. Years of training were to end in this way. A few moments later Derek's aging, portly father broke through security and ran to his son's side. He put his arms around him and spoke words of encouragement, "I'm here son. We'll finish together." The son lifted his face up in agony and sobs, but persevered onwards. With his dad's loving

> The power of community is the power of the Trinity and penetrates to the depths of our hearts, moving us to stay in the race despite tremendous pain, injury, and sacrifice.

arms around him, running alongside him, and an audience of thousands cheering, clapping, and crying with him, Derek made it across the finish line. Why do scenes like this move us so deeply? Why does writing these lines cause my tears to flow? Because, the power of community is the power of the Trinity and penetrates to the depths of our hearts, moving us to stay in the race despite tremendous pain, injury, and sacrifice. If this man had not had his father and the huge crowd of witnesses, he likely would have lain down on the asphalt and given up.

A. Training for Leaders and Peers

Research suggests that a key way of reducing posttraumatic stress even before the trauma is to engage in behaviors that enhance stress management and increase the quality of social supports. The level of social support as well as the perception of organizational support during and after a crisis affects one's coping ability and overall resilience (Forbes & Roger, 1999; Keane, Scott, Cavoya, Lamparski, & Fairbank, 1985). A specific goal of any crisis intervention or prevention program should be to improve and affirm one's support system. Training in development of interpersonal skills, conflict management, team building, crisis preparation, and stress management is an effective strategy for reducing posttraumatic stress and enhancing cross-cultural workers' ability to cope with the inevitable traumatic stressors in international settings. Coaching organizational leaders to provide support to trauma victims is one the unique roles trained caregivers have in international mission settings.

In a community-based approach of providing trauma care, peers, leaders, and mental health professionals work together to assist personnel in crisis, giving them the opportunity to talk about what they have been through and how it has affected them. This type of care is not imposed or required, but made available. As people express their concerns and receive support, they are encouraged to cope with trauma rather than using avoidance as a defense mechanism. Avoidance has been identified as an important risk factor in the development of PTSD. The Mobile Member Care Team (MMCT) has developed crisis response trainings for leaders and peers designed to build on natural caregiver abilities. These trainings contribute to more resilient mission communities. MMCT does this by focusing on the attitudes, beliefs, knowledge, and skills needed to provide effective care in traumatic situations.

B. Attitudes and Beliefs for Community Support

The attitudes and motivations of caregivers within a community are extremely important. Caregivers' core beliefs about suffering, pain, and healing impact the quality of care. Questions for caregivers to ask themselves before entering into helping relationships include:

- What are my motivations for helping this person?
- What are my attitudes and beliefs about pain?
- Can I sit with pain or do I have to fix it?
- Can I tolerate contradictions and unanswerable questions without speaking the obvious?
- Can I hear rage against God without taking offense?

Job's friends made an attempt at providing supportive community when they learned of Job's suffering. But, ultimately their belief systems did not allow them to bring the kind of support that nurtured emotional healing. Their responses (after 7 days of wonderful silence), were no comfort to Job.

They told him what he already knew intellectually, even as his heart was starved for words of truth that would bring some resolution. "Look, I have seen all this with my own eyes and heard it with my own ears, and now I understand. I know as much as you do. You are no better than I am" (Job 13:1-2, NLT). It can be helpful to remind sufferers of truths they may have forgotten or that may be dimmed by pain. An attitude of respect and humility that acknowledges the person's experience and understanding is better than speaking obvious words as though they were fresh insights.

Job's friends also felt that they needed to defend God, as they accused Job of being an unrepentant sinner and exhorted him. Confess and repent! As if this would produce an instant cure! Job replies, "As for you, you smear me with lies. As physicians you are worthless quacks. If only you could be silent! That's the wisest thing you could do...Are you defending God with lies? Do you make your dishonest arguments for his sake? Will you slant your testimony in his favor? Will you argue God's case for him?" (Job 13:4-8, NLT).

Walter Wangerin writes eloquently about words that pour forth from those in deep pain. He advises helpers with reflections on godly comfort. When those who are suffering are asking passionate questions, remember that these questions do not come from an "inquisitive mind but from a disappointed soul." Questions asked in anger often don't have answers because "they aren't questions, they are accusations." You can recognize when the griever is aiming their fury in the wrong direction and gently redirect them – encourage them to take it to the Lord. (Wangerin, 1992, 216-221).

> Remember that these questions do not come from an inquisitive mind but from a disappointed soul.

I once had a pastor for whom grace was elusive. He believed depression was essentially self-pity, and that the primary role of a pastor was to give that person "a good swift kick in the behind." God confirms Job's perception that his friends have not pleased God by misrepresenting him as a harsh, judging, punishing deity. God says to Eliphaz, "I am angry with you and your two friends, for you have not spoken accurately about me, as my servant Job has...My servant Job will pray for you, and I will accept his prayer on your behalf. I will not treat you as you deserve" (Job 42:7-8, NLT). What an interesting turn of events, the one in deepest pain spoke more accurately about God than the "comforters," and ended up interceding on behalf of his friends.

The book of Job doesn't speak to his friends' motivations for saying what they did. However, since cold comfort has been passed down through the generations, we can speculate... Being faced with helplessness and horrible suffering in someone can produce feelings of fear, powerlessness, and desire to escape. Words of judgment, accusation, and impatience can push the person further from us, so that we do not have to take the pain into our own hearts. Platitudes and solutions come from the illusion that logic and reasoning have the power to shortcut the long journey of grief. Here are some additional principles mentioned in *From Mourning into Dancing* (Wangerin, 1992) that offer insights into the attitudes of genuine, effective helpers:

- You are not expected to fix the mortal break but to companion the broken.
- Do not expect gratitude, meek obedience, rational behavior, or thanks; expect nothing for yourself.

- Know the grief process, but know the griever even more.
- Make peace with your own death and with death itself.
- Your presence is more important than any solutions you might propose; stay with them, abide.
- When they repeat themselves or tell the same story again, remember that there is healing in expression, and the point is not for you to learn something you hadn't known before.

In a proactive way, we can contribute to healthy communities that foster healing through an environment nurturing those who have experienced trauma. Jean Vanier writes about the power of genuinely Christian community (Vanier, 1989). Some *characteristics of healthy Christian communities* are summarized in a table on page 78. Communities that develop and nurture these elements will be a safe place for victims of trauma to recover and heal.

To help church or mission communities grow stronger, MMCT has found it helpful to ask missionaries to choose the top three elements done well within their community. This gives an opportunity to affirm what is being done well, while also noting areas needing growth and improvement. Celebrating strengths in a community increases its ability to weather inevitable storms.

C. Knowledge and Skills for Community Support

Crisis training ideally includes knowledge, skill building, logistical help, psychological first aid, crisis assessment, crisis debriefing, and help for children.

Logistical Support

When the Crums (Story 5) described what was most helpful in the aftermath of their violent robbery, the first thing mentioned was finding a house available in Nairobi. Ann (Story 3) wrote, "The support structure within our church provided the practical support that I needed both medically in the aftermath of the accident and financially as I began the process of rebuilding my life."

Practical and logistical help with finances, medical care, housing, meals, child care, future employment options, work continuity, paperwork and other tasks related to safety, security, routine, and normalcy, will all contribute to the healing process and communicate hearty care. These details must beattended to before the person will have mental and emotional energy to meaningfully process the trauma.

> **CHARACTERISTICS OF HEALTHY CHRISTIAN COMMUNITIES**
>
> 1. **Belonging** – a place to fit in, be accepted, and appreciated rather than feeling left out or rejected
> 2. **Openness** – able to be honest, candid, and genuinely share; welcoming towards new people
> 3. **Caring** – kind, thoughtful, gentle, considerate of those who have needs
> 4. **Cooperation** – bringing skills and resources together towards a common goal; teamwork
> 5. **Healing and Growth** – provide comfort to sad or distressed members; strengthen the struggling; develop each other's strengths and abilities
> 6. **Relationships With Friends and Enemies** – willing to be friends with the different; working towards reconciliation after mistreatment
> 7. **Forgiveness** – asking for forgiveness when another was hurt; forgiving when wronged
> 8. **Patience** – enduring and persevering when bothered in smaller ways, or when not getting one's own way; not complaining or speaking badly of others or the situation
> 9. **Mutual Trust** – relying on each other; relying on others just as they can rely on you, to do your best; understanding that each one is able to let others down; give grace when this happens
> 10. **Using Your Gifts** – contributing gifts and talents towards the good of the community; encouraging others in using their gifts

Sleep is often disturbed in the days and weeks following a trauma. Getting adequate, restful sleep may be very difficult. Victims may feel physically exhausted, yet too restless or anxious to surrender to sleep. Good sleep hygiene tips are good practical help. A physician may need to advise regarding the appropriateness of sleep aid medication. Although many prescription medications are available in developing countries over the counter, people should be discouraged from self-medicating to numb emotions. Keeping paper and pen near the bed allows a person to write down thoughts keeping him or her awake. Deep diaphragmatic breathing and progressive muscle relaxation contribute to physiological relaxation and reduce tension. Regular exercise, early in the day or a few hours before bedtime, can help release pent-up tensions and improve sleep. Hot baths and moist heat on the neck or other tense areas will reduce general muscle tension.

Psychological First Aid

Psychological First Aid (PFA) describes a series of responses recommended for caregivers to provide to those experiencing trauma (The National Child Traumatic Stress Network and National Center for PTSD, 2006). Psychological First Aid gives guidelines for anyone who provides crisis response. The basic objectives of PFA are:

- Establish a human connection in a nonintrusive, compassionate manner.
- Enhance immediate and ongoing safety, and provide physical and emotional comfort.
- Calm and orient emotionally overwhelmed or distraught survivors.
- Help survivors to tell you specifically what their immediate needs and concerns are, and gather additional information as appropriate.
- Offer practical assistance and information to help survivors address their immediate needs and concerns.
- Connect survivors as soon as possible to social support networks, including family members, friends, neighbors, and community aid resources.
- Support adaptive coping, acknowledge coping efforts and strengths, and empower survivors; encourage adults, children, and families to take an active role in their recovery.
- Provide information that may help survivors cope effectively with the psychological impact of disasters.
- Be clear about your availability and (when appropriate) link the

survivor to another member of a disaster response team or to local recovery systems, mental health services, public sector services, and organizations.

Crisis Assessment

Assessment skills (observing and recognizing the behavioral, affective, somatic, interpersonal, cognitive, and spiritual (BASICS) responses of a trauma victim will equip the helper to ascertain how the victim is doing and what further supports he or she needs. Assessing a person's risk for complications following trauma is an essential element of crisis intervention. See Section 1 D for more details of the BASICS assessment.

Critical Incident Stress Debriefing (CISD)

Critical Incident Stress Debriefing (CISD) is a structured way for lay caregivers to support trauma survivors. It has been used for years with firefighters, police officers, rescue workers, and missionaries continually exposed to traumatic events, as a method of helping people to process the impact of an event and receive additional social support. CISD is most commonly associated with the Mitchell model (Mitchell, 1983). This model is a structured process led by trained facilitators (not exclusively mental health professionals) that can be offered soon after a psychologically traumatizing event. The CISD process involves telling the traumatic story, exploring thoughts and sensory experiences, sharing emotional reactions, teaching common reactions after trauma, and coaching in coping skills. The purpose of CISD is "to prevent unnecessary aftereffects, accelerate normal recovery, stimulate group cohesion, normalize reactions, stimulate emotional ventilation, and promote a cognitive grip on the situation" (Dyregrov, 1997). It is not a substitute for therapy. It is one method of crisis support intended as part of a more comprehensive critical incident stress management program. With specialized training, peer caregivers can provide immediate, on-site care and make referrals to mental health professionals when there are signs of pathology.

CISD became controversial when some research indicated that it was not helpful, and could even be harmful. While many of these studies are methodologically flawed, nevertheless they bring to light that this powerful tool must be used wisely and carefully. As we have trained peers to debrief one another for many years, we have identified five areas that could contribute to harm for recipients (lack of choice, poor timing, re-traumatization, vicarious traumatization, and superficiality). These potential pitfalls should be avoided in debriefings provided in cross-cultural settings. If the following recommendations are followed, CISD can benefit trauma victims through social support, opportunity for emotional expression, assessment, and links to resources:

1. Improve the process of educating people (leaders and victims) about what CISD is and is not, and give trauma victims multiple opportunities over time to receive debriefing.
2. Before a CISD is provided, debriefers should assess the victims' level of fatigue, practical support needs, sense of being overwhelmed, and anxiety levels, in order to determine the right timing. Consult with a mental health professional if there are any questions about anxiety level.
3. When participants being debriefed express very intense emotions, help to instill a sense of safety, security, and calm before they leave the session. Debriefers should not force a person to express intense emotions, but also should not cut them off or communicate that expression is wrong or detrimental. For group debriefings, consider breaking into smaller groupings according to intensity of traumatic exposure. That way, people do not have to hear graphic details of events they did not face directly. Also, children do not need to hear all the details of adults' thoughts and fears during a shared event.
4. CISD is but one part of a broad spectrum of crisis intervention. Follow up and assess if the person needs intervention beyond a one-session debriefing. Do not underestimate the value of practical helps and ongoing support.
5. When leaders recognize their critical role in providing support, they can facilitate spiritual, practical, and emotional care that may have an even more lasting impact than debriefings.
6. Those of us providing debriefings in cross-cultural settings need to do more research on the validity and value of CISD for trauma victims.

For a more detailed discussion of CISD and critical research, see the article entitled "Critical Incident Stress Debriefing for Cross Cultural

Workers: Helpful or Harmful" at http://www.mmct.org/#/resources/crisis-response.

Acknowledge and Reframe

People in crisis situations often make negative, hopeless, or disparaging statements. Maintaining a distorted self-critical outlook can hamper the process of healing. A helpful skill is called *acknowledge and reframe.* When applying this skill, a caregiver listens for self-critical comments, then gives perspective, or "reframes" irrational thinking. By doing this he or she prevents potentially harmful attitudes or behavior based on inaccurate judgments. Essentially, distorted statements should not go by unmodified. Survivors of critical incidents may:

- Be overly self-critical
- Catastrophize about the incident
- Dwell on negative aspects
- Get caught up in "If only..." thinking
- Lose self-confidence

Saying, "Hey, you couldn't have done anything about that" is at times all that is needed to help someone move past self-criticism and regain confidence. Sometimes this type of statement doesn't help. Avoid telling someone they should not have certain feelings; which leaves the individual feeling unheard. On the other hand, calling their feelings normal may seem patronizing. Due to the unique makeup of each individual, responding to distorted thinking is very challenging. In some situations anything we might naturally say falls on deaf ears and a more strategic response is needed.

When using the *acknowledge and reframe* intervention, listen without judgment, acknowledge the feeling as understandable given the circumstances, and then offer a slightly altered, more balanced or rational, point of view. This intervention affirms the feeling of the individual but changes its frame of reference and meaning. Steps for acknowledge and reframe interventions:

1. Identify the feeling or belief being expressed.
2. Imagine the circumstances in which the individual experienced these feelings.

3. In some way, verbally acknowledge and affirm the normalcy or understandability of the feelings given the situation. Provide an additional perspective that gives the person another way of viewing what they have experienced.
4. Once you have made your intervention, let the statement stand. It should not require a verbal response. Silence probably means they are thinking about what you said. Hopefully you have altered their point of view. If the silence is prolonged, say something like, "So what happened next?" Or, "Tell me what else was going on for you."

For example, someone who has been robbed might say, "If only I had known they were bandits, I wouldn't have stopped the car. I should have known when I saw what they were wearing." An acknowledge and reframe response could be, "When things like this happen, we tend to judge ourselves. At the same time, it's pretty hard to know when people dressed as soldiers at checkpoints are legitimate. It's a tough decision to know whether or not to stop."

Some other examples of acknowledge and reframe interventions:

- It's painful when we do everything we know how to, and it still turns out this way.
- These moments are rough. When it doesn't turn out the way you intended, it's really hard for anybody to deal with.
- It's not easy to make quick decisions in a time of chaos and confusion.

Education about Triggers and Grounding

Learning more about how the body and mind respond to trauma is empowering for those who come up against frightening things they don't understand. Caregivers who know common, typical reactions to trauma can reassure and bring a sense of calm and reorientation.

Triggers are experiences associated with some aspect of the trauma, and can activate a post-trauma response (intrusive memories or anxiety reactions). One way to explain triggers is, "During powerful events like these, the brain records sights, sounds, smells, and so on, that occurred at the incident. Often, like an early warning system, if we bump into a similar sensory experience later, a part of our mind wants to be prepared for the worst. We don't always know what those triggers will be, but it can help to anticipate them" (Schiraldi, 2000; Snelgrove, 1999). Examples of *triggers* are listed in a table below.

TRIGGERS

- **Visual:** Seeing a person approaching the car with hands out of sight reminds one of robbers during a carjacking.
- **Sound:** Hearing the sound of firecrackers and misperceiving it as gunfire.
- **Smell:** Smelling alcohol on someone's breath reminds one of her abuser.
- **Taste:** Eating Chinese food reminds one of what he was doing when he heard news of his wife's death.
- **Physical or Body:** Feeling someone grabbing from behind - gives one a vivid memory of assault.
- **Significant Dates or Seasons:** Anniversary of a death; a date comes and goes that would have carried special meaning prior to the trauma; seasons carry memories and sensations that remind one of trauma.
- **Stressful Events or Arousal:** Increasing political tensions trigger memories of a previous coup or evacuation.
- **Strong Emotions:** A mother feels anxiety about her child not being home yet, and this triggers a memory of her husband's kidnapping.
- **Thoughts:** A bad performance evaluation triggers the thought, "I am a failure," the same thought that occurred on the scene of an accident when "I" was unable to help.
- **Behaviors:** Getting in the car reminds one of being in an auto accident.
- **Out of the Blue:** When one is tired or generally stressed, an intrusive thought may come suddenly and without provocation.
- **Combinations:** Triggers can be stimulated by several categories at once: the sight of a man in army clothes with a gun, combined with the time of day, driving in a car, and sound of his voice, all trigger memories of civil unrest.

Grounding is a technique for helping persons get reoriented to the present reality if a ***trigger*** causes trauma replay or physiological arousal. Coach them to calm themselves down by intentionally focusing on their immediate surroundings (what they can see, hear, and feel). Have them describe those things in a methodical, detailed fashion. For example, "I see the brown tiles of my ceiling, the blue curtains on my window, and the multicolored tile on my floor. I hear the sound of the fan in my room and a bird outside my window. I feel the soft chair fabric on my legs and a breeze blowing across my face." This anchors the person in present reality, presumably safer and calmer than the traumatic memory. For more detail on this skill, see Section 5 B.

D. Community Support for Children

Children are often invisible victims after a trauma because they resume normal activities and may not talk about what happened. Adults sometimes wrongly assume that children have not been significantly impacted. Parents and caregivers have a critical role in helping children to successfully cope with their reactions. The following is a list of actions that will (and will not) help. More elaboration can be found in *Sojourners: The Family on the Move, A Book of Resources,* by Ruth J. Rowen & Samuel F. Rowen (Farmington, Michigan: Associates of Urbanus, 1990, 165-176).

Doing these things will help:
1. Listen intently when children casually mention fears or want to talk about them.
2. Watch for the emotional, cognitive, or physical signs of traumatic responses. Examples of these include lowered performance, withdrawal, irritability, and nightmares.
3. Accept that their fears are real to them, even imaginary ones. Allow them to have those feelings. The real and the imaginary both need to be given the same consideration. A helpful distinction can be made between their feelings of fear and the actual amount of current risk or danger.
4. Educate children about the situation. They may be lacking complete information. Inform them of the situation if it has to do with things that directly concern them such as schooling, friends, food, or wild animals. The unknown causes fear. Use books, pictures or videos to help them understand.

5. Comfort them and give them the support they need as long as they have fears. Many fears will be overcome in a few weeks to several months; however, during this period, be extra sensitive to their feelings and give extra support.
6. Teach them that God promises to be with us. Isaiah 43:5 says, "Have no fear, for I am with you." The promise is that God will be with us at all times, even in difficult situations.
7. Pray with children regarding their fears.
8. Give an extra measure of love and security during this time. Extra family time together would be beneficial.
9. Look for positive experiences in relation to the fear which will help it to dissipate. If the fear is of dogs, spend some time with a friend's dog that is gentle and friendly. Allow the child to begin playing with the dog at his or her own pace.
10. Be sure both parents agree on how to handle the situation.
11. Talk with other parents whose children may have experienced similar fears and find out how they handled it.
12. Consult your family doctor if you think he or she could help determine the best way to overcome fears that cause sleeping or eating disorders. Often bedwetting and nightmares are a result of fears deep-seated in children.
13. Remember that all children develop fears while growing up and whether they develop into more serious problems or not, can depend largely on how parents handle the situation.
14. Talk with children after a crisis to let them tell their story and reveal any wrong assumptions, fears, or personal blaming. Parents and other adults can help their children see the crisis with a different perspective.
15. Help children develop some sense of security through their own actions. For example, a child who is afraid of the dark can benefit from using their own flashlight to illuminate the darkness.

Doing these things will NOT help:
1. Laugh and tell the child it is silly to feel that way.
2. Ignore their trauma reactions and hope that they will go away.
3. Fuss over the fear and give it lots of attention.

4. Compare the child with brothers or sisters who may not be afraid.
5. Instill fears in the child by telling him or her about all the tragedies happening in the world every day.
6. Allow children to see your fears uncontrolled. Fears are mimicked.
7. Display a lot of apprehension in ways that would confirm their fears.

Other tips for interacting with traumatized children:
1. Preschool kids may not be able to verbally express their trauma reaction. An indirect approach is more effective. You can help them draw pictures, play with toys, or use puppets to re-create what happened. Another idea is to have them draw or cut pictures out of magazines showing how they feel.
2. Let the child talk about things at her or his pace and in a nonlinear way, rather than asking a lot of direct questions.
3. Just because a child appears indifferent does not mean that he or she is not affected.
4. How children cope is greatly influenced by what they observe and sense from parents. Therefore, it's important for the parents to get help and work towards emotional recovery and stability.
5. Children will find fantasy answers to unanswered questions. If parents are upset but no one explains to children why, they may think they have done something wrong and are to blame. If a child is told something bad has happened but not what, he or she may imagine a worse than actual scenario.
6. Give clear, simple, and truthful explanations of what happened. If someone has died, you may want to break the truth gradually. Using euphemisms such as "he's asleep," or "he has gone away," or "Jesus needed him more than us," may cause more harm than benefit. A child who equates death with sleep may develop significant anxiety about going to bed or falling asleep. Delayed grieving may trouble children led to believe the deceased may come back. Telling a child that Jesus needed the person more than we do may create resentment toward God.
7. Protect children from repeated exposure to trauma that comes from hearing adults tell the story over and over, or watching violent images on TV.

8. Ask a child what he or she thinks happened, and why, to discover if any erroneous connections or conclusions have been made.
9. Watch for signs that children are blaming themselves for what happened.
10. Try to reestablish routine, structure, sense of safety, and trust as soon as possible. The child may go back to school but with somewhat lower parent-teacher expectations for concentration and achievement. Family routines should be reestablished (mealtimes, patterns just before bedtime such as reading a story and praying, disciplinary practices, and shared tasks).
11. Temporary separation from parents during critical events may lead to separation anxiety later, which includes intense fears of being apart from parents and that something bad will happen to Mom and Dad.
12. Help children develop coping skills and invite them to participate in the process of coming up with ideas for reducing anxiety and increasing competence with managing fear (memorize scripture, listen to music, or pray).
13. If working with children in groups, divide them according to age or developmental level (preschool, primary school, teenagers).

E. Organizational Support

Role of Leaders

Leaders play a key role in preventative care. J. Fawcett asserts that team cohesion and trust in competent leadership—factors that must exist before the crisis—are important elements in promoting healthy post-crisis adaptation. In recommending pre-crisis training for leaders, Fawcett mentions team cohesion, morale, and consultative leadership style. These increase social support and reduce stress. A workshop that focuses on helping participants to build trust, manage stress, listen well, and address relational conflicts, will contribute significantly to quality relationships and teamwork between leaders and staff. A crisis workshop designed for leaders can build skills in understanding normal crisis response, providing crisis care, proactively building and enhancing trust, and reducing stress. World Vision has found that the level of organizational support is more important than victim debriefings (J. Fawcett, 2002). Specifically, staff reported that presence of a senior manager during and after a critical event was perceived as organizational support and care, and was a significant factor in how everyone coped. Leaders can make a crucial impact through phone calls, e-mails, and personal visits communicating support, concern, care, and commitment to help. Given the pressure and responsibility on leaders, any preventative program must consider their emotional needs before, during, and after crises. Ron Brown writes,

> If the mission leadership does not acknowledge in some way the trauma that a worker has endured, then an elephant enters the room. The trauma suffered by a worker can have an enormous personal effect yet the description of this same event might make a fairly minimal emotional impact on mission leadership as the e-mail describing the trauma is quickly scanned. The onus is on the leader to acknowledge the event and to actively find out how the worker is coping after a trauma. After a very traumatic event, one missionary family was back in their homeland for a short time. They spoke in glowing terms of their organization's leader who came, along with his wife, to visit them. 'It was more than an e-mail message. He came with his wife'. That action spoke volumes, and they felt that the pain they had endured had been validated by the visit of a key leader. This contrasted with another family who, after a very tense and traumatic robbery, did not hear anything from their leadership. 'It was as if they (leaders) didn't care'. The family felt very much on their own, and they felt hurt by the lack of leadership response. (Brown, 2007, 316).

Leaders are in a unique role to give people time off, tweak the budget for more financial resources, write a letter to supporters, or arrange for meals. When MMCT evacuated from Côte d'Ivoire, we had to leave behind all of our furniture, office equipment, and personal belongings. As we set up a new house and office in Ghana, we were faced with financial and logistical obstacles. Our leaders supported us in many ways but two practical ways stand out to me. One submitted a request for special funding (three months of our rent in Côte d'Ivoire was paid for, which provided substantial financial assistance). Another leader and colleagues went to back to Abidjan, packed our possessions, and shipped them to Ghana. These actions speak volumes of care and concern, and definitely facilitate the healing process.

Organizational Plans

"A prudent person foresees danger and takes precautions. The simpleton goes blindly on and suffers the consequences" (Prov 22:3, NLT).

Recently a Cameroonian woman crisis manager complained to me of having a hard time getting her supervisor to budget for staff care in times of crisis. His response, "Are you trying to wish a crisis on us?" After their entire staff was evacuated from a war zone and attrition levels soared, he regretted his short-sighted stance.

A proactive organization will approach crisis readiness with contingency planning, trust-building, stress management, budget planning for member care, staff vacation plans, stricter personnel screening for high-risk areas, and crisis training for all staff. Leaders and managers can use the Cross Cultural Worker Stress Inventory (see Appendix 2.D) or the Headington Institute Self Care Inventory at http://headington-institute.org/Portals/32/Resources/Test_Self_care_inventory.pdf to assess staff stress levels at times of transition or crisis. Contingency planning and safety training are also good organizational tools for crisis preparedness. Crisis Consulting International (www.cricon.com) provides ongoing consultation, hostage negotiation, and crisis contingency training for mission agencies.

Organizations cannot be expected to have all the knowledge, skills, or staff needed for every emergency situation. Therefore, networking for cooperative care is highly recommended. This has been done with schools for missionary children (MK's) and member care efforts. MMCT is an example of networking: Staff, advisory council members, governing board, and funding sources come from many sending organizations. The Child Safety Network trains helpers and provides assistance where child abuse is suspected.

For additional organizations seeking to resource providing quality staff care, see Appendix C.

F. Professional Support

Training

Alexander Pope, in *An Essay on Criticism* (1709) wrote, "A little learning is a dangerous thing; drink deep, or taste not the Pierian spring: there shallow draughts intoxicate the brain, and drinking largely sobers us again."

Caregivers entrusted with listening to and coming alongside the wounded are given a sacred trust. God has given us gifts and strengths, the most valuable being the Holy Spirit to guide us through helping those in crisis. Training opportunities may be limited in certain cross-cultural settings. Leaders and caregivers must proactively seek quality training in caregiving skills. This could include MMCT's Crisis Response Training in West and East Africa, clinical and pastoral counseling courses, online training, selected readings, or workshops offered by trained counselors on short-term visits.

Consulting

If a caregiver observes symptoms going beyond normal or common reactions to stress or trauma, then a professional consult by email, phone, internet video-conferencing, or a face-to-face visit can determine the best course of action. Counselor-consultants can help caregivers gather information, prepare emergency plans, and make referrals. Establishing a relationship with a counselor prior to crisis puts contact information, travel availability, and areas of expertise at hand.

Assessment and Counseling

Many organizations use professional counselors to do pre-ministry assessments to determine applicants' psychological readiness. Likewise, assessment can take place at other times, such as home assignment or other transition, to determine how the person is managing stress or if there are lingering post-trauma effects. Done proactively, this may prevent serious complications requiring long recovery times.

Some cross-cultural workers have home countries where counselors abound. For others, to find a counselor, especially a Christian counselor, is a challenge. Several areas of the world have counseling centers for cross-cultural workers, but they are few (see Appendix C). MMCT provides short-term counseling in Africa. However, spiritually mature, Christian professional counselors with sufficient cross-cultural and life experience, who are willing to leave their jobs, raise support, and live overseas, are difficult to recruit. Some come for short-term visits. If a relationship can be established with frequent (annual) visits, then trust can be built. Workers can benefit from counseling "checkups," or working through serious issues that peer caregivers cannot address.

Need for Professional Support

Certain traumatic situations have a high risk for PTSD, indicating the need to involve a professional counselor (rape or any type of sexual assault, murder, suicide, an attack that threatened someone's life, or trauma impacting a child). Symptoms requiring consultation include: suicidal thoughts or actions, clearly self-destructive behaviors; any symptoms of a psychological conditions (severe depression, bipolar disorder, PTSD, or psychosis; substance abuse or addiction; child abuse or neglect; and any persistent or pervasive pattern that severely impairs performance or relationships). In the absence of a counselor, a caregiver with honed observation skills will note when someone is behaving abnormally and not responding to support. A consultation could clarify the significance of such observations.

SECTION 3
Personal Resilience
Karen Carr

Resilience is having strength to fulfill the call God has given us, even when it will be painful and difficult. Resilience is staying fixed on a higher purpose, motivated by love of God, our neighbor, and the world, and supported by friends. While others can let us down, we are all carried by the One who called us. What gives us this strength? There are a number of themes that have emerged from my crisis response and counseling work in West Africa. These themes are about prevention: as we grow and develop, we are better able to withstand trauma. They are also about cure: the foundation for a deep, cleansing healing process after trauma.

A. Knowing Our Call

One study found that "a strong personal conviction of God's direction" was a key factor in missionary retention. Brown describes this by saying,

> Sending agencies must continue to grapple with how the concept of 'the call' is expressed today. Do missionary candidates apply out of a desire to do something good in the world or because of a set of felt needs or from a sense of injustice? If so, how do those sentiments translate or morph into a strong conviction that holds strong during troubles and trials? How is that call developed? Where do new recruits develop their sense of call? Maybe the deeper question is how God speaks and calls people today to follow him in mission work. Whatever the language or semantics used, sending agencies who assign people to high security alert nations must feel satisfied and confident through the screening process that new recruits are called to serve in such places. By ensuring a firm call at the beginning, and testing that conviction in ministry, we will definitely contribute to resiliency after trauma (Brown, 2007, 318).

Henri Nouwen writes. "Knowing that the place where you live and the work you do is not simply your own choice but part of a mission makes all the difference. When difficulties arise, the knowledge of being sent will give me the strength not to run away but to be faithful. When the work proves tiring, the facilities poor, and the relationships frustrating, I can say, 'These hardships are not a reason to leave, but an occasion to purify my heart'" (Nouwen 1990, 109).

"We are all called to do, not extraordinary things, but very ordinary things, with an extraordinary love that flows from the heart of God" (Vanier, 1989, 298). After our evacuation from Ivory Coast, our team relocated to Ghana and began the process of starting over in a new country. In those days of reflection, I realized that some of what I had feared (exposure to extreme stress) had happened, and I was still just as motivated by love as before. I realized that God's call on my life was a constant that external circumstances did not sway. Internal struggles would sometimes bring the call into question, but trauma solidified my reason for being there. People who choose to be in a high-risk area and are motivated by a desire for adventure, an addiction to adrenaline, a sense of guilt, or to have fun, will quickly be disillusioned. Such motivations do not usually contribute to staying power or resilience in the face of suffering.

B. Praise, Gratitude, and Joy

In I Chronicles 20, we learn that a vast army is marching against King Jehoshaphat of Judah. This news terrifies him. In crisis, Jehoshaphat does some interesting things. He begs God for guidance and orders a communal fast. He prays publicly and affirms God's power and sovereignty, remembers the history of God's faithfulness, and confesses his own sense of inadequacy and helplessness. God tells Jehoshaphat's people to go into battle assured of God's presence, encouragement, and victory. Jehoshaphat and his people respond by praising God. They take praise from the relative safety of their homes, right onto the battlefield. They lead the army's charge with singers who are singing, "Give thanks to the Lord; his faithful love endures forever." At the very moment they began to sing and praise, the Lord caused the armies of Ammon, Moab, and Mount Seir to start fighting among themselves.

I confess that as I look over this account of Jehoshaphat's response to the threat of annihilation, the part I identify with is when he felt terrified. Yet, anytime I have turned to praise in the midst of crisis, I have sensed a turn in the battle. These song lyrics by gospel songwriter Kurt Carr (no relationship to this author; www.lyricsmania.com, last accessed 9/9/2012) express comfort found in the armor of praise.

I've lost some good friends along life's way
Some loved ones departed in Heaven to stay
But thank God I didn't lose everything
I've lost faith in people who said they care
In the time of my crisis they were never there
But in my disappointment in my season of pain
One thing never wavered, one thing never changed

Chorus:
I never lost my hope
I never lost my joy
I never lost my faith
But most of all
I never lost my praise

I've let some blessings slip away
And I lost my focus and went astray
But thank God I didn't lose everything
I've lost possessions that were so dear
And I've lost some battles by walking in fear
But in the midst of my struggle, in the season of pain
One thing never wavered, one thing never changed

C. Grace Versus Performance

How did Jesus avoid burnout? What can we learn from him so we can mentor others? Jesus demonstrates a pattern illustrated in The Cycle of Grace (Lake, 1966, 133).

The Cycle of Grace

The Cycle of Grace illustrates the source of our sense of purpose and meaning. It begins with an affirmation of God's love for us and **acceptance** of who we are. We are **sustained** by this ongoing nurture for our well-being and spiritual life. This flows into awareness of **significance**, from which we draw direction and strength and are able to **achieve** things which result in the healing and nurture of others.

THE CYCLE OF GRACE

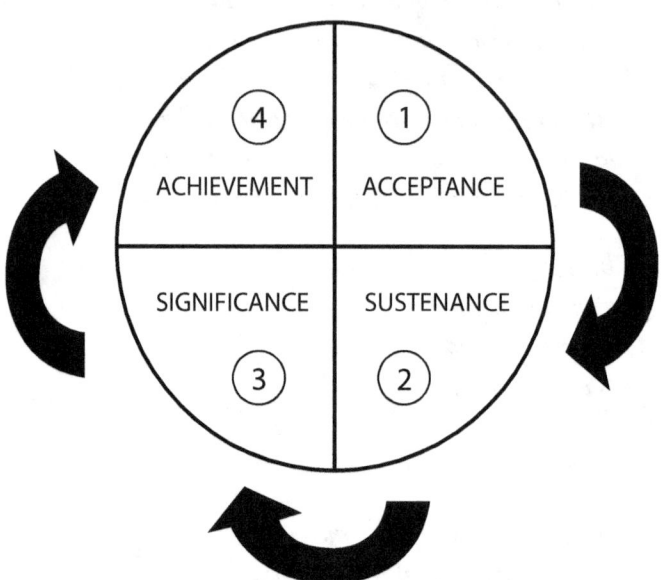

Jesus knew that he was accepted by his Father, who told him he was dearly loved and brought great joy (Lk 3:21-22). We, too, are accepted as loved, chosen, and valuable people that God delights and rejoices in (Eph 1:4-8; Zeph 3:17; Mt 6:25-27).

Jesus was sustained by being in the Father, obeying the Father's commandments, and remaining in his love (John 14:10; 15:10). Our sustenance comes directly from Jesus, the bread and water of life. If we come to him we will never be hungry or thirsty. He also promises to supply all our needs and give us peace of mind and heart (John 6:35; Rev 22:17; Phil 4:18-19; John 14:27).

As Jesus ministered, his significance and achievement came directly from his relationship to his Father. In the same way, our achievements, including our responses to trauma and coping mechanisms, flow from the input received.

Jesus was aware of his significance as the Son of God and boldly proclaimed that he was the way, the truth and the life, and that no one could come to the Father except through him (John 14:6). We are assured of our significance as heirs, adopted children, and friends with the privilege of sharing in his glory and suffering (Rom 8:15-17; John 15:15).

Jesus' achievements of teachings, miracles, and other great works are connected to his relationship with the Father (John 5: 19, 30, 36). Jesus said that his disciples (us) would do even greater things than he, and that we will produce much fruit if we abide in him (John 7:38; 14:12; 15:5).

How does this Cycle of Grace relate to helping traumatized people? Most people in full-time Christian work have a strong work ethic and a drive to bear much fruit for the Lord. Supporting churches and organizations sometimes contribute to this internal pressure by focusing on results (number of converts, or planted churches) rather than their workers' spiritual walk. This drives people to focus on achievement, often neglecting other aspects of the cycle of grace.

Many people start with achievement, move to significance (from accomplishments), and then go on to sustenance (often to a point of exhaustion), and finally to acceptance (feeling they have failed and are not worthy of God's approval). If the cycle is lived out in reverse, then it is a Cycle of Frustration, an Anti-Grace Cycle. For example, a man named Thomas feels a strong sense of God's acceptance when he becomes a missionary. He chooses a difficult field where there are few Christians. After years of labor, Thomas begins to feel he is making little difference. He cannot see results, not a single convert! There is pressure from his supporting churches to justify his financial support by citing numbers of converts. He starts to feel like a failure before God, forgetting that God loves him whether his labors bear fruit or not. Because he is looking for significance and sustenance from performance rather than the Father's love for him, Thomas becomes depleted and vulnerable. He resorts to late-night internet pornography after his wife has gone to bed. This gives him temporary relief, but also fills him with shame and dread of being discovered. Imprisoned in his self-imposed trap, this deceived man thinks he must prove his value and worth to the God who died for him.

If someone has been living the Cycle of Frustration rather than the Cycle of Grace, he or she will fall when trauma occurs. Imagine how the cycle of frustration plays out if there is an evacuation, a relationship conflict, a death, or chronic stress or burnout. The enemy can fill our head with lies about who we are and why we are here.

As leaders and caregivers we can provide member care by gently helping people turn from a Cycle of Frustration to a Cycle of Grace. We can call them back to the truth of God's Word: acceptance and sustenance comes from the Lord, and the output of significance and achievement flows from this source. Good leadership and member care affirms that truth.

D. Forgiveness

A missionary working with women who escaped forced prostitution asked me how she could persevere in this caregiving role without being consumed by hatred for the male abusers. There was a time in my missionary career when I was full of righteous anger because I had seen and heard so many traumatic stories of injustice and abuse. A man was pistol-whipped, kidnapped, and shot while trying to escape. A woman was kidnapped, forced to give up her mission's money, and struck on the head. A girl was gang-raped by robbers. Story after story filled my heart with bitterness toward strangers I never knew and would never meet, who had hurt missionaries I had come to love. I did not let go of my anger towards the offenders and furthermore felt I had every right to hold on to it.

After two years of accumulated toxic emotions, I was diagnosed with ovarian cancer. Following surgery and chemotherapy I was declared healed by the medical profession. Spiritually, I was still sick, and one day in church there was a gentle nudge from the Holy Spirit "Forgive the men who did those things." I protested and argued that I did not know them, and it wasn't me they had injured, so why should I forgive them. "That is your cancer and you will be sick until you forgive them," was the response. In obedience and tears I spoke words of forgiveness, releasing them from the prison I had built for them and myself. Immediately I felt a burning in my abdomen where the tumor had been.

Since then I have practiced regular, if not daily, forgiveness as I continue to hear horrifying stories. "He does not constantly accuse us, nor remain angry forever. He does not punish us for all our sins; he does not deal harshly with us, as we deserve" (Ps 103:9-10). Because we have been given grace that we do not deserve we can give to others what they do not deserve. It's not humanly possible, but by God's grace we can forgive people who don't ask for it, and have hurt those we love. I find this harder than forgiving people who have hurt me directly.

My answer to the missionary who asked how she could keep working with victims of forced prostitution? Forgive daily.

E. Proactively Building Community

This section title, Personal Resilience, may be misleading. It sounds individualistic, as though outside of community. Resilience only happens in the context of relationship to God and others. It happens in the process of suffering, as we submit to the refining fire of our Lord's crucible.

Missionaries who proactively build community will find their personal resilience growing as well as the community resilience, which ultimately leads to biblical caregiving in times of trauma.

The Mobile Member Care Team is intentional about building community. We developed specific ideas all of us considered essential. A few of these ideas apply to a team; many apply to friends or marriage partners.

Attitudes:
- Giving preference: yielding my way or preference for the sake of the other
- Sharing concern for each other's families: call them by name, pray for them, meet them
- Generosity
- Inclusiveness
- Speaking the truth with grace

Practices:
- Prayer
- Spontaneous prayer
- Prayer and Refocus Time: Sunday evenings we each answer four questions: What went well? What didn't go well (about the previous week)? What do I want? What do I need (for the coming week)? Then we pray for each other's concerns.

- Quarterly Prayer Retreats
- Friday prayer for Africa, missionaries we serve, and ministry concerns
- Have fun: laugh and play together
- Care for each other when we are sick
- Touch: frequent hugs, handshakes, high-fives, and reassuring touches on the shoulder
- Service: help each other with practical things even when it means giving up something "I" want to do
- Read Scripture together before midday meals
- Acts of Kindness: take coffee to someone in the morning, make meals, offer to do something that will free up another's time
- Farewell and welcome: sing "May the Peace of the Lord Christ Go with You" or other songs of blessing when one leaves or returns
- Vacation with each other (sometimes)
- Exercise together: take walks, bike, swim
- Practice forgiveness
- Invite families and individuals over for evening meals, hosting together
- Debrief each other when we return from trips
- Team Covenant: We read it together regularly. It includes elements of decision making, communication, loyalty and commitment, conflict management, and building trust.

F. Stillness and Surrender

Mike Mason writes about surrender and suffering in *The Gospel According to Job*,

> In retrospect I can see that a large part of my anguish was rooted in the fact that there really was nothing I could do to control what was happening to me. I was absolutely helpless, and it is this, perhaps, that is the soul of suffering, this terrifying impotence. We Christians do not like to think about being absolutely helpless in the hands of our God. With all our faith and with all His grace, we still prefer to maintain some semblance of control over our lives. When difficulties arise, we like to think that there are certain steps we can take, or attitudes we can adopt, to alleviate our anguish

and be happy. There are no easy answers to suffering - there is no such thing as getting a grip on oneself or pulling oneself up by the bootstraps. The only bootstrap in the Christian life is the cross (Mason 1994, x-xi).

Allergies and asthma have been a minor irritant most of my life. As a missionary in Africa, I was away from the pollens and allergens of Virginia and symptoms disappeared. But, after living in Ghana for about six years, my resistance to the molds of a humid tropical climate began to diminish. Allergy symptoms returned, soon followed by mild asthma, easily controlled with antihistamines and an occasional puff of Ventolin.

In early 2010, my respiratory system could no longer stay ahead of the battle. Lung inflammation made my breathing difficult and labored. My immune system was compromised from intense ministry and heavy travel. I got malaria for the first time in 10 years of living in Africa. At a local clinic the medical staff treated me for an asthma attack, malaria, and an upper respiratory infection, and sent me home. The next day my breathing became even more labored and I experienced something brand new for me – panic. I began to hyperventilate and didn't know what was happening. When I breathed in I could not feel the satisfying sensation of receiving oxygen. Weak and dizzy, my fingers and hands began to tingle and go numb. Friends carried me into the clinic, and I thought I was going to die. I was put on oxygen, given shots, put on an IV, and surrounded by concerned and caring faces.

Something interesting was going on in my mind and emotions as I was being half-carried into the clinic that day. I was aware of people in the hallway looking at me with concern and worry. And my main thought was, "What's wrong with you? Don't be so weak." I was embarrassed by my frailty and lack of control. Even as I had these thoughts, I stepped back from them with a perspective of compassion and laughed that I could be so self-critical in a crisis moment like this. Am I not the one who exhorts others to give grace to themselves? A different kind of battle was brewing inside of me. Months later I understood it better.

After stabilization, I was admitted as an inpatient. The doctors and nurses were kind but I sensed that some were afraid to touch me or get too close. My teammates camped out in my room and took turns staying with me overnight. If my breathing became difficult, one of them went to find a nurse. The first night was the most difficult. I didn't sleep at all and felt that every breath was an effort requiring my concentration. I wondered if I would make it through the night. The next morning I felt the panic rising again and hyperventilation once again contributed to my breathing difficulties. I felt that my body was betraying me as breathing in gave me no sensation of having sufficient air. Later I came to know terms like *air hunger* and *air trapping* that helped me to make sense of what was happening in my lungs.

After being released from the hospital, I continued to have difficulty breathing, and consulted with pulmonologists in Ghana and the U.S. Blood tests showed I had picked up a secondary infection, most likely from unsanitary conditions in the hospital. I had been on high doses of prednisone and antibiotics for weeks. My illness was beginning to feel like an endless journey. I could see it was taking a toll on my teammates, and that brought feelings of guilt and frustration. I found myself feeling more intensely about things than the situation merited. I would cry in despair over what normally I could easily brush off. I was restless and feeling driven to produce and accomplish something. My body and emotions were outside my control. Some of this was due to side effects of medication, but also negative self-judgment related to even having those symptoms.

As these things were happening, the Master Gardener was tilling hard ground in my heart, preparing it for seeds of a deeper intimacy with him. In the stillness and rest required by my illness, I read, prayed, and reflected. I was intrigued by the many references to breath and breathing in scripture.

One day, when I was laboring to breathe deeply, I recalled the story of Elisha in 2 Kings 4:32-37. The child of the widow had died and Elisha lay down on the child, placing his mouth on the child's mouth, his eyes on the child's eyes, and his hands on the child's hands. The child was restored to life. As I prayed I sensed that the Lord was doing the same, giving me breath and life.

Will Collier's book about the writings of Fenelon titled *Let God* confirmed themes the Lord was teaching me. We all take breathing, the essence of life, for granted and hardly think about. When God formed man from the dust of the ground, he breathed life into the man's nostrils, and the man became a living person (Gen 2:7). Deep and satisfying breathing, just like sleep, requires surrender. Fenelon wrote,

> Abandon yourself entirely to God. Recklessly abandon yourself to God as long as you breathe on this earth. Let loose. You are in

good hands. You can be self-abandoned because you will never be God abandoned ... Give way to God. Surrender. Allow him to wreck the beautiful self-image you have spent so much time creating. Let God dig into the most hidden corner of your heart where this self-obsession lurks. ... Feel the alive pleasure of no longer clinging to your own so called beauty, but hoping deeply in (and for) the beauty of Jesus (Collier, 2007, 5).

Part of my self-image that had to die was that I was strong, courageous, and exempt from anxiety. Once I was able to admit and acknowledge anxiety, I was free to explore how it was driving me in other areas and undermining my relationship with the Lord and others. Sometimes my high productivity, achievement orientation, and need for closure were anxiety driven. Recognizing this, breathing more slowly, and voluntarily entering a place of rest and stillness brought healing and freedom. Fenelon wrote to a friend who needed to stop trying so hard,

> Even though you are perceptive and have a great mind, God will allow the chaos to converge in such a way that none of your natural abilities are any help...This isn't the time for deciding or for doing. God isn't asking you to do anything. Just wait. Right now, do nothing. Later after things have calmed down and you are more at rest, you can quietly and peacefully consider your circumstances and evaluate the truth of your situation. Then, when you aren't so ruffled, you can get a simple sense of what might be best for you. Again it will be simple stuff. Gradually go back to simple living, simple listening, simple praying, simple humility. Don't rush. Give yourself time. Have ears wide open to God, and have ears closed shut to self (Collier, 2007, 56-58).

In Wendell Berry's *Whitefoot,* he wrote about a mouse caught in a flood, rapidly floating down a swollen river on top of a log, vulnerable to predators. Berry comments, "If you had seen her, you might have thought she was patient. She was capable of patience, I think, but now she was simply doing nothing, which was all there was to do" (Berry, 2009, 30).

In my journey back to health, I wrote in my journal, "When we are restless and agitated and anxious, what does God say? 'Be still and know that

I am God. Lie beside these still waters. Drink in my presence. Trust me to produce fruit even when you do nothing. Ask me what I want you to do and don't do more or less than that. You will know you are doing my will when you have peace and joy in your spirit. That's your litmus test. When you are driven by anxiety, it's not coming from me.'"

After a few months back in the U.S., I recovered sufficiently to return to Africa and reenter full-time ministry. I live with knowing my respiratory system is compromised. I have to remain vigilant to early warning signs of asthma relapse, take preventative medications, and avoid certain allergens. But, I do not have to live in fear. So, in surrender and trust, I take risks and live life to the fullest. I breathe.

SECTION 4
Healthy Stress Management
Frauke Schaefer

When Tom and Nancy (not their real names) prepared for their first term in mission, they looked forward to serving as houseparents for children they could love and care for in a country where many were poor and uneducated. They expected cultural adjustment and poor living conditions. They did not expect that after an intense first year of adjustment, a devastating earthquake would hit the area. They also did not imagine that the project director would become unable to fulfill his role, and that Tom would need to take over leadership. He would not have signed up voluntarily for this role, but with extra effort he nevertheless did a great job. There were unending needs on the project, and the couple usually lent a hand, working most of their waking hours. Not surprisingly, both Tom and Nancy were soon stretched beyond healthy limits, burnt out, and in need of effective stress management if they were to continue the ministry they loved.

There are many stories like Tom and Nancy's in home and international ministries. Dedicated and often heroic people manage to respond to human needs in spite of limited means and personnel. These people with a purpose keep on helping, promoting justice, and advancing the kingdom in difficult circumstances. However, extended periods of high demand or severe trauma take a toll on these earthen vessels of heavenly purpose. Burnout, depression, and posttraumatic stress can be the result. Fortunately, there are practical ways to reduce the stress of ministry.

A. Healthy Practices for Resilient People

Physically healthy people can practice stress management strategies in most environments. By doing this they can be in "better shape" as they face ordinary and extraordinary life challenges. Regularly practicing those strategies creates an emotional buffer for periods of intense difficulty. When overstress and burnout have already taken hold, these practices will usually decrease severity, if there is enough energy and motivation left to put them into practice. When energy and motivation are lacking, and the person is too distressed, overwhelmed, or suicidal, professional help including medications is the only realistic option to effectively improve the situation.

Many pastors and missionaries are eager to learn more about stress management strategies. These simple practices can be integrated into daily life. Whether it is to improve wellbeing, address general stress, traumatic stress, anxiety, or depression, stress management can make a difference. Stress management is a suitable alternative when a person is reluctant to "just take medications to feel better." If there is not sufficient relief after several weeks of applying stress management strategies, persons should consult a medical professional. At that point they also may be open to consider medications without passing judgment on themselves. They know they have tried their best. There are some situations where stress management alone is not enough and a professional counselor or physician should be involved immediately.

STRESS MANAGEMENT STRATEGIES SAFELY APPLIED

SAFE
- To enhance resilience
- To reduce distress in people functioning sufficiently
- To assist people with enough energy and motivation to apply the strategies
- To improve sleep for those with insomnia
- To improve feelings of sadness decreased joy or energy
- To improve difficulties controlling feelings such as anxiety, irritability or anger

NOT SAFE BY ITSELF*
- If a person is tired of life or has thought of hurting him-or herself
- If a person is thinking of being destructive or hurting another person
- If persons are seeing or hearing things that are not really there, irrationally feeling like somebody is after them or out to get them, or have other strong and unrealistic fears
- If a person is abusing alcohol or drugs (including prescription drugs, such as "nerve medicine," sleeping pills or painkillers)

These people need to see a medical professional immediately!

B. Resilience – What It Means

The term *resilience* has been used increasingly in recent years. What does it mean? Originally used in physics, resilience describes:

> The property of a material that can return to its original shape ... after deformation that does not exceed its elastic limit. (wordnetweb.princeton.edu/perl/webwn)

According to this, if an external force is applied to a material, it has a capability to return to its previous shape not too long after impact. The term resilience has also been used for human beings. According to the Resiliency Center it is:

> The ability to recover ... from disruptive change ... without being overwhelmed or acting in dysfunctional or harmful ways. (www.resiliencycenter.com/definitions.shtml)

After disruptive change a resilient person will be impacted for a while, but then move towards restoration and return to regular functioning. A modern resiliency model by Richardson (Richardson, 2002) shows how a person affected by trauma may return to the previous level of functioning, at a lower, or even a higher level. Trauma impacts the psychological homeostasis of a person. The impact leads to a level of disruption, the severity of which is buffered by protective factors: Community support, good mental health and stress management, along with a solid theology of suffering. Reintegration processes lead to varied functional outcomes, depending on psychological and spiritual factors as well as the quality of support. Researchers observed that aside from weakening or restoration to the previous state, someone could also become stronger in the midst of struggle with adversity, leading to reintegration at a *more* resilient level than before. The Bible describes this possibility: "And the God of all grace, who called you to his eternal glory in Christ, after you have suffered a little while, will himself restore you and make you strong, firm, and steadfast" (1 Pet 5:10 NIV). Though restoration is ultimately God's doing, there are biological conditions that will assist us to "bounce back" and become strong. (Please see *Richardson's Resiliency Model* on the following page.)

RICHARDSON'S RESILIENCY MODEL

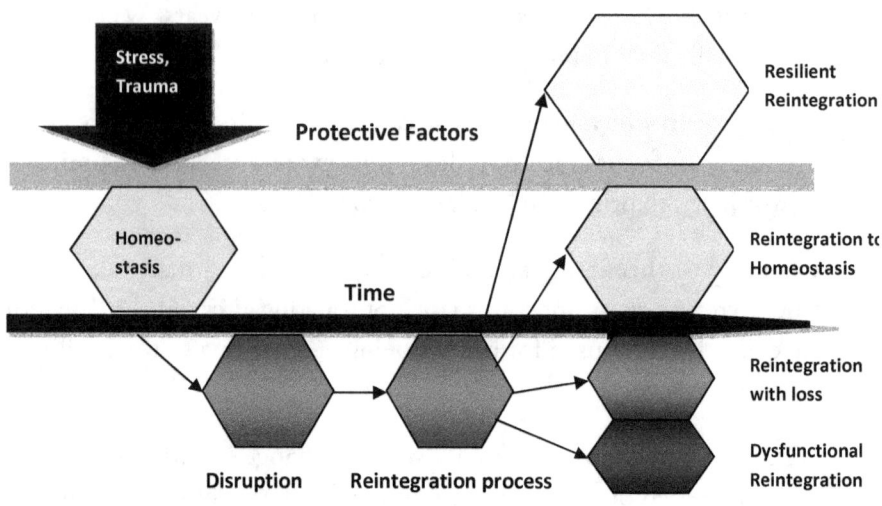

C. Healthy and Unhealthy Stress Response

Natural and effective stress response mechanisms help human bodies adapt to stress. If is senses a threat, such as a physical attack, hormonal signals from the brain go to the pituitary gland, which in turn produces signals to the adrenal glands. The autonomous nervous system can be activated in a flash. Stress hormones (cortisol, adrenaline, and norepinephrine) become available immediately. The physical stress response mobilizes energy, provides focus, and increases wakefulness. The body is ready for fight or flight, whatever is appropriate.

After threat has decreased (danger has passed, the person fled from the attacker or used self-defense strategies), the stress hormone response needs to shut down and return to normal. An effective recovery makes the body resilient and more adaptable. However, if the stress response stays activated, bodies will be exposed to continuing high levels of stress hormones. Scientists call accumulation of physical stress "allostatic load." When allostatic load increases, human bodies are exposed to chronic elevated stress. With further adversity, the stress response will become weaker and less efficient, since it is already partially activated. As chronic stress accumulates, the system is less able to adjust. It cannot produce sufficient additional stress hormones. This inability to adjust to stress makes bodies and minds less resilient. Effective stress management helps the shutting-down process of the stress response. Effective shutting-down reduces chronic elevated stress or "allostatic load," which in turn improves the ability to adjust to new stressors. This adaptability increases resilience in high stress environments.

If the stress response is in constant overdrive, body and mind will start to show signs of chronic high stress. Immune defense will decrease, making it harder to fight off infections, colds, diarrhea, or malaria. Blood pressure and heart rate may remain elevated, and cholesterol levels may increase. Sleep may become disrupted. The ability to think clearly about complex matters, focus, and make good decisions will suffer. Memory may deteriorate; muscles may be tense; one may feel hot, sweaty, dizzy, have headaches or stomach troubles; one may feel on edge and irritable, with emotions shifting frequently and becoming harder to control; one may suddenly be in tears or raise the voice in irritation. These signs of chronic high stress increase the risk of burnout.

At the end of my turbulent first term in Nepal I accumulated chronic stress. At first I felt only muscle tension in my neck and shoulders and a constant sense of emotional stress. Then I started to have difficulties going to sleep. It became harder to concentrate, but I still could manage and so soldiered on. One day, I suddenly could not hold back tears while working in a clinic. On medical examination I had an elevated heart rate and blood pressure. My cumulative stress and lack of effective management had led to a degree of burnout needing attention.

The challenges of ministry at home or abroad are best met by keeping the stress response subtle and adaptable. After trauma and crisis the stress response can be reduced by engaging in good self-care, enabling brain and body to bounce back physically and emotionally, and the soul to grow spiritually.

D. Strengthening Biological Resilience

Any activity that decreases baseline stress levels will increase biological adaptability and resilience. The most effective stress management strategies are regular aerobic exercise, sufficient sleep, eating resilience-enhancing foods, and having a balanced lifestyle with regular downtimes.

Regular Aerobic Exercise

Have you noticed how relaxed your body feels after a brisk walk, jogging, biking, or swimming? Physical and emotional relaxation are common benefits from aerobic exercise. Aerobic exercise is the type of exercise that raises heart and respiratory rates for a sustained period of time, while allowing comfortable breathing. For example, while exercising aerobically, it should still be possible to talk to a friend running or biking alongside. Research on the effect of exercise on anxiety, depression, and sensitivity to stress shows that people exercising regularly at an aerobic level reap mental health benefits (Salmon, 2001). However, those who overexert and push themselves too hard cause anaerobic effects, and may actually mentally get worse. Physically fit people recover much quicker from stress, clearly indicating improved resilience. Interestingly, laboratory mice performing wheel running *after* a major stressor showed a reduction in stress response (Mills and Ward, 1986; Starzec, Berger and Hesse, 1983). This result likely also applies to humans. Regular exercise increases protective factors to counteract the damaging effects of stress on brain cells. People who stop exercising lose the beneficial effects within about two weeks (Salmon, 2001).

Simple aerobic exercises include brisk walks in the neighborhood, jogging or running, biking, swimming, jumping rope (good for indoors, too), and tennis. There are also great aerobic team sports such as volleyball, basketball, badminton, soccer, and football that involve a lot of running. About thirty minutes most days of the week are sufficient to "do the trick," increase resilience, and reduce mild to moderate levels of anxiety and depression. People unaccustomed to exercise can start with whatever they can do comfortably, gradually increasing time and effort. For stress management purposes, staying in the aerobic zone is more important than speed. Muscle power and aerobic threshold will gradually build with gentle pushing and allow for increasing speed while staying in the aerobic zone. After rest and rehydration, you should feel energized rather than exhausted, a good sign of successful aerobic exercise.

A depressed person will find it hard to "get going" with exercise due to lack of energy. Such a person can start with short times and moderate exercise, such as walking for ten minutes, then building up gradually to thirty minutes. For caregivers a great way to assist a stressed or depressed person to "get going" is to take a short walk together. As depressed and anxious people focus on the immediate discomfort of exercise, caregivers can help them focus on the benefits they will gain (or have gained in the past). This will increase motivation. In addition, combining exercise with a pleasant activity such as listening to music, talking to a friend, or seeing pleasant sights, can enhance motivation.

Sufficient Sleep

The pressures of ministry can tempt us to "save time" by sleeping less. Cutting down on sleep may sometimes be unavoidable, but it is risky long-term. Physical and mental consequences result after even a few shorter nights.

There are many causes for disturbed sleep. People serving in ministry usually have full schedules. On top of this they may get contacted at odd hours with urgent matters. Medical mission personnel in remote areas of less developed countries are often the only ones available in an emergency. They need to respond whether it is good for their own health or not. Sleep disruption can also come from heat, noise, mosquitoes, the needs of young children, or menopausal hot flashes. Obstructive sleep apnea is a condition common in those who snore or are overweight. Rest is disturbed by the struggle to breathe and lack of sufficient oxygen. Medical consultation, possibly a sleep study, can help identify the cause(s) of insomnia.

Adults normally need about seven to nine hours of sleep a night. Typically, they fall asleep within thirty minutes, wake up once or twice a night, and fall back asleep in less than thirty minutes. Most people know how many hours of sleep they normally need for good performance and stress management. A rule of thumb would be the time of sleep they need to wake up refreshed after a few days on vacation.

Researchers have compared stress hormone levels and stress-response recovery times in people who slept a sufficient amount, with those in people who slept a few hours less. Stress hormone levels were significantly lower in those who slept sufficiently. Also, in the sleep deprived it took longer for stress hormone levels to get back to normal. Longer recovery times clearly indicate that sleep deprivation decreases resilience (Leproult, et al., 1997).

Disturbed sleep is common in people under stress, after trauma, or in burnout. Loss of sleep is often a first indicator that stress is taking a toll on body and mind. As caregivers of people in high stress roles and environments, we should always take great care to inquire about sleep patterns. Sleep was the remedy God applied to Elijah when he was exhausted after prolonged spiritual battle. God had him sleep, eat, drink, and sleep again until his strength returned (1 Kings 19: 5-8).

There are many resources available to improve sleep with simple, practical strategies called "sleep hygiene." You can find online resources about sleep enhancing strategies in Appendix C *Books, Online Resources, Training Opportunities, and Counseling Centers.*

Eating Resilience-enhancing Foods

Can food increase resilience? To some degree, but less so, compared to aerobic exercise and sufficient sleep. When Daniel and his friends lived in the idolatrous environment of the Babylonian exile, they requested permission to only eat vegetables, and drink water, rather than to defile themselves with the meat and wine of Nebuchadnezzar. As opposed to their warden's concern they became stronger than others around them (Dan 1:8-16). Population-based research studies show that people who follow a "Mediterranean diet" are less depressed than others. Mediterranean food includes fruit and vegetables, cereal, bread, nuts, legumes, fish, and low saturated fats such as olive oil, with only small amounts of meat or whole fat dairy (Sánchez-Villegas et al., 2009). Research notes the mental health benefits of Folic Acid (about 400mcg/d; Coppen and Bailey, 2000; Coppen and Bolander-Gouaille, 2005). Also recommended are Omega 3 Fatty Acids (two servings of fatty fish per week; fish oil, walnuts, and flax seeds), and likely Vitamin D (400 to 1000 IU), in combination with sun exposure of more than 30 minutes a day.

Foods with high sugar content (candy, cake, doughnuts, ice cream, white bread, and potatoes) increase stress hormone levels. Why is that? A steep increase in blood sugar induces a strong insulin response. Eventually, this leads to blood sugar "crash" (hypoglycemia or low blood sugar), which in turn activates hormones very similar to a stress response. This is why about an hour after a high sugar and carbohydrate meal, a person can feel vaguely anxious or irritable and at the same time hungry, craving more of the same. Foods with lower sugar and carbohydrates, high fiber, and combined with healthy fats, cause a more gradual increase of blood sugar, a gradual increase in insulin, and avoid a blood sugar "crash." To reduce their baseline stress hormone levels, people need to eat predominantly complex carbohydrates rich in fiber such as fruits, vegetables, and whole grain products. These foods may not always be available in remote areas. Many missionaries, therefore, have taken on vegetable gardening with great personal benefit. Their harvest often inspired the surrounding community to plant vegetable gardens and to eat healthier also.

People under stress feel drained and easily fatigued. For those determined to keep going, the most promising quick fix appears to be a caffeinated drink. Caffeine does increase alertness and a sense of renewed energy in minutes. However, this comes at a price. Caffeine reduces the effectiveness of the enzyme *adenosine,* which breaks down stress hormones in our bodies. The impairment of adenosine causes the "caffeinated feeling" of restlessness and jitteriness in people under high stress. This agitated feeling is due to accumulated stress hormones that cannot be broken down as normal. The higher the baseline stress, the more pronounced this caffeine "side effect" will be felt. Caffeine lingers in the body for up to twelve hours, sustaining high stress hormone levels. Caffeinated drinks in the afternoon or evening can affect sleep. Decreasing or avoiding caffeine will help to minimize already high stress levels, especially after trauma. Without relying on caffeine, the common afternoon fatigue can be relieved by moving around, drinking fluids, or having a small amount of chocolate.

Keeping Balance

Stress responses wind down at the end of the day, when people slow down, enjoy socializing, play, or have fun. While having a good time, the stress system recovers. Sabbath-keeping has gained more attention among people of faith in our increasingly nonstop world that measures importance primarily by accomplishment. For ministers, Sunday is often the busiest day of the week. Pastors and missionaries have professional responsibilities all week, with church duties on weekends. Work never seems to stop. This is certainly "against the grain" of our design and against the life principles of our Creator, who worked intently and creatively, and then stopped on the seventh day to rest and delight in his Creation. The Creator shifted into being with himself as Father, Son, and Holy Spirit, and connecting with who and what he had created. He experienced deep delight and connectedness. Here is permission to honor the rhythms of work, rest, and delight!

A weekly downtime of rest and delight is helpful and often lifesaving. It allows the stress response to bounce back and returns the body to a more adaptable and resilient baseline. Annual vacations de-stress in an even more profound way. Some people may feel important and indispensable if they "can't afford" regular times out. However, this will erode their adaptability and resilience over time as they deprive themselves of the God-ordained recovery time necessary to bounce back from the effects of ongoing stress. Good, ongoing care for people in ministry often starts with encouraging them to take time out for rest. This encouragement can start by allocating the resources necessary for regular times of renewal. The point being, they "can't afford" not to.

Downtimes

After trauma bodies are flooded with stress hormones. Reminders of the event can be like earthquake aftershocks, bringing back the original horrors full force. Zahava Solomon, a Jewish psychologist, studied the effect of frontline treatments for combat stress in Israeli soldiers. Those who suffered stress reactions were treated in *proximity* to their place of service, *immediately* after the stress reaction occurred, and with the *expectation* of recovery. Even twenty years after the combat stress reaction, soldiers treated like this had lower rates of mental distress and were functioning better than their untreated peers (Solomon et al., 2005).

Therefore, allowing people in ministry downtimes when suffering post-traumatic stress will have long-term benefits for their health and functioning. How can the principles of proximity, immediacy, and expectancy be applied to mission workers with stress reactions? Some organizations already provide downtimes for staff after trauma or particularly demanding times of service. These organizations reap the benefit of high functioning workers, rather than high attrition rates and burnout. Some workers in Southern Sudan get out of this high-stress environment every few months to rest and recoup in a safer neighboring country. Locations for such downtimes need to be sufficiently safe and restful, and are best if in proximity to the location of service. Sending missionaries home for downtimes can put new stressors on them since they may need to address expectations of supporters; it would also take them out of their immediate support network on the field, and decrease expectations of returning to their location of service soon.

E. Specific Stress Management Tools

Accumulated stress often creates muscle tension because of difficulty relaxing or slowing down. Here are some easy and effective techniques to respond to that.

Progressive Muscle Relaxation

Progressive muscle relaxation decreases stress-induced muscle tension by increasing awareness of the tension and building skills to release it. Muscle groups are tensed for a short time (progressing from one group to the next) and then relaxed, while the person notices how each group feels when relaxed (Jacobson, 1938; Rimm and Masters, 1979). Noticing muscle tension is the first step to consciously releasing it. Stressed people often tense shoulder, neck, or lower back muscles. Physically letting go will also prompt the mind to follow suit and relax.

Written instructions can be found on the Internet at: www.amsa.org/healingthehealer/musclerelaxation.cfm.

An audio instruction can be particularly helpful for practice. Examples can be found at: www.cmhc.utexas.edu/stressrecess/Level_Two/progressive.html or www.youtube.com/watch?v=HFwCKKa--18 .

Slow-Beat-Music and Singing

In a research study, stress levels were measured for open-heart surgery patients listening to calming music. While they listened, their cortisol (stress hormone) levels were significantly lower than those of patients who only rested (Nilsson, 2009). When patients undergoing hernia surgery listened to calming music, their stress response decreased and they reported less postoperative pain (Nilsson, 2005). Calm, slow-beat-music of any style appears to decrease the stress response. This music puts listeners in a calm inner space. As attention is drawn to pleasant sounds, rhythms, and tunes, they calm the agitated body and pleasingly distract the mind. Whoever appreciates music should make plenty of use of his or her favorite slow-beat-music, especially when stressed. When traumatic memories trigger a stress response, slow-beat-music is one strategy to emotionally exit the memory and relax.

Like deep breathing exercise, singing slows breathing and supports a more diaphragmatic, relaxed style of breathing. Singing is an artful way of voiced exhalation. In distress it can also become a "beautiful way of groaning." As the music connects with our souls so the slow voiced exhalation affects our bodies. American trauma expert Bessel van der Kolk hypothesized during a workshop I attended recently, that singing (in a church choir) may be a good way to increase trauma resilience. It is worth considering how songs, chants, or humming a tune could be used in coming alongside traumatized people. The Christian community has a vast tradition of hymns and contemporary songs, which can soothe, comfort, and calm in stressful moments, if appropriately used.

Imagery

Imagery is a way to emotionally enter a relaxing and comforting experience. Suitable for imagery practices are a safe, relaxing vacation spot; a pleasant, restful garden; a scene of spiritual significance; or an image from the Bible (Psalm 23's resting in green pastures, for instance). As one enters healing imagery, specific sights, sounds, scents, and physical sensations need to be vividly imagined. As these sensations become strong in one's mind so will the relaxing and comforting effect of the imagery.

F. Medications and Resilience

Often Christians are concerned that psychotropic medications could "coddle" them, leading to dependency on "crutches." Jonathan Davidson, a researcher at Duke University, examined the effect of the anti-anxiety and antidepressant medication Sertralin (Zoloft), one of the selective serotonin reuptake inhibitors (SSRI), on resilience. Some aspects of resilience improved with the medication. People felt more confident. They also had a better sense of control, improved ability to handle themselves and their feelings, and increased ability to adapt to change. Since they were less overwhelmed, they felt that coping with stress made them stronger. Davidson also found aspects of resilience that remained the same with or without medication. Not surprisingly these unaffected characteristics were belief in God, a sense of meaning, ability to make decisions, and a sense of determination (Davidson et al., 2005).

Generally, medications are needed when people do not have the energy or emotional control to apply their usual coping skills. Examples of this include someone feeling overwhelmed for a long time despite efforts to improve, or losing control over emotions. People with angry outbursts, repeated crying, or "freaking out" will benefit from medications. If there are suicidal thoughts, a referral to a trained professional is needed. Medications can help to "turn the volume down" on strong feelings a person is unable to deal with constructively. In this way medications can help establish a sense of control and improve functioning. One will still feel emotions, but no longer to an overwhelming degree.

People taking medications still need to work through their emotional issues, but will be less inclined to avoid or resist this work. Once a need for anti-anxiety or antidepressant medication has been established by a physician, the person does best to stay on it for at least six to twelve months. This allows the person to work through stressful issues, increasing long-term *psychological* resilience. It also provides a time frame for the brain to recover from the effects of high chronic stress, increasing long-term *biological* resilience. When the physician suggests that medications be gradually tapered off, the patient is in a better place to do this successfully. It is then often possible to "get rid of the crutches" because new psychological and biological resilience has been gained. As spiritual resilience is very little affected by medications, we need to "dig deeper" to strengthen or restore this aspect of strength and vitality. The *Spiritual Resources* chapter of this book presents aids for effective "digging."

SECTION 5
Managing Severe Traumatic Stress
Frauke Schaefer

A. The Brain Responds to Trauma

The body's reaction to trauma goes beyond a biological stress response. Neurobiologists have in recent decades shed more light on how the human brain reacts to severe trauma. These insights are invaluable for understanding how to manage severe traumatic stress.

Deep brain structures, the amygdala and hippocampus, take center stage in survival situations. As part of the limbic system, they guide emotion and behavior for safety and survival. This part of the brain works at an instinctual, unconscious level and responds to sensation rather than to language or conscious thought. The amygdala assesses sensory perceptions from the body for their significance, and indicates detected significance by emotions. For example, it alerts the body to danger, and sets a flight–fight response in motion when needed. In dangerous situations, the amygdala functions like an alarm system. It also stores experiences, especially dangerous ones, as memory images connected with strong emotions. These memory images coupled with strong emotions aid the body in reacting immediately and effectively to threats.

The hippocampus saves memories and factual details (when and where something happened), then categorizes and stores them in short-term memory. It also makes memories available to higher cortical brain structures that allow conscious processing. Learning from experience requires at least a functioning short-term memory. Unfortunately, high stimulation of the amygdala interferes with hippocampal functioning. A person with high amygdala stimulation has strong emotional and physical distress (arousal, somatic flashbacks), but is unable to further process an event (van der Kolk, *Psychobiology*, 2007). Once arousal is under control, the hippocampus can categorize, store, and connect information to the brain cortex for cognitive and verbal processing. This is necessary for understanding, integration, and making meaning. Several modern therapeutic and healing prayer intervention strategies support relaxation by creating physical and emotional experiences of safety and connection (grounding, imagery), which decrease amygdala arousal, making way for effective processing of emotionally charged traumatic memory.

Psychological trauma is like an emotional scar that causes the brain's appraisal system to overreact to stimuli, triggering physical stress, flashbacks (stressful images), or physical sensations as if major trauma was happening. The person may be unaware of the trigger, but notice the reaction in mind and body. In fact those who have not stored traumatic memory in higher brain structures may be unaware that a trauma-related sensation has caused alarm in their body. Those without conscious recall of parts of the trauma can be left with confusing memory gaps. Increased ability to manage arousal and traumatic stress can pave the way to restoring those gaps.

Researchers studied brain activity in people with active traumatic flashbacks when their trauma stories were read to them. There was ample activity in the right-brain hemisphere where emotional significance is evaluated. In contrast, the left-brain hemisphere, including the parts responsible for language, showed very little activity (van der Kolk, *Psychobiology,* 2007). When exposed to traumatic memories, brains can be so overstimulated that they are literally "unable to think" at a level necessary to comprehend and integrate the experience. Based on this, it is necessary to provide tools for managing overstimulation, hyperarousal, and flashbacks in preparation for any verbal processing of a traumatic event. Connecting to a traumatized person in a gentle, respectful, calm, and if needed, firm manner is a first step toward reducing her or his state of arousal.

B. Skills for Emotional Control

Since effective processing of trauma is possible only when a person is able to manage hyperarousal and flashbacks sufficiently, skills for emotional control are essential. The following skills have been used successfully in coping with the strong emotions caused by traumatic stress.

Deep Breathing

The fight–flight response activated with trauma-related triggers releases stress hormones into the body. Anxiety makes breathing shallow and rapid; muscles of the chest move and extend upward. Shallow, rapid breaths can lead to hyperventilation or dizziness. Deep, slow diaphragmatic breathing is a quick, safe, and effective way to decrease a stress response. It is like putting on the brakes after the accelerator was pushed too far. Just a few slow, diaphragmatic breaths often settle intense arousal. Deep breathing should be practiced prior to a stressful situation. Here is one way to practice:

1. Sit comfortably in a chair, rest your feet firmly on the ground, and place your hand(s) on your stomach. (You can also practice deep breathing standing up or lying down.)
2. Breathe in, imagining air flowing into the lower part of your abdomen. Hold the air for a brief moment.
3. Slowly exhale through your mouth; you may count to eight to help slow exhalation. Pause for a moment until you need to take the next breath.
4. Take several deep breaths and notice the changes in your body. Once practiced, deep breathing can be used in any circumstance or posture.
5. As an additional help, you may think of breathing in new (God's) strength on inhalation, and letting go of tension while exhaling.

When assisting somebody in acute distress, try breathing deeply together. Crisis is not a time for detailed instructions, but a companion providing an example will lend great support.

Grounding Techniques

Grounding techniques are helpful to counteract trauma-related triggers and flashbacks. As mind and body are highjacked by memory images (flashbacks), intense emotions, and physical alarms of the amygdala, the person can return to the present moment (here and now) by grounding his or her senses in immediate safe surroundings. Grounding can work like this:

- "Notice how your feet feel touching the floor. Notice how your body feels resting on the chair. Notice any physical sensation that feels neutral or comforting."
- "Notice what you see in the here and now. (Notice some details: Which items around you are green, blue, or yellow?) Notice what

you hear (details). Notice what the chair, table, clothes feel like when touched (details), and perhaps, notice what you smell. This is (day of the week, date), in (place). This is a safe place."

- In addition, consider a favorite strong scent such as cinnamon, lavender, perfume, cologne, or coffee to bring awareness back to the present moment. Some people carry a small sample of scent in their handbag or pocket and sniff it when triggered. Since the olfactory system (sense of smell) is part of the limbic system, scents with positive associations can reduce the effect of flashbacks. On the other hand, flashbacks can be triggered by scents associated with trauma, such as smoke, oil, the burning of a fire, or the scent of cologne associated with a rape. It is important to help the person select a scent with only pleasant and relaxing associations.

Imagery Techniques

Imagery techniques are used to consciously direct one's attention to relaxing, safe, and enjoyable sensations. When trauma-related sensations cause distress, redirecting the mind to pleasant sensations helps to relax and reduce the stress response. Typically, trauma survivors are relieved when they realize they do not need to suffer through flashbacks, but have tools to control, reduce, or stop them.

The following imagery techniques have been applied with good results:

1. *Safe-place Imagery*

The safe-place relaxation exercise is particularly useful in overcoming traumatic stress. It fills the mind with pleasant, relaxing sensations, literally crowding out unpleasant trauma-related ones. It can reduce or stop flashbacks. The following is an instruction for safe-place imagery:

- "Find a memory in your mind of a place that you have experienced, where you can feel completely safe, and your body is calm and relaxed. You are there by yourself. God may be present. It may take a while to find that place. Make sure you feel completely safe and relaxed there."
- "Once you have found your safe, relaxing place, imagine entering it. Notice what you *see*. Become aware of details. Notice what you *hear*.

What characteristics do the sounds have? Or, do you 'hear' silence?
- Notice what you *feel on your skin*. Is it warm or cold, any movement of air? Can you *touch* things around you? What do they feel like? Do you notice a pleasant *scent or smell*? What is it like?"
- "Linger in your safe place for a while; enjoy the relaxing, pleasant sensations. Let them fill your mind until they are strong and your body feels good and relaxed."
- "When you are ready to leave the safe place take a deep breath, open your eyes, and return to where you are now."

The safe-place imagery needs to first be practiced when there are no flashbacks or triggers. Once this is mastered, it can be applied to stop flashbacks and trigger reactions.

2. *Image-Stop-Technique*

This skill is used to control traumatic flashbacks lasting more than a short moment. Flashbacks may be stable images or a moving picture. Changing the flashback from overwhelming, horrible and inescapable image to something that can be mentally observed with some detachment from a distance achieves a greater sense of control. This reduces emotional impact.

- "Visualize the flashback image as you would normally view images or movies at home (scrapbook, TV, computer screen)."
- "Gently shift your awareness from the middle of the image to the edges. Imagine a picture frame, TV screen, or the edges of your computer around the image or movie."
- "Imagine the flashback image as a picture in a scrapbook. Mentally close the scrapbook and put the date and year on the front, so you can find the image again when you are ready." Or, "If it is a flashback movie, imagine using a remote control or computer keys to change the images: press fast forward, backward, switch off the sound, change the color, or edit with a photo-shop program."

3. *Imagery Rehearsal*

Imagery Rehearsal has been studied in trauma survivors who have disturbing nightmares. It was very effective after only a few focused practice sessions. The results were so impressive, they were published in the *Journal of American Medical Association* (Krakow, 2001). The Imagery Rehearsal technique assumes that intentional imagery while awake can influence the type and frequency of nightmares. Key elements of Imagery Rehearsal are:

- Write down a disturbing nightmare (start with a less disturbing one).
- Change the nightmare in any positive way you wish, and write down the changed dream.
- Rehearse the changed dream in vivid imagery for ten to fifteen minutes.
- Share the old and new dream with another person (a trusted caregiver, peer responder, counselor, or mental health professional).
- Rehearse the new dream for five to twenty minutes daily, but never work on more than two distinct dreams each week. Start with the least distressing nightmare and gradually proceed to more distressing ones.
- If Imagery Rehearsal unexpectedly increases emotional distress, stop and consult a mental health professional.

In less severe cases, encourage persons with nightmares simply to change the bad dream in any way they like and write down the new version. They then rehearse the altered dream daily until the nightmare is no longer bothersome.

Strategic Distraction

Simple distraction helps when intense pain, hurt, or anxiety floods in and cannot be dealt with effectively. Distraction should not become a regular habit, but has its place in managing distress. Safe activities with physical sensations are particularly suitable as they provide natural grounding in the present moment: Wrapping oneself in a blanket and enjoying a hot or cold drink, leisure reading, taking a warm shower or bath, looking at something pleasant or beautiful, or listening to calming sounds (waterfall, creek, soft music).

If one is angry or anxious, physical activity will relieve stress and generate strong, normal physical sensations. Examples include yard work, lawn-mowing, chopping wood, gardening, housecleaning, baking and cooking. Games that do not demand a lot of focus can be a welcome distraction, too. Movies can work, but need to be used with great caution as they can contain violence and trauma triggers. If social situations are a trigger, talking to a "safe" person can help inner upheaval subside.

Basic Anger Management

Anger is a common concern after trauma. If a person "goes from 0 to 100" in a fraction of a second it makes controlling anger difficult. Fortunately, most people are able to identify physical sensations that indicate when anger is rising. Examples include muscle tension, sense of heat, or higher pulse rate. Once aware of the indicators, people can remove themselves from a situation and calm down before further action. "Time out" can be as simple as leaving the room for as long as it takes to reduce anger to a manageable level. Walking away for a moment, and taking a few deep breaths can further decrease inner tension. Regular exercise often helps cut down intense, angry reactions.

Trigger Identification

Triggers are sensations that activate a person's flight-fight response. These could be any sensations associated with past trauma, such as the sight of clothes reminiscent of a robber, sounds or smells associated with a car accident, or types of touch or other sensations linked to a rape. It may take a little detective work to understand why a person is triggered by an otherwise normal situation. But, effectively "spotting" triggers is part of overcoming their effect.

The more people become aware of trauma-related triggers they react to, the easier it is to actively "take care of their flight-fight response" by using grounding skills, deep breathing, and strategic distraction. Educating recently traumatized people about triggers and common reactions equips them to "spot" triggers. This enables them to accurately interpret physical and mental arousal and react with effective use of skills. Equipped with information, handouts, and grounding strategies, they will feel more confident.

C. Avoiding Avoidance

As described earlier, when the amygdala identifies a serious threat it puts body and mind in survival mode, ready for effective fight or flight. Reactions are instinctive and physical rather than thought through. As the fight-flight reaction subsides, other brain functions such as short-term memory (hippocampus) and complex processing (executive frontal brain cortex) become available enabling deeper understanding, coherence, and decision making. While a person is in fight-flight mode, it is impossible to think in more complex terms. It is a state of uncomfortable physical arousal and a strong sense of fear and danger. This is hard to tolerate. The instinctive impulse is to spring into action to overcome or avoid the threat.

While action or avoidance is helpful in immediate danger, it is a "false alarm" when a trigger leads to a flashback. The more uncomfortable the response to trauma-associated sights, sounds, smells, and other sensations, the more likely the person is to avoid such stimuli. Someone may avoid driving for a while after a severe car accident, or may avoid driving on the road where the accident happened. If a truck was involved, then trucks could become triggers. Passing trucks could be so intolerable that driving is avoided completely. Only when people gain confidence in dealing with their distress will they gradually overcome avoidance.

Considering the pain of trigger reactions, there is good reason to avoid certain sights, sounds, physical sensations, or talking about the traumatic event as long as somebody is very distressed and easily overwhelmed. Pushing a person to talk or engage in activities that trigger traumatic memories when they do not have the necessary management tools would re-traumatize him or her without any gain. If, however, a person feels confident and equipped to cope with triggers, she or he is in a good place to talk about the trauma and take steps to overcome avoidance behaviors. The trauma will need to be faced eventually for healing to occur. Applying the wisdom of Ecclesiastes 3: There is time to avoid (distract, stabilize) traumatic memories, and there is time to face them. When a traumatized person is overwhelmed, it is time to avoid, distract, and stabilize. When a person has natural or acquired coping skills and is ready to face the trauma and related triggers, it is time to do so. Jerry Sittser attests to the necessity of facing traumatic loss in *A Grace Disguised* with a powerful metaphor:

> The quickest way for anyone to reach the sun and the light of day is not to run west, chasing after the setting sun, but to head east, plunging into the darkness until one comes to the sunrise (Sittser, 2004, 42).

When a person continually avoids darkness (emotional pain) the way to the sun (healing and well-being) will be protracted. Some will need to make a conscious decision to take a 180-degree turn from immediate pain relief by avoidance, and instead face what is uncomfortable in order to attain deeper long-term relief and restoration. Skills in managing traumatic stress will help a person take this step. Sittser describes his choice:

> I discovered in that moment that I had the power to choose the direction my life would head, even if the only choice open to me, at least initially, was either to run from the loss or to face it as best I could. Since I knew that darkness was inevitable and unavoidable, I decided from that point on to walk into the darkness rather than try to outrun it, to let my experience of loss take me on a journey wherever it would lead, and to allow myself to be transformed by my suffering rather than to think I could somehow avoid it. I chose to turn toward the pain, however falteringly, and to yield to the loss, though I had no idea at the time what that would mean (Sittser, 2004, 42).

Convinced of the value of facing emotional pain, counselors and other supporters may feel an urge to draw someone into talking about their trauma or loss before they are ready. It is important to wait until the person is willing to talk. The interim is best used for supporting, stabilizing, comforting, and equipping with coping methods. Once the person is ready to talk about the trauma encourage him or her to pause, breathe, or take a break whenever needed. The confidence gained by navigating in and out of traumatic memories without being overwhelmed is worth more for the healing process than a complete narrative.

Some people find it helpful to process by journaling. This is a great tool! Those prone to avoidance may need nudging to journal. They may want to first talk with another person about difficult aspects of their experience. Others may be drawn into working too hard at processing their event, not allowing sufficient time for comfort, relaxation, support, and normal activities of life. The latter group risks exhausting their limited emotional resources. They will need encouragement to slow down, take their time, and engage in normal, stabilizing, or comforting activities and then continue processing. Facing pain takes a physical toll, and needs to be offset by regenerating activities. As a physical body needs the rhythm of working and resting, so does the soul.

It needs to move in an alternating rhythm of facing pain, and regenerating, or distracting.

There are many ways to avoid pain. One is to keep preoccupied with thoughts about how the situation could have been prevented. These thoughts tend to start with "if only," and can lead to self-accusation or guilt, which can then dominate the mind, leaving no room for facing pain. Another means of avoidance is to allow too much distraction (TV, play, overeating, drinking, drugs, and inappropriate relationships or sexual activities), so that pain is crowded out or numbed. For others, anger feels easier than vulnerability, but it deflects the pain. Withdrawing from all but the closest and safest friends and family may be necessary for a time, but continued withdrawal will prolong agony.

Fortunately, resilient rebound from trauma is far more common than lasting posttraumatic stress (Bonnano, 2004). Though the majority (50-60%) of the American population goes through one or more severe traumas in their lifetime, only 5-10% develop PTSD (Ozer, 2003). Among a group of missionaries working in West Africa, 85-90% had one or more severe lifetime traumas, but only about 5% developed PTSD (20% had either full PTSD or posttraumatic stress symptoms; Schaefer, 2007). This suggests that the West Africa missionaries were more resilient than the general American population. Certain types of trauma have higher rates of PTSD (physical assault, rape, and war trauma). Also, high-risk environments are a factor. Missionaries in less stable locations (high rates of poverty, crime, and civil unrest) developed PTSD more frequently. This indicates that very high levels of ongoing stress may eventually even exhaust the reserves of those with excellent coping skills. This said, a large number of traumatized persons gradually improve over three to six months from impact. Despite lingering symptoms and struggle, even more improvement can be expected during the remainder of the first year. For many, the first or second anniversary after the crisis are turning points toward improvement and return to a "new normal" way of life. Each situation and person is unique, and no judgment should be passed on people with a longer course of recovery. Only a small number will suffer long-term distress. With good support this number can be further reduced. If a person seems to be doing well after trauma, it is good to follow up after about three months to see if recovery continues. If not, additional support by a trained counselor or professional may be needed.

D. Dissociation—Numbing and Amnesia

Dissociation is a way the brain protects the mind from unbearable distress by detaching from some aspects of the trauma. During dissociation the thalamus, a part of the midbrain, shows reduced activity. Normally, the thalamus receives sensory input from both the body and the external world. Then it connects this information with the cerebral cortex, allowing conscious processing. This thalamus–cortex interaction helps the person integrate sensory (bodily), emotional and cognitive data, process them effectively, and experience himself as coherent. Dissociation protects the mind, but at the cost of disintegrating perception, memory, and sense of self (Frewen, 2006; van der Kolk, *Dissociation*, 2007). The normal integrated conscious experience of self is disrupted when people dissociate. Though the process allows distancing, it leads to a disintegrated state of mind. When dissociation continues beyond the immediate phase after trauma, it will start to hinder effective reintegration. Flashbacks can be considered as dissociated perceptions. Other common ways dissociation is experienced are amnesia and numbing.

When dissociation occurs, some of the experience is not available. Therefore, the person cannot remember parts of the traumatic event, however hard he may try. This is amnesia, and it can be troubling and confusing. Crisis responders need to be aware that this memory gap has been established for a reason. It is part of the trauma story the person was unable to face at that time. Once the person has acquired tools to regulate distress and regains stability, her or his mind may fill in the memory gap and process it, leading to reintegration of the person's experience. If the memory gap continues and is troublesome, the person would benefit from professional counseling.

Emotional numbing occurs in another type of posttraumatic dissociation. The brain processes this type of dissociation in a very different manner. It is a state of high vigilance and increased pain tolerance (Frewen, 2006; van der Kolk, *Dissociation*, 2007). People who experience emotional numbing feel detached and not really present, as if they had "left their body;" they feel "frozen" and emotionally "shut down." This type of dissociative process called depersonalization functions like an anesthetic. Depersonalization keeps people from feeling pain when others would feel a lot. Supporters will notice these people as seeming unusually numb and calm for what is occurring (or being discussed). They appear disengaged, detached, or absent. A person talking about a horrible event in an emotionless manner may be dissociating rather than "coping." In such a state, normal coping or processing is impossible. This "shut-down" emergency state of mind avoids distress overload but does not aid reintegration. Though dissociation relieves distress in acute crisis, it is never the state of mind to process troubling events constructively.

E. Supporting People in Panic: De-escalation

After the sudden death of a loved one, assault, sexual violation, deadly disaster, or other similarly intense traumas it is not unusual for painful emotions to reach such intensity that they are impossible to control. Some people may cry uncontrollably or have a panic attack. Panicked people are agitated, pacing, crying, wailing, shouting, or hyperventilating. Their heart beats fast, their muscles are tense, they sweat; some are nauseous to the point of vomiting.

Supporting people in panic starts by remaining calm ourselves. We can control our own stress by taking a few deep diaphragmatic breaths (see *Deep Breathing* in Section 5 B), briefly praying, and focusing our mind on God's presence, help, and strength. We might pray quietly, asking God to provide comfort and safety. If we stay calm, our support and guidance can provide stability for the person in panic. The supporter's emotions directly influence the assisted one's, for better or worse.

We can help panicked people by asking them to take a few deep breaths. This works best by deep breathing together. If the person continues to hyperventilate (rapid, shallow breaths) we can offer a paper bag to hold and breathe into. This helps calm the troubling physical sensations that go along with hyperventilation. After the person is breathing slower (or into a bag), we can ask: "Which part of your body feels better now?" This turns her or his attention away from physical distress to positive sensations, and will allow further relaxation.

The following *de-escalation techniques* can help in difficult situations:

- Try to appear calm and self-assured, even if you do not feel that way. Consciously lower your tone of voice, speak firmly and perhaps somewhat slower.

- Always be respectful even when redirecting or setting limits. The agitated individual is very sensitive about feeling shamed and disrespected.
- Do not smile, since this can be misinterpreted as mockery or anxiety.
- Be cautious with touch (ask permission first), or do not touch at all since this can feel uncomfortable or intrusive to an agitated person.
- Allow the person physical space to pace, and do what you can to prevent physical injury.
- Do not raise your voice over a screaming person. Wait until the person takes a breath, then talk. Speak calmly at average volume.
- Speak in an authoritative, firm, but always respectful tone.
- Never argue or try to convince, since agitated persons are not in a state to be reasonable.
- Try simple steps, such as providing some water (in an unbreakable container) or a blanket, or gently directing attention to an action step.
- If possible, take the person to a place with shelter from upsetting stimuli.

F. When to Consider Medications

Emotion regulation and de-escalation skills will go a long way, but occasionally the support of medications is indicated.

Panic

If panic does not subside with support, or if it recurs intensely, a consulted physician may prescribe tranquilizers (such as alprazolam, lorazepam, clonazepam, or diazepam). These medications should only be used short-term, as they may cause dependency.

Insomnia

Agitation following a crisis can keep body and mind on alert all through the night. If insomnia lasts for several days, it leads to fatigue and decreased ability to cope. Avoiding caffeine and alcohol are important steps to improve sleep, along with relaxing and distracting activities before bedtime. If this is not sufficient, over-the-counter medications (Benadryl, Melatonin, and

Valerian Root) or sleep-enhancing herbal teas are a next step. If these do not bring about six to seven hours of sleep most nights, a physician should be consulted about an appropriate sleep aid. These should generally not be taken long-term. Address the underlying cause of sleep disturbance and develop healthy sleep habits ("sleep hygiene").

Depression, Anxiety, and Posttraumatic Stress

When more severe depression, anxiety, or posttraumatic stress leads to significant difficulties functioning at home or at work, it is time to consider an antidepressant or antianxiety medication with a health care provider. In most situations an SSRI (Selective-Serotonin-Reuptake-Inhibitor) or SNRI (Serotonin-Norepinephrine-Reuptake-Inhibitor) will be prescribed. These are medications such as sertraline (Zoloft), citalopram (Celexa), escitalopram (Lexapro), fluoxetine (Prozac), paroxetine (Paxil), venlafaxine (Effexor), desvenlafaxin (Pristiq) or mirtazapine (Remeron). They improve depression, anxiety, and posttraumatic symptoms after two to four weeks of regular intake. This period is necessary for serotonin or norepinephrine levels in the brain to increase. The health care provider will consider overall mental and physical health, as well as potential side effects, in selecting the best medication.

G. Managing Suicidal Impulses

After the devastating accident in Tanzania that killed her husband and severely injured her son and herself, Ann Hamel recounts:

> As the reality of what happened sank in I was overwhelmed. All of my life I had seen God as my heavenly Father. I willingly left the comfort and security of life in America to serve Him in Africa but I trusted Him to take care of me and my family. As I grappled with what had happened, I regretted that any of us had survived this horrible accident. Death seemed preferable to the life that I had before me. My pain was so intense that I only thought of how to escape it. I looked at the IV drip and asked our physician friend to put something in there that would end my life. I didn't want to face a future without my husband and without God. (Story 3)

Right after Ann realized what happened she was so overwhelmed with pain, loss, and spiritual struggle that death appeared preferable to life. She not only wished she were dead, but also considered practical steps to bring that about.

After devastating crises, suicidal thoughts can befall even the strongest and most spiritual of us. The righteous Job laments the devastating pain of his life. His distaste for life after successive disasters was grave, indeed. He wished intensely he had never been born, and cursed the day and circumstances of his birth (Job 3).

Supporters need to be aware that suicidal thoughts and urges to act on those thoughts can occur when people are overwhelmed with pain, loss, depression or anxiety. It is important to listen for indications of suicidal thinking. It needs to be our normal practice to ask people directly whether or not they feel "tired of life" or "wish they were dead." Asking will not plant dangerous ideas in someone's mind. In fact, asking the question in a caring manner provides an opportunity to talk about thoughts or urges they have been too afraid or ashamed to discuss.

Suicidal people feel trapped and helpless, either because of the situation or the intensity of their emotions. If a person voices suicidal thoughts, take safety measures immediately! Professional assistance needs to be pursued to determine the severity of risk. In the U.S.A. this is a mental health professional. If there seems to be an imminent risk of self-harm, bring the person to a local emergency room or call 9-1-1.

In the absence (or delay) of access to a professional, a trusted and mature supporter (or team) should stay with the person at all times. The presence of supporters in itself often alleviates fears and the urge to self-harm. Supporters need to make sure that any means for self-harm are inaccessible, in particular those the person may be thinking about. This includes removing potentially harmful medications, knives, guns, ropes, or other items that could be used for self-harm. Access to alcohol, which can impair self-control, should also be monitored. Normally, people in distress want both to escape the overwhelming distress through death, and also to continue living. Suicidal thoughts often frighten the person who has them. Supporters can usually connect with the part of the person that wants to live and support this inclination. In this way, supporters become allies in the fight to survive any death wish.

H. Concluding Remarks

Supporting those with severe traumatic stress can be a daunting task. In countries where health care, including mental health, is readily available, support will most often be provided by health care professionals and emergency or disaster workers. In countries where professional support is limited, peer responders, member care representatives, mission leaders or colleagues may be at the forefront providing "psychological first aid." For all of these, as well as pastors and church members with special interest in post-trauma support, understanding principles of managing traumatic stress will help in companioning people on the road to recovery, often alongside professional support.

Many cross-cultural workers in less developed countries use *Where There Is No Doctor* by David Werner (Werner, 1992) for medical first aid. This book provides information about essential health care at the grass roots level in an easy-to-understand format. Since 2003, *Where There Is No Psychiatrist* by Vikram Patel, with a similar concept became available. A similar book focused on crisis care would be a great and much needed addition.

SECTION 6
Spiritual Resources in Dealing with Trauma
Frauke and Charlie Schaefer

When a drunk driver devastated Jerry Sittser's life by killing three family members and injuring others, Jerry was bewildered by confusing thoughts and a host of intense feelings (Story 4). Pain, grief, sorrow, anger, fear, and puzzlement were often overwhelming. His slow recovery was aided by certain strengths that supported him through this crisis. Jerry's faith was strong. He also leaned on solid, close friendships, and a strong connection to a Christian community. Friends listened to his feelings without trying to change them. Knowledge of psalms of lament reminded Jerry that voicing strong, raw emotions before God is acceptable. Jerry also needed to make sense of the traumatic incident and its impact on his overall understanding of life and God. He grappled with serious questions: Is there a God? Is God truly in control? Is there a universal morality? He entered a process of "wrapping his mind around" a world that had changed profoundly for him.

In retrospect, many years after the accident, Jerry points at the trauma-induced scar on his life that became a mark of grace. He noticed that his emotional life had deepened, that he had new clarity about what really matters, and renewed determination to dedicate himself to what matters most. After much doubting and grappling, Jerry found renewed confidence in his faith. He came to know God and his grace in a new, deeper way.

As with Jerry, severe trauma abruptly forces people out of their emotional and intellectual stability. In *Facilitating Posttraumatic Growth*, Calhoun and Tedeschi (Calhoun and Tedeschi, 1999, 2) metaphorically describe severe trauma as events with "seismic" impact on a person's worldview and emotional functioning. Like an earthquake, trauma vehemently shakes up, and often shatters the person's understanding of the world.

Trauma, in this chapter, refers to experiences that people go through or witness involving either serious injury, death, or threat of dying. Either they themselves are affected, or their family and close friends. Reactions to severe trauma typically include fear, helplessness, or horror. Examples of such traumatic events are accidents with physical injury or death; natural disasters resulting in threats of injury or death; diagnoses of life-threatening diseases; miscarriage or stillbirth; and violence, such as robbery, carjacking, rape, and exposure to civil unrest or war. There are other traumatic situations such as unemployment, loss of property, homelessness, divorce, and ongoing high levels of stress that take a toll. These are not the focus of our considerations here. However, much of what we discuss also applies to these painful issues.

Trauma shakes up a person's deepest convictions about the purpose and meaning of life, and raises questions about one's view of God. Christians in ministry, whose relationship with God is the foundation of their lives, can be especially challenged. Questions can erupt such as: Why does God allow suffering? Is God indeed good when he apparently allows evil? Is belief in a loving and all-powerful God consistent with the suffering in the world? Trying to make theological sense of world tragedies, including the incomprehensible massacre at Virginia Tech in 2007, Philip Yancey asks, "What good is God?" (Yancey, 2010). Tragedies challenge the concept of God we have known and relied upon. Does God care? Will he respond to our needs and the needs of those we care about? Can we bring our confusion, disappointment, or frustration before God? Or, would God be angered and abandon or punish us in the midst of our deepest pain? Does God want us to only trust and defer to him? Or, can we still face him with honesty and dignity? Trauma can alter our sense of vision and purpose in ministry. After loss, hurt, or betrayal it is common to wonder: Is it worth it? Are *they* (the people ministered to) worth it? Does it make sense to give up so much? Can ministry have any meaningful impact here? How can God want me to continue when I am weak and failing?

When trauma pushes us into emotional turmoil and confusion about life's deepest questions, shaking our very foundations, we become vulnerable. Previously comforting beliefs can take a beating. As we struggle through puzzlement, pieces of our belief system eventually become rearranged. Crisis creates an opportunity for new construction and more solid foundations. Picture what occurs when houses are rebuilt after a natural disaster. Some parts of the old house may come to good use in the new one. Some may not be useful any more. Some foundations may require rebuilding. Rebuilding can result in a structure that is less solid, equally solid, or even more solid than the one before. Similarly, after the personal and spiritual reconstruction process following a crisis, people might emerge more fragile, as strong as before, or stronger and more resilient. Considering this process of shattering, struggling, and reconstructing, the questions arise: What characteristics increase resilience in the face of trauma-induced emotional and spiritual challenges? Are there ways to better prepare for them? What factors determine how we move through this emotional and spiritual vulnerability?

Resilience describes a person's ability to "bounce back" after an impact. It assumes a trauma-induced "loss of shape," which will be restored later. Resilient persons regain their prior constitution after the impact. Many factors determine resilience: biological, psychological, social, and spiritual. This chapter focuses on spiritual factors that enhance resilience.

Our *Christian faith* is relational in nature, a personal, covenantal bond between us and God who created and loves us. In Jesus Christ, God suffered and died on the cross for our sins so that we can receive newness of spiritual life. God lives in us and transforms us through the Holy Spirit. We want to love and honor God as we pursue his kingdom purposes in the power of his Spirit. We ultimately expect to be eternally connected with him in love and worship. The purpose and meaning of our lives are built on this relationship with God; this is described scientifically as "intrinsic religiosity." Trauma can break this essential relationship. Christians may experience this breaking like the proverbial rug being pulled out from under them. Spiritual resilience is determined by the probability that one's connection with God will be restored and even strengthened after an impact.

Certain *spiritual characteristics* make us more resilient. An acquired healthy biblical theology of suffering provides a sturdy framework of support through inevitable struggles after trauma. A practiced ability to forgive will facilitate letting go of debilitating anger, hurt, bitterness, and resentment after violent crises. Familiarity with accepting and expressing strong feelings in relationship with God and others will allow connecting, healing, and regaining hope more quickly after adversity. Security and openness in a few relationships, particularly with other believers, will provide a much needed safe place to sustain in vulnerable times.

For a person in the midst of the "seismic impact" of posttraumatic struggle, certain *spiritual resources* help the rebuilding process, often establishing deeper foundations. Experiencing God's presence in "the valley of the shadows," however weak or veiled, is key to assuring Christian believers of the enduring relationship with the author and sustainer of their lives. Expressing strong feelings in lament to God is a way to reconnect with him. Finding a path from anger and bitterness to true forgiveness frees the person from being trapped in an ongoing, self-destructive bond to the painful past. Experiencing God's grace can help someone rebound from the self-condemnation that trauma can cause.

Those who go through struggle and rebuilding well will reap growth in the process. *Posttraumatic growth* describes positive changes after trauma, changes in how we see ourselves and relationships, and how we understand God, the world, or life's purpose and meaning. Posttraumatic growth increases future resilience.

In this section we will first look at *spiritual characteristics* that increase the resilience of Christians *before* they venture into a high-risk situation. We will consider how these characteristics can be strengthened in preparation for challenge. Then we will look at *spiritual resources* that will help *in the midst* of spiritual struggles after trauma. Those who prepare others for ministry may find the "Spiritual Resilience Checklist" (pages 146-7) helpful in orientation programs or as a tool for assessing spiritual resilience in candidates for ministry. Those caring for people *after* trauma will find particularly relevant resources in the second section of this chapter. The distinction between spiritual characteristics and spiritual resources is not clear-cut. They influence each other. Spiritual characteristics affect the resourcefulness of people as they move through struggle. And, familiarity with spiritual resources such as lament and the forgiveness process will improve spiritual resilience.

1. SPIRITUAL CHARACTERISTICS OF RESILIENT PERSONS

A. A Sound Theology of Suffering

After unexpected suffering, people are not only challenged to cope with immediate distress and practical problems, but also need to somehow "make sense" of everything. However, what happened may not "make sense" in light of the person's beliefs and expectations. Basic assumptions generally help to attribute meaning to events from a larger framework. Assumptions, as part of a worldview, provide a sense of order, security, orientation, and control. They help interpret new and unusual experiences, which aids adjustment. Religious faith is the overarching framework a believer has to understand the world and find meaning. It provides a lens for understanding the purpose of events and of life as a whole. This understanding generates motivation and vigor for purposeful living.

When an event does not "make sense" within a person's current understanding, confusion, disorientation, a sense of unfairness, unpredictability, and vulnerability will result. The once clear life purpose may turn to uncertainty. Energy and focus gained from a prior clear purpose may be weakened or gone. The person may instead feel like a sailboat adrift on a vast ocean without its compass.

Research Model of Religious Coping after Trauma

Research-based models of coping after trauma have determined that discrepancy between prior assumptions and the understanding of a new event causes distress. The more discrepancy between assumptions and understanding increases, the more distress. This can mean a keen sense of disorientation, loss of control, predictability, or comprehensibility of the world. Crystal Park, a researcher of religious coping, found that reducing discrepancy increases the likelihood of recovery. Discrepancy reduction is possible by changing how the event itself is understood, adjusting global beliefs and goals, or both (Park, 2005). Large discrepancies challenge people to redefine or remodel many of their prior assumptions. Redefining facilitates adjustment, and allows integration of a specific negative experience into a person's global understanding. Better integration will bring about lower levels of depression, higher levels of subjective well-being, and posttraumatic growth.

Theology of Suffering and Discrepancy

A sound theology of suffering will help reduce discrepancy by means of biblically realistic expectations of God. It will also help restore a sense of ultimate security and control. For Christians this sense of security is often found in accepting that God is ultimately in control. A biblical theology of suffering offers reassurance that God is still "good" and "working things out for good." A minister, missionary, or Christian disciple will be less confused in crises when she or he has already grappled with a personal theology of suffering. Teaching missionary and clergy candidates a theology of suffering is fine, but their personal heart-level exploration of beliefs about suffering is the most solid foundation for their resilience. This would involve personal study of relevant texts, small group discussions, and asking difficult, controversial questions. Otherwise, it will remain shallow head knowledge and will not provide sufficient emotional and spiritual support later. To support such a process Scott Shaum has prepared a *Worksheet: Toward a Theology of Risk and Suffering* (Appendix A).

Even equipped with the best theology of suffering, people in ministry will face heart-level struggles after severe trauma. In the midst of these struggles their self-understanding and grasp of the purpose of life will usually deepen. Though there is a real risk of alienation from God during these struggles, fortunately, for most they will bring about the possibility of coming to know God in a new, deeper way.

B. Intrinsic Religious Motivation

Trauma challenges faith and how we know God. The outcome is influenced by the centrality of faith in a person's life. As a Christian's faith grows stronger, it becomes the lens through which trauma is viewed. Faith is also a deep reservoir of spiritual nourishment when we are in need. For a Christian, the degree of love for God and the extent to which personal purpose and meaning is found in relationship with God is key for resilience.

Religious motivation is the most important spiritual characteristic determining how Christians experience trauma. Motivation is distinct from beliefs and practices that make up overall faith, although they are interrelated. Motivation describes the drive behind a Christian's faith in God. Christians pursue faith for many different reasons.

There are two kinds of religious motivation: viewing religion as an end in itself, or as means to another end. *Intrinsic religious motivation* views relationship with God and its sense of purpose and meaning as an end in itself. Christians with this motivation love God because he is God, because he loves them, and because he has died for them. These thoughts inform their choices.

Another motivation for Christians to pursue their faith is it is a means to fulfill other personal desires. They view participation in religion as just one part of life, and value the benefits that come with it. For example, religious practice and commitment can provide security, community, happiness, comfort, health, and prosperity.

These two kinds of motivation are not opposite ends of a continuum, nor are they mutually exclusive. Christians might have both at the same time; with one stronger than the other. Intrinsic religiousness tends to be stronger in those who have solid beliefs and commitments to their faith; whereas, seeking fulfillment of other desires through the practice of faith is not tied to the strength of the person's belief and commitment (Donahue, 1986).

Shadrach, Meshach, and Abednego's response to King Nebuchadnezzar is a good example of how religious motivations influenced decisions (Dan 3). The three young men had been appointed over the affairs of Babylon through Daniel's God-given interpretation of the king's dream. They knew their power and wealth had come through their relationship with God and other believers, and that God was capable of intervening and providing. Nebuchadnezzar threatened to throw them into a fiery furnace if they did not serve his gods or worship the golden image he created. However, Shadrach, Meshach, and Abednego demonstrated that their greatest motivation to worship God was intrinsic, not for status and safety. They would serve God regardless, with the knowledge that God could deliver them. Their motivation was the belief that God was the only one worthy of worship.

> Nebuchadnezzar answered and said to them, "Is it true, O Shadrach, Meshach, and Abednego, that you do not serve my gods or worship the golden image that I have set up? Now if you are ready when you hear the sound of the horn, pipe, lyre, trigon, harp, bagpipe, and every kind of music, to fall down and worship the image that I have made, well and good. But if you do not worship, you shall immediately be cast into a burning fiery furnace. And who is the god who will deliver you out of my hands?" Shadrach, Meshach, and Abednego answered and said to the king, "O Nebuchadnezzar, we have no need to answer you in this matter. If this be so, our God whom we serve is able to deliver

us from the burning fiery furnace, and he will deliver us out of your hand, O king. But if not, be it known to you, O king, that we will not serve your gods or worship the golden image that you have set up" (Dan 3:14-18, ESV).

Deep spiritual resources assured Shadrach, Meshach, and Abednego that God would be with them regardless. When they came out unscathed, King Nebuchadnezzar also began to worship God because he recognized the deliverance of those who chose death over worship of a false god.

When our lives are out of control, belief in God's purpose and promise to be with us (intrinsic religious motivation), can provide steadiness and comfort. Karen Carr experienced this in the weeks following her evacuation from fighting in Ivory Coast. She wrote:

> I cried, I asked questions that didn't have answers like, "Why did God allow this to happen?" I went back to the roots of why I was there (God gave me a love for missionaries and called me to this work). Those roots were deep and enduring and assured me that God would equip me to do the work he had called me to do. It wasn't about my strength or energy or will, really. It was about knowing that this was exactly what I was supposed to do. Motivated by love for the people I was helping and joy in doing so, I could keep on going (Story 1).

When trauma makes us feel helpless, we look for security trusting in God's control, care, and love. Sometimes violence, loss, and tragedy do not make any sense at all. They seem impossible to reconcile with God's love, as initially was the case for Jerry Sittser when he lost three family members (Story 4). Our belief that God loves us and is working his purposes in and through our lives is a steadying source of comfort, hope, and purpose as we endure pain.

Trauma has the potential to cause distress in the form of depression, anxiety, and powerlessness. Research shows that people with intrinsic religious motivation tend to be less depressed by trauma and are more apt to recover sooner (Smith, McCullough and Poll, 2003). They also feel a greater sense of purpose and influence over outcomes, rather than helplessness. Religiousness and mental health are more powerfully linked as one moves from institutional religiosity (extrinsic motivation, participation in church services or activities, ritualized prayer) to personal devotion (intrinsic motivation, emotional attachment to God, devotional intensity, and colloquial prayer) (Hackney and Sanders, 2003).

Engaging Intrinsic Religiousness

Intrinsic religious motivation contributes strongly to better long-term mental health for people who have come through highly stressful life events (Smith, McCullough and Poll, 2003; Schaefer, Blazer and Koenig, 2008). People with strong intrinsic motivation are more likely to make positive changes and grow during the struggle after trauma. They tend to have greater personal strength, deeper personal relationships, greater appreciation of life, and more spiritual growth. These benefits are so remarkable that the American military advocates attention to soldiers' spirituality in cases of Post Traumatic Stress Disorder (PTSD) (Pargament and Sweeney, 2011). This underscores the importance of engaging spiritual resources for resilience and healing when caring for Christians after trauma.

Most Christians in ministry have a strong intrinsic religious motivation when they start out. Their roles play out the purpose and meaning provided by their faith. However, the challenges and pressures in certain ministry positions may erode some of that strength. Since intrinsic religiosity fosters resilience, Christian ministry leaders need to assess, maintain, and strengthen it. Leaders can look for intrinsic motivation by asking about candidates' sense of call and the reasons behind their desire to serve. They can listen for purpose and meaning coming from candidates' relationship with God. To maintain and strengthen intrinsic religiosity, ministry leaders can encourage activities to nurture love for God and awareness of God's presence, such as community worship, music, and prayer. They can foster sharing among staff members about God's work. Mutual support and caring is a tangible expression and reminder of God's love. The priority of personal devotions can be modeled and promoted. Bible studies around topics such as God's character, forgiveness, and grace are reminders of God's love and challenge ministers to incorporate those principles. Christian ministry workers might take regular spiritual retreats with worship, contemplative prayer, spiritual direction, and applied Bible study. Fasting with prayer is another discipline that can draw us away from busyness to focus on God.

Even after trauma, intrinsic motivation can be strengthened. As a caregiver, pay special attention to how someone's experience has affected their faith. How did he or she previously find spiritual focus and comfort? A caregiver could encourage the person to spend some time in those familiar ways. Caregivers can listen for healthy religious beliefs and practices, and urge taking refuge in them. Continued participation in worship, prayer, and personal devotion is desirable. Others may join supportively in these practices as the person reaches out to God. Caregivers can elicit responses from traumatized persons about how they believe God has been acting in their lives, even in their pain. Talking about their experiences of God helps people to be more aware of God's presence. Demonstrating an active interest in their spirituality and not avoiding the issues gives the traumatized person an invitation to talk and to grow.

ACTIVITIES THAT PROMOTE INTRINSIC RELIGIOSITY

- Participating in community worship and prayer
- Sharing within the community about God's involvement in their lives
- Experiencing God's love through mutual support and caring
- Engaging in personal devotions
- Participating in Bible study that seeks to know God's character, forgiveness, and grace
- Joining spiritual retreats with worship, prayer, spiritual direction, and Bible study
- Taking part in individual and communal practice of fasting with prayer

---

C. Facing and Sharing Uncomfortable Feelings

Acknowledging and voicing uncomfortable emotions is essential for dealing constructively with trauma-related distress. Unfortunately, that is not a characteristic of all present-day conservative Christian churches or organizations. There may be expectations that those who are "right with Christ" and have "enough faith" do not have negative feelings. Consequently, people expressing sorrow, pain, sadness, doubt, or anger (in the American context often described as "negative" emotions) can attract disapproval or even condemnation from fellow believers. Struggling believers may buy into this and think their feelings are due to weak faith or being a "bad" Christian. Others may assume their feelings are sinful or shameful. Understandably, these people hide negative emotions or, even worse, deny them.

In the second part of this section we will explore lament in the spiritual tradition of Israel and, in a broader sense, all people of God. In lament, believers bring agony, sorrow, sadness, anger, and desire for revenge before God. This may happen privately or in community. The spiritual tradition of lament shows that feeling and expressing pain is not a mark of weak faith, being a "bad" Christian, sinful, or shameful. In fact, courage and trust that our relationship with God is anchored in his faithfulness are the virtues needed to confront and communicate troubled feelings in God's presence.

Promoting authentic Christian church and mission communities that welcome expression of all kinds of emotions lays a solid foundation for surviving rough life events. It allows for spiritual growth to spring forth from honest wrestling. Practice grounds include small groups, intercessory teams, and healing prayer ministries.

D. Knowing and Extending Forgiveness

Interpersonal crimes such as assault, robbery, carjacking, rape, or terrorism generate powerful feelings of anger and desire for justice. Initially, a solid "fight response" is necessary for self-protection. However, lingering hostility will drain emotional and physical resources needed for healing. Research has found that long-term hostility and resentment is linked to greater mental, emotional, and physical distress (Luskin, 2002, 77-93). In contrast, those able to extend forgiveness after violent trauma are less distressed.

How are people able to forgive? Christians believe they are forgiven for their wrongdoing, since Jesus Christ took the just punishment for it upon himself. Having received forgiveness opens minds and hearts to offer the same to others. The Lord's Prayer infers that forgiving others is connected to having first been forgiven. Commitment to the regular practice of forgiving "debtors" and "trespassers" is great preparation for extreme situations that put forgiveness to the test. Most people have some grievances with parents, siblings, spouses, or friends, which provides practice opportunities.

> **ABILITY TO FORGIVE**
>
> People will be better prepared to forgive, if they have
> - accepted and continually received forgiveness from God and others,
> - a biblical understanding of the forgiveness process, and
> - extended forgiveness to others on a regular basis, not harboring resentment.

E. Knowing and Receiving Grace

Christians in ministry typically have a strong desire to please God. They are often hardy and "strong" people. Many hold themselves to high professional and personal standards. This is good, unless they get swept away into heroism or perfectionism in which redemption is manufactured without the power and grace of the Redeemer. Stand-alone heroism increases vulnerability to feeling like a failure when things go wrong. A sense of not being "good enough" or "worth it" is the result. Shame, self-condemnation, and withdrawal from God and others can result. In survival mode after crisis, people will not always make the best possible decisions, nor will they be in "good shape" when affected by confusion, stress, and depression. In fact, they may be weaker than ever before. Accepting vulnerability and weakness without undue self-contempt is both reasonable and resilient.

Knowing and receiving grace can help people rebound. If a church or mission acknowledges normal human failure and weakness, and supports its members compassionately, it will provide an environment for receiving grace. Along with this, members need to be aware of their own limitations. Accepting these limitations and looking to God's grace will help to rebound quicker and to put more trust in God. Harsh self-judgment erodes emotional strength. True perfection in the Christian sense comes from the one who said, "My grace is sufficient for you, for my power is made perfect in weakness" (2 Cor 12:9, NIV).

F. Supportive Relationships With Other Believers

Human resilience depends on the ability to closely connect with at least a few other people. Openness and vulnerability allow for the kind of depth in relationships that encourages truly facing and moving beyond struggles.

Such close connections grow in friendships, prayer partnerships, spiritual mentoring, and small groups. In these relationships, people support each other "in the thick of things." Research has shown that Christians become more resilient by regularly engaging with their faith communities in worship and mutual, caring support.

Resilient people are more *inter*dependent than *in*dependent. When life hits hard, they entrust themselves to others and accept help and support. People in ministry are often "on stage," which makes it risky to be vulnerable. They frequently have high workloads, with only limited time for nurturing friendships. Though many want and appreciate close relationships, not everyone gives forming and maintaining those bonds a priority. Understanding the importance of keeping personal and ministry life in balance nowadays leads more Christian workers to allow themselves the time and pleasure for close relationships with at least a few others. In these kinds of relationships vulnerability is lived and practiced. Though all good close relationships provide support and comfort, those where faith and purpose are shared are the ones in which Christians can most honestly wrestle and pray, allowing understanding to deepen when trauma raises questions about the foundations of faith.

G. Strengthening Spiritual Resilience in Preparation for Risk

In this section we have reviewed the important spiritual characteristics of people who are more resilient when faced with trauma. Fostering these qualities in individuals, churches, and mission organizations better prepares them for the emotional and spiritual impact of trauma. A summary of these characteristics appears in the *Spiritual Resilience Checklist*.

SPIRITUAL RESILIENCE CHECKLIST

Sound Theology of Suffering
- ☐ Has the person (have I) grappled with his or her (my) theology of suffering and are the resulting assumptions biblical?
- ☐ Does our (my) organization encourage and promote a sound theology of suffering?

Intrinsic Religious Motivation
- ☐ Does the person (do I) have a habit of attending community worship and prayer?

SPIRITUAL RESILIENCE CHECKLIST continued

- ☐ Does the person (do I) have at least two close Christian friends for mutual support and sharing openly and deeply?
- ☐ Does the person (do I) have a regular habit of personal prayer and studying the Bible? Does the person (do I) have a regular practice of participating in spiritual retreats, contemplative prayer, and receiving spiritual direction?

Ability to Face and Share Uncomfortable Feelings
- ☐ Is the person (am I) authentically and honestly talking about difficult life experiences and surrounding feelings?
- ☐ Does our (my) organization support honest sharing of uncomfortable feelings, or are there indirectly communicated messages that "good Christians" should not have certain feelings?

Knowing and Extending Forgiveness
- ☐ Does the person (do I) have experiential knowledge of receiving forgiveness from God and from others?
- ☐ Is the person (am I) aware of the forgiveness process and able to distinguish forgiving from excusing or glossing over injuries?
- ☐ Does our (my) organization encourage and promote giving, experiencing, and knowing forgiveness?

Knowing and Receiving Grace
- ☐ Does the person (do I) have a deep experience of being loved and valued by God?
- ☐ Is the person (am I) accepting of human brokenness as a common experience and able to love others (myself) when the brokenness is visible, rather than being overly condemning?
- ☐ Does our (my) organization encourage a culture of openness, vulnerability, and support as its members deal with their brokenness?

Supportive Relationships with Other Believers
- ☐ Does this person (do I) have at least two close Christian friends?
- ☐ Does this person (do I) give growing and maintaining close relationships a measure of priority over ministry work?

2. RESOURCES FOR THE SPIRITUAL STRUGGLE

Strengthening spiritual resilience is an excellent preparation to better handle what may lie ahead. Preparing well includes reflecting on a personal theology of suffering, deepening spiritual life and motivation, understanding and practicing forgiveness, growing in sharing uncomfortable feelings, and giving priority to building friendships with other Christians. However, in the midst of tests and tribulations even more is necessary.

In the vulnerability and confusion after a traumatic crisis, it is necessary to rely on God and others in a new way that does not come naturally when life "works out." This necessity most often leads to new discoveries. However, some get stuck in the challenge. Suffering can either "burn" people spiritually or become the Holy Ground of deepening faith. This ground can be a place of a transformation upon which shattered fragments reassemble into a new, God honoring order.

How can people meet the challenges of a crisis, experience transformation, and grow spiritually? Reliable spiritual resources are necessary to support a person in the "valley of the shadow" of spiritual struggle (Ps 23:4, ESV). This section is about those essential spiritual resources for the struggle after trauma.

A. Knowing God's Presence

There is nothing more important and comforting for Christians in crisis than to realize that God is right there with them. The Bible is full of assuring reminders that God is always with us. The number of these passages is evidence how much humans need this assurance. It is often hard to be aware of God's presence in frightening situations. Trauma survivors know that in spite of their firm belief that God is with them no matter what, there were times when it was hard to hold on to that belief and to actually feel it. Some will not find God's presence for a season and others may seem to lose their sense of connection to God forever. Fortunately, most will know God's presence again before long. Those who support Christian believers in crises recognize that people experience God's presence in very different ways.

When Allan and Betsy (Story 2) were in a life-threatening health crisis their friends and church community gathered around them immediately. They provided practical support, prayer, shoulders to cry on, and company in lonely moments. Their friends were often simply present. They acknowledged their pain and literally lived through the crisis together with them. Being surrounded by caring people was the most tangible evidence of God's presence Betsy had ever known. For Allan, God's presence started in a solitary moment when his glance fell on a Holy Trinity icon. This moment brought to him a vision and promise that he, Allan, was invited into the fellowship of the Holy Trinity as he started traveling a road with no clear end in sight.

In another scenario, Amanda (not her real name) and her husband worked in medical mission in a developing country. Both loved their children dearly. Confusion and darkness fell over Amanda when they suddenly lost a child due to serious illness. Amanda initially lost her connection to God. She also lost closeness to caring people in her ministry context and circle of friends. People attempting to get close were mostly shut out. Only a few were allowed into her inner world of hurt, disappointment, and bitterness. Her husband was allowed in, but he was eyed with suspicion and sometimes greeted with irritation. Amanda's heart was crying out for understanding in the midst of hurt and anger, and this was hard for her to find. So, she did not want to talk, keeping to herself with brooding thoughts and dark feelings. This dark place with the pain of her longing and the refusal to accept her child's death seemed to be where she could still connect with her lost child, and feel some sense of control over what otherwise appeared completely out of her hands. She wondered whether letting go of the pain would betray the child she loved. When Amanda realized that God was in pain with her, grieving the loss of her child, deeply understanding her experience, a small light began to shine into her darkness.

God's presence signals that we are not lost even in the most chaotic and painful situations. It confirms that our lives are under divine control, even though they seem out of control to human senses. Knowing that God is present assures us that he understands the pain. But how can God's presence become real in the confusion and darkness that follows trauma? How can his presence be experienced when it is hard even to conceive of it?

B. Knowing God's Presence: Through Others

Many have testified to the powerful way a caring community has helped them to feel that God was with them. The tangible presence of caring people conveys love and comfort that point to the love of God.

Ability of Caregivers to Be Present

Many desire to "be there" and "be present" with trauma victims. Still, entering into their world can be daunting. Being with someone in pain means allowing ourselves to be affected by the pain and confusion the victim feels, though to a lesser extent. Because of this the temptation for caregivers is to "fix" the pain. Fixing relieves the pressure of wanting to help the other feel better. It makes supporters feel useful and more in control. But, fixing does not reach deep enough to heal. Most of us remember a time when a well-meaning person offered quick, spiritual-sounding advice or a shallow comment intended to comfort. It didn't work. We felt pacified, dismissed, or misunderstood. Many also remember precious moments when somebody entered into our pain by listening well or touching gently. Vulnerable sharing and attentive listening can create a connection that is rarely known otherwise. The shared grief and pain in the caregiver's expression acknowledges and validates that of the afflicted and makes it easier to bear. When supporters join people in their pain, confusion, and vulnerability, they step onto "Holy Ground." There they join with the person in reverence to the Lord in what he may be doing.

Ability to Receive Support

Caregivers will be familiar with situations when they were more than willing to "enter into" someone else's emotional and spiritual distress and "be present," only to be locked out. What can be done if the door is closed or even slammed shut in the caregiver's face? Self-examination is a good place to start, including considering whether or not they are the best ones to offer help in that situation (please refer to *Caregiver Self-Reflection When a Person Withdraws* on the following page).

If attempts to reach out to the person do not open the door, the reason may not have anything to do with the caregiver. Some traumatized people feel so vulnerable or so overstimulated, that all they can do is withdraw. Each attempt to get close might feel to them like an intrusion, and may be met with irritation. Patterns of response caused by past hurts often are activated by a new traumatic incident. Also, past experiences with others will affect how traumatized men and women receive and interpret helpers. Common reasons for withdrawal are a strong sense of vulnerability, shame, unresolved anger, or depression.

> **CAREGIVER SELF-REFLECTION WHEN A PERSON WITHDRAWS**
>
> - Could I be unduly concerned about making the person feel better rather than listening, understanding, and being with him or her?
> - Did I offer suggestions too quickly when the person was not ready to receive them and perhaps felt misunderstood or hurt?
> - Am I overly focused on talking to the person rather than reaching out in a more holistic manner, such as offering items or help they need? How can I provide them with comfort?
> - Am I the best person to reach out to this person in need? E.g., if a woman has been raped, the presence of a woman would generally feel safer to the victim than a man. Is there another person more trusted by the traumatized person than I?

To complicate matters, not all who withdraw actually want others to leave them alone. A person who suffered severe loss once said, "Though I refused invitations and attempts of other people to talk to me, I also did not want them to give up on me." Though she refused, she needed to know that her friends and family were still interested, attentive, loving and caring for her. Being gradually convinced, she eventually opened the door an inch at a time.

Interpersonal violence may cause victims to be especially mistrustful. They need to rebuild trust slowly. The children's story, "The Little Prince," by Antoine de Saint Exupéry, can help us picture the gradual process required. The little prince is trying to build a relationship with a shy, fearful fox. The fox instructs him to be patient and use a cautious, gradual approach: "First you will sit down at a little distance from me. ... I shall look at you out of the corner of my eye, and you will say nothing. ... But you will sit a little closer to me, every day . . ." (de Saint Exupéry, 2000). A strategy of regular contacts, however short and seemingly insignificant, often helps with somebody who has withdrawn. Don't take angry outbursts personally; rather understand this as a defensive wall that makes the person feel less vulnerable when "holding it together" is difficult.

C. Knowing God's Presence: Intercession

By presenting the person and situation before God in prayer, Christian believers take on a priestly role. Even if the one in crisis feels unable to approach God personally, the support team bridges that gap by bringing him or her before God in prayer. Letting him know that others are praying on his behalf often provides special comfort. In addition to human prayers, Christ himself steps into the gap and intercedes in the spiritual realm. The Holy Spirit also is active by bringing one's deepest concerns, even those expressed in groans, before the Most High (Rom 8:27, NIV). Realizing that others pray can encourage those in pain, especially when they feel a rift in their connection with God.

Early in his ministry, Paul ran into strong opposition in Lystra and was eventually stoned. He was dragged outside the city and others assumed he was dead. The biblical account says, "But, after the disciples had gathered around him, he got up and went back into the city" (Acts 14: 19b–20, NIV). This very short account is a powerful image of what happens when believers "gather around" a person in pain. Gathering, with or without words, creates an instant sense of connection, nurture, comfort, order, and hope. It is like a form of concrete prayer when believers act out God's intent to be close to those who suffer; and its effects are powerful.

D. Knowing God's Presence: Rituals

Religious rituals symbolize and enact spiritual reality. They render supernatural reality in a concrete way, involving minds, hearts, and senses, thus bringing the spiritual realm close. Rituals are particularly beneficial at times when holding on to spiritual truths is difficult. During life's storms, rituals can become an anchor for distressed souls. Rituals also connect members of a community. Familiar rituals can be used or new ones created for special purposes. Which rituals are particularly helpful in supporting Christians after trauma?

Holy Communion

Since a person in crisis may feel distant from God, taking communion individually or with a group can help one literally taste God's presence. People often feel buoyed in their faith and assured of God's faithfulness when they receive communion. During communion they may meditate on the suffering of Christ and realize that he knows and understands their suffering. Those who feel guilt can release it in the knowledge of flesh and blood given for them. Taking communion together can renew the connection to one's community of faith.

Candlelight Vigils

Candlelight vigils are sometimes used to protest injustice, stand witness to suffering, or commemorate lives lost in accidents, natural disaster, massacre, or disease. They often symbolize sorrow for the deceased. In this sense, candlelight vigils are enacted lament. They can be held in silence with memorabilia and pictures at hand, or with prayer, song, and other expressions of lament.

Tributes for the Deceased

Tributes for the deceased are common. They can be expressed in a variety of ways: writing notes or cards, presenting flowers, favorite items, evidence of accomplishments, or displaying pictures of the deceased. Today, electronic tributes can assist mourning in a scattered community; examples are a website or Facebook page in honor of the deceased. Such tributes can also be very comforting for the family.

When loss has affected a certain geographic community, a special meeting can be arranged to remember and support each other in grief. Providing a ritualized expression of sorrow and grief will help people express their feelings and move beyond them with the resonance and support of community.

Forgiveness Rituals

Letting go of resentment and bitterness against those who caused harm is hard. Performing a symbolic act of willingness to forgive can help people overcome inner resistance, or make forgiveness more "real" for them. Despite their desire to forgive, people may find themselves "taking back" forgiveness again and again. A forgiveness ritual can help remember a special moment of willingness, and encourage walking the same path of forgiving again... and again.

The Mobile Member Care Team in West Africa introduces missionary peer-responders to a simple, powerful forgiveness ritual gleaned from Dr. Rhiannon Lloyd's Healing-the-Wounds-of-Trauma workshop. A large, plain wooden cross is constructed, a reminder of the one who bore our pain and graciously forgives us. People are invited to write on slips of paper issues of pain and resentment they wish to release. They can share those with another believer if they wish. Otherwise, they fold up their note and, one by one, take a hammer and nail it to the cross. Doing this, they symbolically let go of their resentment through intentional forgiveness.

Leave-taking Ritual

Needing to leave a home or area abruptly due to natural disaster or civil war does not allow much time to grieve. A leave-taking ritual assists the process. A floor plan of the home is roughly drawn. A lighted candle can symbolize a final walk through important rooms of the house. In each room, participants commemorate special events and offer thanksgiving. Then the room is released into God's hands and to new owners.

Home Restoration Ritual

Homes that have been burglarized or robbed can feel "soiled" and invaded by something evil. A restoration ritual can reclaim the atmosphere and character of the home. One way to do this is to use fragrances or fresh flowers and enjoy them in the house together. The home can be restored with words such as: "This is a home of kindness and generosity, of welcome and hospitality, of friendship and relationship, a home for cooking and sharing, and a home dedicated to God and his people." The scents, words, and prayer re-consecrate the house. Prayers for protection could follow, along with prayer for those violated and, if appropriate, for the burglar or robber.

E. Obstacles to Knowing God's Presence

Caring support, intercessory prayer, and rituals bring God's presence and love closer to those in crisis. However, some perceptions and emotions can jeopardize or even block awareness of God's presence after a major life event. These include the sense of being punished or abandoned by God, and feelings of guilt and shame. Caregivers need to address these potential obstacles.

Sense of Being Punished by God

When a woman's husband suddenly died, she thought this was due to an omission on her part, and therefore surely punishment from God. So, she withdrew from God and those around her. After earthquakes and tsunamis, spiritual leaders have been asked whether the disaster was divine punishment. Sometimes leaders have said that the disaster was indeed God's wrath for disobedience and spiritual inattention. Research shows that people who perceive suffering as God's punishment have more difficulty coping and suffer more depression and posttraumatic stress. The Bible indicates that suffering came with the fall and can be a consequence of human disobedience. But when Jesus was asked about a man born blind, "Who sinned, he or his parents?" He answered: "It was not that this man sinned, or his parents, but that the works of God might be displayed in him" (Jn 9: 2–3, ESV). Jesus' perspective on this issue is present and future directed, not focused on blame for past actions.

It is human nature to seek causes and explanations for suffering. When a person assumes that their wrongdoing caused the suffering, it is often an attempt to feel more secure and try to avoid problems in the future. By identifying a cause for the problem, people gain a sense of security, control, order, or justice. However, interpreting something as a punishment from God for personal wrongdoing comes at a very high price of guilt, shame, and distance from God and others. In contrast, Jesus speaks of God as revealing himself *in the midst* of a disturbing situation. This perspective draws one closer to God and turns attention to possibilities now and in the future. Caregivers can gently question notions of punishment, and encourage reflection on what God may be doing in the midst of the "mess."

Sense of Guilt and Shame

Recently traumatized people say things like, "If only I had done this, that, or the other, then it would not have happened," "If only I had realized and paid better attention," "If only I had taken time to drive the car more slowly," or "If only I had reacted more appropriately, my friend would not have been killed." An anxious woman unable to successfully resuscitate her unresponsive husband, once said: "If only I hadn't been so shocked and started the CPR (cardiopulmonary resuscitation) earlier, then my husband would not have died." Overwhelmed by realizing what happened, people ponder in hindsight how the incident could have been avoided, then move on to accuse themselves of omissions or commissions. The resulting self-accusation, guilt, and shame can drive a wedge between them and God.

If a person needs help overcoming false guilt and shame, rational discussion is apt to lead nowhere. An *"acknowledge and reframe"* strategy helps best in such situations. Caregivers can *acknowledge* the person's wish that the event never happened, and *reframe* that the bereaved did "the best they could." For example, one might tell the woman who "failed" her husband, "I know how much you wish you could have saved him. Anyone in your situation would have been in shock. You did the best you could in that moment and more than most others could." In this way it is possible to gently encourage people to accept grace for themselves. If the person is taking responsibility appropriately for an aspect of the trauma, that can be acknowledged, too, and then guide her or him onward toward forgiveness and grace. (Karen Carr elaborates in Section 2 C of this chapter about the *Acknowledge and Reframe* skill.)

Sense of Being Abandoned by God

After her family's van collided with a truck in Rwanda, Ann felt that God had abandoned her (Story 3). If God promised to keep her family safe, and yet allowed this tragedy, she reasoned that he must have left the scene when the accident happened. When God does not act as expected people might think he has left them. When shock numbs emotions, or when someone drifts into depression, the usual emotional cues of God's presence (peace and joy) are missing. It is then possible to feel abandoned because of the inability to feel these emotions. Believing that God has intentionally withdrawn makes it hard to take steps to reconnect with him. A person that feels abandoned may withdraw into sadness, loneliness, or despair.

Research indicates that those who feel abandoned by God have a harder time coping (Pargament et al., 1998). What can caregivers do? They can explore why the person feels abandoned by God. Is it the person's inaccurate understanding of what God should have done (theology of suffering), or could it be due to emotional numbing or depression? With such knowledge supporters are better equipped to address underlying concerns. Inappropriate expectations can be gently questioned. Or, an explanation can be provided about shock-induced numbing or depression-induced lack of joy and peace, but that lack of feelings does not mean that God is absent. The caregiver could then help the person find ways to reconnect with God, such as through the Lord's Supper, or lament.

F. Lament

While emotional distress and spiritual confusion after trauma threaten trust in God and awareness of his presence, some will feel that their relationship with God is disrupted. When pain, confusion, anxiety, sorrow, regret, and anger all erupt at once, some recoil, some are shocked and frozen, and others urgently cry out to God for help. In such a situation God remains the one we need the most. However, we may not feel comfortable expressing certain feelings to him. Here is where the practice of lament can become the turning point for healing.

Defining Lament

Lament is a "strong expression of sorrow, regret, or complaint to God in prayer or song, either individual or communal" (Fuller Youth Institute, 2008). As documented in the psalms, the Israelites prayed and sang to God in a great variety of life situations. Psalms expressing raw emotions such as hurt, confusion, upset, anger, hate, and abandonment have been distinguished as "psalms of lament" or "psalms of disorientation" (Brueggemann, 1984). Researcher Keith Meador found that highly religious people generally are more likely to express their emotions openly compared to others (Meador et al., 1992). Honest emotional expression facilitates coping with distress.

Looking more closely at the essential elements of lament in the Old Testament as well as the New, the following stands out:

1. *Recognition:* A clear recognition and honest acknowledgement of hurt.
2. *Invocation:* God is called upon to pay attention.
3. *Presentation:* Presenting to God a *specific* situation and voicing

conflicting feelings such as pain, hurt, abandonment, shame, confusion, being overwhelmed, sadness, despair, anger, and struggle with God's seeming inaction or silence. At times, no words can be found, and crying or "groaning" become the only expressions (Rom 8:22, 23, 26, NIV). Jesus is described as "overwhelmed with sorrow" in Gethsemane (Mk 14:34, NIV). He cries out feeling abandoned ("forsaken") by the Father on the cross (Mk 15:34, using the lament of Ps 22:1, NIV).
4. *Expectation:* God is expected to hear, take the hurt in, and be affected by it. Brueggeman writes, "God takes the hurt of earth into God's own life and *heaven* is thereby transformed" (Brueggemann, 1992, 47; italics mine).
5. *Anticipation:* God is expected to respond according to his promises. "God accepts the groan, takes it into God's own person, and speaks it back to hurting Israel as promise from on high" (Brueggemann, 1992, 52). Anticipation that God will respond in concrete ways generates hope in the here-and-now. Beyond this, a larger perspective of hope opens up in eschatological redemption.
6. *Proclamation:* God is recognized and praised for who he is and for anticipated fulfillment of his promises. Almost all psalms of lament end in praise. In many psalms, lament and praise are intertwined; and the psalmist goes back and forth between them.
7. *Participation:* The community of believers enters into the lament of the individual, receiving the hurt and bearing it with the afflicted. The individual and community together find hope and God's redemptive presence.

In lament we acknowledge distress over a painful occurrence and present it to God and the community; both are expected to pay attention, hear, and resonate. As God receives human pain into his heart and processes it in divine ways, he is expected to act according to who he is and to fulfill his promises now and at the end of time.

Engaging in Lament

Providing models of lament will aid people in praying or journaling personal lament. Biblical examples of the *psalms of lament* and a *simple structure of lament* (please refer to corresponding tables) are a good way to start. Another helpful model can also be found at www.Journey-Through-Grief.com. The most helpful expression of lament depends on the distressed person's temperament. A more extraverted person may sit down and pray aloud to God using a simple structure, or voice concerns to a group. The group can then join the person in lament before God, perhaps prompted by a leader. A more introverted person may prefer to journal and at a later stage verbalize a prayer of lament before God.

PSALMS OF LAMENT

Individual Lament
- Psalm 3, 5, 6, 7, 13, 17, 22, 25, 26, 28, 31, 35, 38, 39, 42, 43, 51, 54, 55, 56, 57, 59, 61, 63, 64, 69, 71, 73, 77, 86, 88, 102, 109, 130, 142, 143

Communal Lament
- Psalm 44, 60, 74, 79, 80, 83

Even with encouragement, modeling, and resourcing, some people will not be ready to express their feelings in words. Groans and cries may be all they have to offer up. After Jerry Sittser lost three family members in one accident, he found himself in this place. He wrote, "Groans became the only language I could use, if even that, but I believed it was language enough for God to understand" (Sittser, 2004, 43). In this place without words, the Holy Spirit is ready to provide support: "We do not know what we ought to pray for, but the Spirit himself intercedes for us with wordless groans. And he who searches our hearts knows the mind of the Spirit, because the Spirit intercedes for God's people in accordance with the will of God" (Rom 8:26.27, NIV).

One word of caution about lament: Walter Brueggemann makes a distinction between "dwelling *on* loss" and "dwelling *in* loss." Dwelling *on* loss leads to closing ourselves off, wrapped in "emotional knots," which can lead to self-pity and weakening of constructive lament. Dwelling *in* loss leads to being honest, acknowledging loss, and attending to it, rather than denying it. People might dwell *on* loss due to a tendency to withdraw, occasionally to attract attention, or for the secondary gain of assuring that compassionate support will continue beyond the need. A trained counselor may need to address psychological issues in such a scenario.

> **A SIMPLE STRUCTURE OF LAMENT**
> - Addressing God
> - Presenting the situation, including feelings, and complaints
> - Affirming trust based on past experience with God
> - Presenting petitions, desires, or needs
> - Presenting enemies and the need for justice
> - Expressing expectation that God will hear and act according to his faithfulness and promises
> - Praising God

Facing Anger and Disappointment

Many Christians will not have difficulty expressing pain, sorrow, confusion, abandonment, or even despair to God, but may be reluctant to express anger. Even encouraged by counselors, directing anger, frustration, disappointment, or accusations at God, may just not "feel right" for some people. However, they run the risk that hidden anger will alienate them from God. Friends and supporters can remind them that "God can handle those feelings," that he is aware of any anger already, and continues to love them in spite of it. Even Jesus cried from the cross, "Why?" to the Father. Psalms of lament expressing anger and disappointment can encourage a person in pain to express these feelings to God. A psalm with complaints, accusation, anger, and questioning of God is Psalm 88. Job also openly questions and even confronts God about the suffering he has allowed. God receives and honors Job's honesty, which actually is a hallmark of trust and commitment to his relationship with God. After allowing Job to talk, question, and complain for a long time, God ultimately reveals his sovereignty and puts Job in his place as a human. Job receives a deeper knowledge of God through this struggle.

Theologian David Kelsey of Yale Divinity School is the father of an eight-year-old son with a serious illness that led to coma and disability due to brain damage. In his book, *Imagining Redemption,* David Kelsey reflects that though he was angry about his family's suffering, it was freeing for him to note that it was not anger *at* God, but *before* God. This allowed him "to recognize that acknowledging anger *before* God was not the same thing as expressing anger *at* God" (Kelsey, 2005, 29; italics mine). He also recognized that "asking Job's questions of God on behalf of Sam [his son] could be one way of being faithful to God in the midst of this awful situation rather than a way of blaming God for this terrible story" (Kelsey, 2005, 29; brackets mine).

Human anger does not come as a surprise to God, since he understands and resonates with it. In a mysterious way those who lament are joining God in his pain over the brokenness of all creation. Honest lament expresses more trust in God than withholding difficult feelings. From this perspective, expressing anger and vulnerability become a way of being faith-full and honoring God, a foundation for rebuilding connection and trust. Reframing anger as *before* God can make it easier for a reluctant person to express it. For example: If a woman, whose son tragically died, would say: "This hurts so much. I just cannot understand how God could allow this to happen," it is anger *before* God (a lament or complaint). However, if she said: "God just does not care. He is unfair. He should not let this happen to a good person like my son," she is angry *at* God, questioning his character. For those who are angry *at* God, offering up their anger as the best and only response at that moment can be cathartic and a starting point for a gradual restoration of trust.

Moments of vulnerable interaction with God after trauma are "holy ground," upon which someone in pain ultimately stands alone before God. This level of vulnerability and pain will at times be hard for caregivers to bear. They can assist, support, and come alongside. However, determining the right timing for anything to happen is "between the two of them." It is likely that more is happening internally than meets the outsider's eye. Supportively waiting for the "right time" allows the caregiver to witness the mystery of God's redeeming power.

Nicholas Woltersdorf, who lost his son to a mountain climbing accident, testifies about this mystery in his book *Lament for a Son*:

> In the valley of suffering, despair and bitterness are brewed. But there also character is made. The valley of suffering is the vale of soul-making (Woltersdorf, 1987, 96-97).

Maintaining the long-term perspective that God is at work in the midst of "messiness," and not on a human time schedule, can help while "hanging in there" with someone in pain.

Jerry Sittser experienced his journey of grief as practicing lament with his whole being:

> I did not go through the pain and come out on the other side; instead, I lived in it and found within that pain the grace to survive and eventually grow. I did not get over the loss of my loved ones; rather, I absorbed the loss into my life, like soil receives decaying matter, until it became a part of who I am. Sorrow took up permanent residence in my soul and enlarged it (Sittser, 2004, 45-46).

Lament helps those who experienced trauma and loss to fully own their emotions and honestly connect with God from a place of vulnerability. Gradually, "enlargement," "soul-making," and renewed perspectives on God, self and life, will emerge. In accepting vulnerable feelings and reaching out in dialogue (or groaning) to God something new is created.

G. Forgiveness

Trauma can be so consuming that we want to know who or what is responsible for so much pain. Sometimes there is no one or nothing to hold accountable. In that case, lamenting our pain and grief is a way to heal by sharing. However, at times another person or a group of people *is* responsible for causing the pain. Perhaps the hurt was intentional or negligent. Either way, we blame them. When holding someone responsible, forgiveness is a key to the healing process.

Challenge of Forgiveness

Forgiveness seems crazy when one is hurt and afraid. It is not easy or even natural. It goes against the world's common values of self-centeredness and competition. Hurt can be so bad that it will never be forgotten. Pain can be too intense to be ignored. Feelings of vulnerability, betrayal, or violation might be overwhelming. Deep feelings of insignificance may result when someone's devastation did not seem to matter to the person who caused it.

Anger and hatred can quickly emerge, giving the injured person a feeling of strength, power over someone else, or hope for justice. Why would anybody want to give up judgment over someone who hurt them? It is natural to desire justice. Whoever caused such tremendous pain should feel at least as much pain in return! Or, it may seem easier to pretend that nothing really bad happened and bury the experience away somewhere. Neither of these common strategies to escape pain helps.

Forgiveness is difficult for many reasons. It is a vulnerable step because it acknowledges having been seriously hurt. It also means letting go of the desire to personally impose justice, judgment, and punishment. That is vulnerable! Forgiveness is especially hard when the perpetrator has not taken responsibility or felt remorse. Forgiveness doesn't seem deserved.

Reason for Forgiveness

Forgiveness seems unnatural when undeserved and brings even greater feelings of vulnerability. So, why forgive? Christians forgive because they have been forgiven (Col 3:13). God commands forgiveness (Lk 6:37). God forgave human sins even though it was not deserved. Willingness to forgive means acceptance of the need to repent and be forgiven ourselves, with submission to God's wisdom.

Forgiveness creates freedom from the burden of carrying debilitating hurt and anger for the rest of our days. From a self-interested perspective, forgiveness is good for health. There is an illusion of strength in holding onto anger and the right to judge; paradoxically, holding on keeps people trapped, making their pain and injury the focus. Research shows forgiveness helps people heal physically, emotionally, and mentally, compared to holding on to hostility and resentment (Luskin, 2002, 77-93). Forgiveness is not only an act of humility and obedience; it also helps free people from the emotional exhaustion of dwelling on their pain.

In Laura Hillenbrand's *Unbroken*, her 2010 bestselling biography of Louis Zamperini, an American World War II flier who became a POW (Prisoner of War) tortured by a Japanese officer nicknamed "Bird," she clearly describes the pain of unforgiveness:

> The paradox of vengefulness is that it makes men dependent upon those who have harmed them, believing that their release from pain will come only when they make their tormentors suffer. In

seeking the Bird's death to free himself, Louie had chained himself, once again, to his tyrant (Hillenbrand 2010, 366-367).

Karen Carr discovered a similar insight that helped set her free from pain after being evacuated from the Ivory Coast. She wrote:

> Most significant was Job 19:25, 'But as for me, I know that my Redeemer lives, and he will stand upon the earth at last.' It helped me to consider that the many injustices might not be redeemed in my lifetime, but they would indeed be redeemed (Story 1).

Forgiveness provides freedom from anger and resentment that chain the unforgiving to their pain.

Process of Forgiveness

Forgiveness is not about ignoring or minimizing pain by forgetting it, nor excusing the one who caused it. Excusing is for lesser pains, accidents, or slights. Excusing and forgetting are for insignificant, unintentional hurts that probably will not happen again. Lewis Smedes (Smedes, 1984, 61-66) described excusing as a social lubricant that allows people to move more easily through minor hurts, such as someone accidentally stepping on your foot or forgetting your name. However, severe, extraordinary, or repetitive hurts cannot be dealt with in this manner. Excusing those would disregard their significance and the threat they pose to safety. This type of greater hurt needs to be dealt with appropriately or it will continue, which means acknowledging the hurt and holding the one who caused it responsible.

Deep hurts damage trusting relationships. That damage needs to be acknowledged for true healing to occur. The hurt cannot be excused or avoided. Forgiveness cannot begin until the hurt and the broken relationship are clearly recognized. That relationship cannot go back to what it was without forgiveness and reconciliation.

The full extent of the damage needs to be acknowledged. The loss and hurt must be *felt*, a fearful and difficult process. At times seemingly insurmountable pain might be overwhelming. Admission of hurt also risks self-condemnation for failing to keep ourselves safe or to protect something or someone important to us. By understanding and accepting loss, we acknowledge the risk of being deeply hurt again, which is necessary for taking protective steps in the future. One example of this occurs in an abusive relationship. The abuse must be acknowledged and appropriate steps taken in order for the cycle of violence to be broken.

Acknowledging pain and vulnerability is the first step to forgiveness and healing. Accepting our own humanity can free us from self-condemnation for allowing the injury to occur. It also helps to accept the humanity of others. The "monsters" responsible for the pain are also humans subject to weakness and sinfulness. Acknowledging and accepting others' humanness does not free them from responsibility for their choices. However, accepting our and their humanity is another step toward letting anger go and beginning to heal.

Dan and Connie Crum found some humor in a friend's insight that helped free them from their pain after being assaulted, having their lives threatened, their children frightened, and losing their home. Dan Crum wrote:

> A friend at church told me, 'The problem with thieves is that they are always out of money and on the run.' I laughed. Somehow, that helped me realize I could move on, free from seeking justice in order to quell my anger, because the thieves were still trapped in their own evil schemes. That was a form of justice to me and I felt free to stop focusing on them and get on with my life. What a release! (Story 5)

Although anger often results from hurt, holding judgment over others does not keep anyone safe. What may feel like strength or safety actually chains people to their pain. Dwelling on judging hurtful people inhibits the restoration of relationships. Security does not come by holding onto the right for justice or vengeance. Forgiveness means choosing to give up that right, even though someone else is still held responsible. The right to justice is laid down, entrusting it into God's hands (Rom 12:19), and heartfelt freedom is picked up.

Acknowledging hurts and broken relationships increases the probability of change in the relationship. The relationship will not be restored to exactly what it was before. God commanded forgiveness even if the perpetrators have not taken responsibility for the pain they caused. Forgiving is not the same as forgetting. Even after forgiveness, intentional changes might still need to be made for future security: locks on doors, guards on hearts, preparation for future disasters. Even though the Crums had forgiven, they still needed to end their relationship with a neighbor who had betrayed them.

Forgiveness is a process that takes time. Anger might reoccur when painful moments are remembered. New experiences can reawaken forgiven hurts, such that they must be let go once again. Forgiveness is a journey with many twists and turns in simultaneous relationships: with others, ourselves, and God.

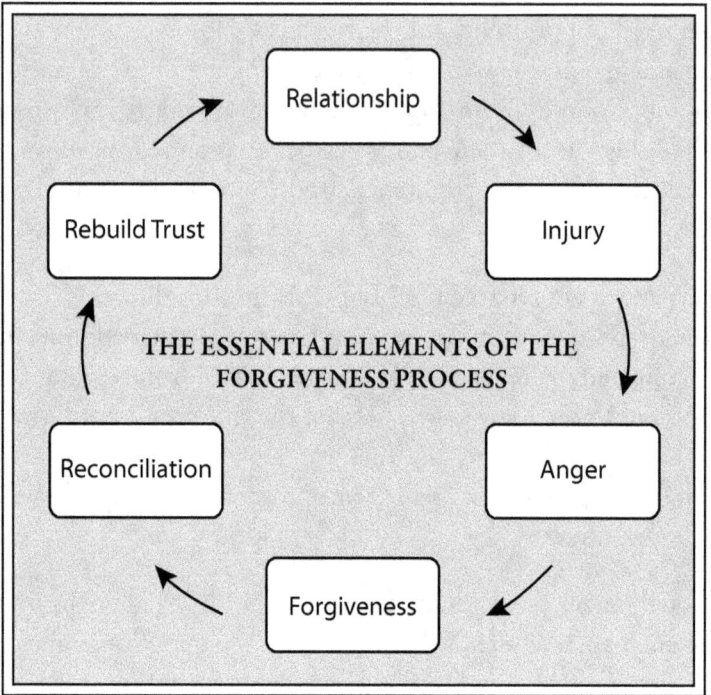

Forgiving Ourselves and Accepting Forgiveness

Sometimes we see ourselves as causing pain, loss, or tragedy. We might hold ourselves responsible for wrongdoing or for not handling something well. We might also blame ourselves because we have impossibly high standards. We blame because knowing the cause decreases our sense of vulnerability. Self-blame increases the feeling of security because it implies that our own improved performance can keep the tragedy from striking again. It seems to put control in our hands, but also puts us under pressure.

Forgiving ourselves and accepting forgiveness are steps toward healing. This must be done with honesty in order to last. We must be fair in assessing our responsibility. Assistance from a trusted friend can help us be reasonable about the amount of responsibility we hold. If it is unreasonable to hold ourselves responsible, then healing proceeds by letting go of blame and lamenting the pain. When we *are* responsible in some way, then forgiving ourselves or receiving forgiveness begins the healing process. If we have caused pain, we must seek and accept forgiveness from the injured person or from God. If we cannot speak with that person or experience God's closeness, a trusted friend can hear our repentance and help us hear God's message of forgiveness (1 Jn 1:9). Accepting responsibility, expressing pain, letting go of self-destructive condemnation, repenting, accepting forgiveness and learning from experience can help us move freely into the future.

Forgiving God

Christians who believe in God's omniscience and omnipotence may blame him for pain or a lack of protection. The idea of "forgiving God" may not be comfortable for Christians who know God is without sin and cannot make mistakes. However, they tend to withdraw from God when they feel hurt, neglected, or abandoned by him. It is possible to be very angry at God, afraid of his interventions, and want to hide from his presence.

Forgiveness is about healing broken relationships, which often benefits the forgiver more than the one forgiven. Forgiving others involves coming to accept human limitations and letting go of the desire to hurt them back and claim justice. "Forgiving God" involves the attempt to better know God's true nature and let go of anger or blame, realizing that God loves faithfully and without fault, even if it is hard to understand. Some Christians describe this process as "surrendering" to God's love, rather than maintaining defensive barriers of anger, resentment and distance. Others might experience "forgiving God" as gaining a greater concept of God's faithfulness, and accepting that God's reasons cannot always be known.

Reconciliation and Restoration

A broken relationship can be restored and healed through the process of reconciliation, which is a step beyond forgiveness. Reconciliation occurs when both parties are ready to speak with each other in order to express their hurt, understand the other's experience and concerns, and take responsibility for pain. After both parties feel understood and have expressed regret, the hurt usually lessens. Based on this, both parties accept and express the responsibility they will take for protecting each other's safety in the future. In this way a relationship can return to how it was before injury. Such a restoration process takes time. After reconciling, trust must be rebuilt through repeated positive experiences before a relationship will again feel safe.

CAREGIVER QUESTIONS TO SUPPORT THE FORGIVENESS PROCESS

- How were you hurt? What did you lose? (Listen and understand the various hurts that occurred.)
- What or who was responsible for the pain? With whom are you angry? Are you angry at someone, yourself, or God?
- How is your anger affecting you?
- What would it be like for you to let go of judging that person? Would you feel vulnerable in some way?
- How can you let go of your anger and condemnation and still keep yourself secure?
- What do you need to feel more secure?
- How can I join you, walk through this pain, and help you be safe?

G. Shame and Grace

There are two ways people manage blame when they feel responsible for something awful that happened. They can attribute blame to wrongful actions. They can also attribute it to a failure of character. When people focus on their actions, they feel guilty and will need forgiveness to find relief. When they focus on a failure in their character or capabilities, they feel shame and will need grace to heal. Shame and guilt are not mutually exclusive; people may feel one or both at the same time.

Shame is an appropriate emotion when our sinful nature is considered. It can indicate a sinful area in our lives where God wants to offer redemption. However, shame can be achingly painful and debilitating when it grows unchecked in our hearts (2 Cor 7:10). Overwhelming shame leads to self-condemnation, and spiritual and emotional death. A shame-filled person might despairingly think over and over, "If only I wasn't so stupid, that wouldn't have happened." Or, someone else might shame us by screaming, "You are so blind and so lazy that you brought this on us ... you are the worst partner I ever had!"

The pain and humiliation of failure, coupled with distress following trauma, can be so intense it becomes obvious to others. Visible emotions can lead to even more embarrassment. Shame is felt because it isn't easy to "just get over" the experience. We may believe we are weak or unspiritual if we can't just "give it to God" and "trust him."

Shame is powerful and debilitating because it attacks our personal sense of worth. Feeling unworthy can cause us to turn down the love and support of God and others. When feeling ashamed, a natural tendency is to pull back and hide, even from God. Adam and Eve hid from God because they were ashamed of their nakedness. Their nakedness was nothing new to God, who created them that way. God knew them in their nakedness even before their sin, just as he knows the failings in our characters and still pursues us. Their nakedness was not a flaw; it was part of his design. God knows the failings of our humanity even better than our family, friends and colleagues and he still loves us.

Healing Shame

Adam and Eve were guilty because they acted disobediently and God imposed consequences. At the same time, God was compassionate with the shame they felt about their nakedness and gave them garments to cover themselves. Knowing our failures and sinfulness, God covers us, too. He loves and values us enough, just as we are, to die for us (Rom 3:23–24; 5:6–8). God promises to continue to transform and perfect us, until "the day of Jesus Christ" (Phil 1:6, ESV). He knows we are never going to be perfect on this side of heaven, and yet he will continue to love us and keep on working in our lives, covering our nakedness.

God loves and values us even while we fail. This is the grace that heals shame, as forgiveness heals guilt. God's grace is the spiritual resource for times when we know our failures brought tragedy. Grace is also what we need when others bury us under criticism. A natural desire to hide makes it difficult to experience God's grace, just as when Adam and Eve crouched down in the garden. In contrast, opening up to the experience of a closer relationship with God and others who love gracefully is most healing.

God's command is to love others as he has loved us (1 Jn 3–4). We are to love others even when their failings are visible (Col 3:12–17). God has provided for shame by enabling and commanding Christian communities to be grace-filled. Grace differs from forgiving someone for actions. A grace-filled caregiver humbly comes alongside a person who feels shame and offers acceptance, compassion, and love, while acknowledging the struggle with brokenness. A grace-filled community provides healing and a tangible experience of caring and dignity. Rather than shame's weakening effect from hiding, resilience is strengthened through grace-filled relationships. To receive the fruits of grace, we must not hide, but instead reach out to God and a grace-filled Christian community.

Healing is not complete until grace penetrates our souls deeply enough that we can fully accept it, often the most difficult aspect of healing shame. Knowing about God's grace and recognizing grace-filled acts from others might not touch the core without acceptance. If we focus only on what we don't deserve, grace from God and others is a confusing, shallow experience. Grace can be played down, or ignored. Some dismiss grace because they believe others don't know how bad they truly are, blocking the healing power of loving acceptance. Shame buries people and traps them. Recognizing our humanity with all its failings and brokenness, we must become willing to open our hearts to the love and value God and others give us. We do not deserve it. That is the point of grace! God and grace-filled people, whom he has transformed, give it freely (Eph 2:8-9). It is so difficult to accept grace because it is vulnerable and humbling to acknowledge the need to accept what is not deserved. Yet, God provided grace as the spiritual resource to heal shame, including the shame that trauma can bring.

3. GROWTH IN THE MIDST OF STRUGGLE

Researchers have observed that posttraumatic struggle can result in either growth or disintegration of persons, relationships, and faith. Generally, the stronger the impact, the greater the change, either as growth or disintegration (Fontana and Rosenheck, 2004). If people are resilient, well prepared, and supported after the incident, they will usually grow.

Like it or not, growth after trauma begins in the struggle immediately after impact. The time of greatest vulnerability and confusion also has the greatest growth potential. This truth was known even in the days of the Old Testament. The psalmist observed: "Blessed are those whose strength is in you, whose hearts are set on pilgrimage. As they pass through the valley of Baca, they make it a place of springs" (Ps 84:4–5, NIV). The "valley of Baca" is a place of misery, weeping, tears, and drought. The psalmist observes that those who trust and seek God (intrinsic religiosity) will find life-giving newness as they walk through misery. Though miseries will always remain miserable, pursuing God and his purposes during misery will result in newness and vitality.

Many Christian songs witness to spiritual change born out of struggle. Stories behind some of the deepest, most precious Christian hymns reveal that they were written in times of hardship. Horatio Spafford, author of "When Peace Like a River" (*Chorus*: "It is well with my soul"), lost his four daughters in a shipwreck. When his ship passed by the place they drowned, Spafford received comfort from God that allowed him to write, "When sorrows like sea billows roll … it is well with my soul." He wrote about peace beyond understanding, renewed focus on God, stronger assurance in faith, and increased awareness of the larger purpose revealed in the history of God with humankind (Osbeck, 1990, 25).

> *When peace, like a river, attendeth my way, when sorrows like sea billows roll-*
> *Whatever my lot, Thou hast taught me to say, It is well; it is well with my soul.*
>
> *Tho Satan should buffet, tho trials should come, let this blest assurance control,*
> *That Christ has regarded my helpless estate and shed His own blood for my soul.*
>
> *And, Lord haste the day when my faith shall be sight, the clouds be rolled back as a scroll:*
> *The trump shall resound and the Lord shall descend, "Even so"- it is well with my soul.*
>
> **Chorus:** *It is well with my soul, it is well, it is well with my soul.*
>
> Horatio Spafford, 1873

William Cowper (1731–1800) faced many emotional struggles that became a gateway of "mercy and blessings." In the hymn "God Moves in a Mysterious Way His Wonders to Perform" he wrote:

> You fearful saints, fresh courage take: The clouds you so much dread are big with mercy, and shall break with blessings on your head (Osbeck, 1990, 202).

The unknown 19th Century author of the hymn "How can I keep from singing" found a new song "above earth's lamentations." As she clung to her Savior, she gained a new glimpse of things that really matter, felt a firmer connection with God, a deepened peace, and new strength:

> No storm can shake my inmost calm, while to that refuge clinging; since Christ is Lord of heaven and earth, how can I keep from singing?... The peace of Christ makes fresh my heart, a fountain ever springing; all things are mine since I am his. How can I keep from singing? (Wikipedia, last accessed 7/14/2012)

Secular researchers have recently taken a closer look at posttraumatic growth in the general population (Calhoun and Tedeschi, 2006). This has led to better understanding of positive change after trauma. Posttraumatic growth has been observed in the following areas: *Changes in self-perception, changes relating to others, changes in philosophy of life, and spiritual change.*

Often people describe increased personal strength, feeling "more vulnerable, yet stronger." Many see new possibilities in life. Examples are: a woman who started an oncology nursing career after her child died from cancer; Dan and Connie Crum (Story 5) pursued training to support missionaries after they had been robbed overseas; and Ann (Story 3) trained as a psychologist and trauma expert after living through a motor vehicle accident that claimed the life of her husband and injured her children and herself. Many describe deeper, closer connections with others. Some independent individuals have opened up to depend on others at the time of vulnerability. Having been in pain, many develop deeper compassion, particularly for those in similar circumstances. Others feel greater freedom to be themselves, and gain courage to be more authentic in relationships. The third area of observed change is a revised philosophy of life. This frequently means increased appreciation for life, closer relationships, and changes in perspective in the existential, spiritual, and religious realm.

Jerry Sittser wrote about his own journey in *A Grace Disguised* (Sittser, 2004). He honestly and artfully describes changes in his own life that resonate with those researchers describe. Jerry provides depth to understanding spiritual change. He describes *"enlargement of the soul"* as he "absorbed the loss into his life, like soil receives decaying matter." His metaphor of decay hints at a new soul-fertility in the midst of death and destruction. The enlarged soul has a *deeper capacity to feel*: "The soul is elastic, like a balloon. It can grow larger through suffering. Loss can enlarge its capacity for anger, depression, despair, and anguish, all natural and legitimate emotions whenever we experience loss. Once enlarged, the soul is also capable of experiencing greater joy, strength, peace, and love." Sittser also observes that sorrow leads to fewer pretenses, *greater authenticity*, and *clearer priorities*: "Deep sorrow often has the effect of stripping life of the pretense, vanity, and waste. It forces us to ask basic questions about what is most important in life. Suffering can lead to a simpler life, less cluttered with nonessentials. It is wonderfully clarifying." Intense suffering "strips us of the props we rely on for our well-being. It knocks us off our feet and puts us on our backs. In the experience of loss, we come to the end of ourselves. But in coming to the end of ourselves, we can also come to the beginning of a vital relationship with God."

Giving up false dependence on our own strength, we experience *new spiritual vitality* by rooting our lives more solidly in God. As we encounter the one true God and know him better, we are transformed. "To our shock and bewilderment, we discover that there is a Being in the universe who, despite our brokenness and sin, loves us fiercely. In coming to the end of ourselves, we have come to the beginning of our true and deepest selves. We have found the One whose love gives shape to our being." To his surprise Jerry Sittser found *grace* in the midst of tragedy: "The tragedy pushed me toward God, even when I did not want him. And in God I found grace, even when I was not looking for it." This grace leads to *peace, contentment and a new centeredness*. His faith took stronger roots in God and his grace: "God has become a living reality to me as never before. My confidence in God is somehow quieter but stronger. I feel little pressure to impress God or prove myself to him; yet I want to serve him with all my heart and strength. My life is full of bounty, even as I continue to feel the pain of loss. Grace is transforming me, and it is wonderful."

A gain after trauma for intrinsically motivated Christ-followers is an even more intrinsically motivated faith, strongly focused on God and his grace. In the worst of times, God draws Christians to himself as they hold onto him and his people with all their feeble might. Here and there in the midst of mud and mire, there is a glimpse of redemption, a hue of the glory to come.

FEATURES OF POSTTRAUMATIC GROWTH

Self – perception
- More vulnerable, yet stronger; deeper capacity to feel
- New meaningful possibilities in life

Relating to Others
- Deeper connections, increased capability for interdependence
- Greater authenticity, less pretense
- Increased compassion

Philosophy of Life
- Greater appreciation of life
- Greater importance of relationships

Spiritual Change
- New appreciation of grace
- Stronger connection to God
- Stronger spiritual vitality and intrinsic religious motivation
- Deeper sense of peace and contentment
- Stronger awareness of things that ultimately matter

---

4. CONCLUDING REMARKS

When trauma strikes, people are affected physically, psychologically, and spiritually. Christians in ministry will encounter significant spiritual challenges along with posttraumatic stress. Their response to these spiritual challenges will affect their ability to bounce back from the impact. A deeper understanding of the spiritual impact of trauma helps to better prepare for crises, and to identify resources for the inevitable spiritual struggle after trauma. Those who are well prepared and sufficiently supported will be more resilient. Despite loss, posttraumatic stress, and struggle, the prepared will grow and deepen in faith.

Churches, mission organizations, and other Christian communities would do well to include these elements of spiritual preparation into their teaching and training. They should also build a general culture of mutual support for times of crisis, which can be complemented with structures specific to the individual and a particular crisis. Supporters and support teams will benefit from being familiar with the essential resources for spiritual support.

> **SPIRITUAL PREPARATION AND TRAUMA SUPPORT**
>
> *Key elements for spiritual preparation are:*
> - A sound theology of suffering,
> - Strengthening intrinsic religiosity,
> - Knowing and extending forgiveness,
> - Ability to face and share uncomfortable emotions,
> - Ability to build close relationships, and
> - Ability to accept weakness and failure.
>
> *Essential resources for spiritual support after trauma are:*
> - Knowing God's presence through the presence of other believers, intercession, practical support, and/or rituals,
> - Lamenting sorrow, pain, disappointment, and anger before God,
> - Forgiveness, and
> - Grace.

Sometimes the consequences of trauma will continue to hurt for the rest of someone's life. People can allow this to draw them closer to God and to the resources in their faith. Christians understand that God's ultimate purpose is the restoration of human brokenness into a freely loving relationship with him as Creator and Redeemer. What ultimately matters most is what draws humans to love God from all of their heart, soul, and mind, and their neighbors as themselves (Mt 22:34-40). In this self-centeredness is overcome. Spiritual struggle in suffering has its place in fostering such love. No one in their right mind, not even the God-man Jesus, would want to suffer unless it was for a really good reason. Suffering makes sense only as part of a fallen world in an all-encompassing process of restoration and redemption. Not that a sufferer is more in need of redemption than anyone else, but sufferers can choose to embrace spiritual growth in the midst of trouble. This choice mysteriously imparts a greater capacity for mercy, grace, and redemptive wonders.

SECTION 7
Prayer That Heals
Ann Hamel

Missionaries are generally a healthy and well-adjusted group of people, deeply committed to God and to his service. However, many are battle weary. They are soldiers on the front lines of a great battle and need special care as they carry the Gospel to the ends of the earth. As Scott pointed out in his chapter on suffering, missionaries live under high duress, by the very nature of their calling. Missionaries go to the most impoverished, disease-ridden and politically unstable areas of the world with the good news. The Bible makes it clear that our world will become increasingly unstable and violent as Christ's Second Advent approaches. As Scott noted, the remaining regions of our world will be reached for Christ at high personal cost. The stories in this book represent the price that we, as the body of Christ, must be willing to pay to fulfill the great commission to go into all the world. It is our responsibility to provide the very best care possible for those who are called to the front lines of missionary service.

Crisis intervention and conflict are the two main reasons mental health professionals are asked to intervene in the lives of missionaries. Research shows that missionaries are exposed to more trauma than those who remain in their homeland. Because trauma impacts one's ability to relate to others and to God, it can, as Frauke and Charlie Schaefer noted in their "Spiritual Resources in Dealing with Trauma" section, "shake up our deepest convictions about the purpose and meaning of life and raise questions about our view of God." Because my relationship with God had provided the foundation for my life since early childhood, I was challenged when my view of God and what I believed he had promised was brought into question by my husband's fatal accident. The spiritual aspects of this complicated the grieving process.

As my work with missionaries has increased over the years, so has my recognition that unresolved emotional trauma early in life compromises one's ability to deal with stress and trauma in the present. Missionaries are vulnerable because they are separated from their family, culture, and social support systems. Wounds of the past and trauma of the present are fertile soil for the enemy of our souls to plant seeds of discord and strife. Without an understanding of both the spiritual and the emotional dimensions of trauma, the benefits of treatment are often short-lived.

While Christians have always believed in the healing power of prayer, science is now recognizing that prayer *does* heal. As a result of research done by Herbert Benson, Jeff Levin, Harold Koenig, David Larson and many others today nearly 80 of the 125 medical schools in the U.S.A. have courses on spirituality and health, whereas prior to the 1990s only three schools offered such courses. In this section we will look at the healing impact of prayer on both traumatic events in the present and unresolved emotional issues from the past. Effective ways of integrating prayer and other spiritual practices into therapy will also be presented.

A. Prayer as a Psycho-Spiritual Intervention

In June, 2003, I attended a Formational Prayer Seminar at Ashland Theological Seminary in Ashland, Ohio, led by Dr. Terry Wardle. At that seminar God touched my life in a way that changed not only how I practiced psychology but how I lived. Although I was a Christian psychologist, like most who were trained prior to mid-1990s, I had a very limited understanding of how to effectively integrate spiritual and psychological concepts into the therapeutic process. I had found in my work with missionaries, that spiritual and psychological issues are often intertwined. Because of my desire to more effectively meet their needs I enrolled in the Doctor of Ministry Program in Formational Counseling at Ashland that August.

Terry Wardle developed the healing prayer methodology called Formational Prayer as a result of his own personal struggles. As a pastor and seminary professor, Wardle applied biblical principles to his own emotional health. He found that pain opens one's eyes to spiritual realities as little else can. Wardle was influenced by the inner healing movement and the contemplative prayer movements within Christianity as he developed and refined his methodology to treat unresolved emotional wounds.

In the mid-1990s Wardle began to use biblical principles useful in dealing with his own crisis to help others. He has written a number of books in which he explains his methodology. One of his first was entitled *Wounded* (Wardle, 1994). However, the one that explains his methodology is *Healing Care/Healing Prayer* (Wardle, 2001). He first called this method Inner Healing Prayer and later changed it to Formational Prayer.

Formational Prayer is a healing prayer methodology developed to position individuals for healing unresolved emotional trauma. Dr. Ed Smith, a Baptist minister, developed Theophostic Prayer; then David Seamands wrote extensively about the healing of memories. Seamands was born in India of Methodist missionary parents and spent most of his childhood there. As an adult, Seamands and his wife returned to India and served from 1946–1962. After returning to the United States Seamands has been a pastor and seminary professor specializing in emotional healing. Missionaries around the world have been influenced by his work. He has written six books that together have sold more than two million copies. Two of the most well known are: *Healing of Memories* (Seamands, 1973) and *Healing for Damaged Emotions* (Seamands, 1981).

Other methods have been developed by LeAnn Payne, John and Paula Sandford, Francis and Judith MacNutt and others. I am most familiar with Formational Prayer, and will focus on it and point out principles common to it and other methods. Each of the methodologies has its own unique theological perspectives and most attempt to base their methods in scripture. While the basic principles of healing prayer are solidly based in scripture, the "techniques" common to the various models generally are not. Although similar to the common practices of Christians throughout history and not inconsistent with biblical principles, there is room for criticism when an attempt is made to base the techniques' rationale entirely in scripture. A look at the historical context and psychological underpinnings of the various methods will help form a rationale for their use.

Historical Development

Agnes Sanford is considered the founder of the inner healing prayer movement. Born in China in 1897 of missionary parents, she was forced to leave China when she was 15 due to political unrest. Sanford struggled with many of the issues common to missionary kids. After graduating from college in 1918 Sanford returned to China as a missionary herself, but came back to the United States in 1925 due to post-partum depression. Although Sanford and her husband wanted to continue in China, her depression became more severe. When she met an Episcopal priest who believed in the healing power of prayer, her depression lifted. The impact of this man's prayers changed the course of Agnes' life.

Sanford lived when the fields of psychology and psychiatry were in their infancy. Sigmund Freud graduated from medical school in 1881, just sixteen years before she was born. Freud published his first major work in 1900. He was an atheist and pioneered in using the scientific method to develop a systematic means of studying the mind.

Carl Jung was a Swiss psychiatrist who was strongly influenced by Freud. Jung was the son of a protestant minister and was very much impacted by his own religious beliefs and experiences. Ultimately he split with Freud. While some Christians are uncomfortable with Jung's theories, Jung never dismissed the importance of religion on mental and emotional health. While Freud was an atheist, Jung attempted to integrate religious and scientific concepts.

In *The Healing Light* (Sanford, 1947), Agnes outlined what she believed the Lord had shown her about healing. She stressed the importance of focusing on God's love and the living presence of Christ within. She believed the power of God can work through one person for the healing of another. For Sanford, visualization was foremost to inner healing and the imagination was an important part of effective prayer. Sanford promoted the use of Jungian psychology and frequently used Jungian concepts and terminology to explain the concepts of inner healing.

Psychological Background

Healing prayer methodologies rarely acknowledge their connection with Jungian psychology. Most have a solid scriptural basis in line with their denominational perspectives. However, as one looks closely at Jungian psychology the relationship is clear. Jung was very much influenced by the work of Rudolf Otto, a German Lutheran theologian. He believed that the sacred was beyond what science and reason could understand. Otto believed the "experience of the sacred" was the hallmark of religion. Jung began to use Otto's concept in the 1930s in his clinical work. He describes a woman who had suffered an extremely abusive childhood and was positively impacted in their session by a "numinous" experience related to the abuse. The experience that Jung describes is what we find with healing prayer. By recalling an incidence of emotional pain or abuse, and inviting Jesus into the pain, individuals often have an encounter that significantly alters their perspective. According to Jung, such encounters are often powerful enough to bring about healing and effect personality change in a way that a cognitive experience alone cannot (Jung, 1973).

All healing prayer methodologies are designed to speak to and activate emotions. They attempt to facilitate re-experiencing a traumatic memory together with the presence of Jesus. Traumatologists teach that psychological crisis is registered in the emotional brain (the limbic system). Neurobiological research confirms that to treat trauma, one must access the emotional brain not just the cognitive brain. Traumatic memories are stored emotionally rather than cognitively. Both the trauma and the presence of God must be experienced emotionally in order for healing to take place. By revisiting a negative experience and allowing it to be transformed, individuals are able to find healing. This is both a Christian belief and a therapeutic reality. The limbic system is the "God part of the brain" and has been called the "transmitter to God" because spiritual experiences take place there.

Biblical and Theological Basis

Both the Old and New Testaments teach that we are to come to God with both mind and heart. In Psalm 46:10 we are invited to "Be still and know that I am God." The New Testament instructs us to keep our minds fixed on Jesus. Ephesians 3:18 says that "we all, with unveiled face, beholding as in a mirror the glory of the Lord, are being transformed into the same image from glory to glory, just as by the Spirit of the Lord."

The plan of salvation is to restore intimacy with God and to heal our brokenness. Pain and suffering are the result of sin but God allows it to be a means of drawing us back to himself. Formational Prayer, as developed by Wardle, is based on the biblical principle that pain and suffering are doorways used by God to enter our lives and to draw us closer. As a result of sin we are all wounded. Wounds are manifested physically, mentally, emotionally, socially, and spiritually. Jesus came not only to secure our place in heaven with him but to heal our wounds and to give us life abundantly (John 10:10).

Some people fear bringing the emotions into religion, and prefer remaining in the realm of the intellect. Yet spiritual leaders throughout history, regardless of denomination, acknowledge the necessity of bringing heart, mind, reason and emotion into the spiritual walk. In A.W. Tozer's classic *The Pursuit of God* (Tozer, 1992) he says that "it is not mere words that nourish the soul, but God Himself, and unless and until the hearers find God in personal experience they are not the better for having heard the truth. The Bible is not an end in itself, but a means to bring men to an intimate and satisfying knowledge of God, that they may enter into Him, that they may delight in His Presence, may taste and know the inner sweetness of the very God Himself in the core and center of their lives" (Tozer, 1992, 9). Later in the book he says: "It is for increasing degrees of awareness that we pray, for a more perfect consciousness of the divine Presence. We need never shout across the spaces to an absent God. His is nearer than our own soul, closer than our most secret thoughts" (Tozer, 1992, 62).

In Calvin Miller's *Into the Depths of God* (Miller, 2000), he talks about communing with God. We are to remember who we are and who God is, when we come to him in prayer. Miller says "God is to be met and listened to, not sat down and talked to. God alone says when he is through talking and the time of our communion is over" (Miller, 2000, 53). According to Miller, God is King and we should enter into his presence and wait on him. We are forgetting who we are and who he is when we enter into his presence and *we* take the lead.

In *The Desire of Ages* (White, 2001), Ellen White talks about the importance of intimacy with Christ. She stresses the importance of letting "the imagination vividly grasp" the various scenes from the life of Christ, particularly the final scenes (White, 2001, 83). The experiences Tozer, Miller, and White are describing are right-brain: relational rather than rational; heart rather than head. This kind of prayer or worship is rooted in the limbic system (emotional brain), not the cerebral cortex (rational brain).

I recommend *Seeing is Believing* (Boyd, 2004) by Gregory A. Boyd, who writes about the role of the imagination in prayer. This book emphasizes experiencing the presence of Jesus as real in order to be transformed into his image. It is consistent with scripture and Christian practices throughout history. Boyd points out that for cultural reasons Westerners have come to equate the imagination with fantasy and make-believe. According to him, imagination is simply "the mind's ability to evoke images" (Boyd, 2004, 72). These images may be either real or make-believe. We may experience reality in life by "imaginatively replicating reality in our minds" (Boyd 2004, 72). Consider our images of atoms and molecules, blood flowing through our veins, or Earth rotating on its axis. We don't see them, but believe their reality based on evidence we *do* see. Therefore, we imagine their reality. Imagined reality is not less real, rather it helps us grasp their reality. In my husband's absence, I imagine a picture of him. It is hard to think of him without imagination; at least a memory of the sound of his voice or the touch of his hand or the smell of his cologne. Imagination helps us experience reality that is not present or visible.

Boyd claims that one of the "most pervasive problems in contemporary Western Christianity is that we mistakenly assume that *information* automatically translates into *transformation*. That "something is true does not in and of itself ensure that this truth will make a significant difference in our lives" (Boyd, 2004, 71). The fundamental Christian belief in an omnipresent God is an abstract theological reality, but most of us do not experience it as a practical reality. Boyd states that we need "to learn to 'fix our eyes on Jesus' and 'set (our) minds on things that are above' if we are to break free from the pattern of the world and be transformed into the likeness of Christ (Col 3:2-3; Heb 12: 1-2)" (Boyd, 2004, 89). "By focusing on the use of Spirit-inspired imagination in prayer, resting in Christ positions people to know Jesus in a face-to-face manner (Ex 33:11) that can be as real as any relationship in life." Boyd says he knows of no other spiritual discipline as "transforming and as healing as the discipline of resting in Christ" (Boyd, 2004, 17).

B. Formational Prayer as a Model of Healing Prayer

The focus of Formational Prayer is finding emotional healing from an intimate relationship with Christ. Psalm 147:3 (NIV) says that he "heals the broken-hearted and binds up their wounds." By entering into an awareness of the presence of Jesus one is ready for God's healing and transformative touch. Formational Prayer is a blend of spiritual formation and inner healing. It functions as a psycho-spiritual intervention with specific steps to facilitate healing of unresolved emotional wounds.

Step One
Experiencing Emotional Safety With Imagery and Awareness of God

Because Formational Prayer is about unresolved trauma, emotional safety is a primary consideration. Even in a secure environment, many who suffer from unresolved emotional trauma have difficulty feeling safe. Therefore, the first step is to ask individuals to "imagine" a safe place, one where they have been or one they create mentally. Once they have imagined this place and allow themselves to step into it, they ask the Holy Spirit to open their minds and senses to the presence of Jesus. Since the "omnipresence of God" is a fundamental Christian doctrine, this step is simply an invitation to become aware of it. The other steps proceed from this awareness. Step one lasts between ten to twenty minutes. Often this step is enough to enable an individual to experience the healing touch of Jesus in their lives. Thomas Keating refers to this prayer as "divine therapy" (Keating, 1999). According to sociologist Margaret Poloma (Poloma, 1991), Christians who practice this type of prayer report a deeper and more meaningful relationship to Christ and more frequent experiences of presence. Practicing the presence of Christ opens the door to the Holy Spirit's transforming and healing power.

Steps Two, Three, and Four
Working Through Layers of Dysfunction

Wardle describes layers of dysfunction in unresolved emotional wounds. These layers include thoughts, feelings, and behaviors. Addressing layers of dysfunction is like pealing the layers of an onion. Our life situation, with its problems and challenges, is like the outer layer of the onion, where emotions are typically readily available and accessible. Jerry Sitter shared that his emotions demanded attention; they could not, and would not, be denied. He knew he "had to face them squarely, plunge into the darkness, and work them through." Jerry appreciated his friends being wise enough to listen to his feelings without trying to change them or deny them (Story 4).

Some individuals bury the pain of trauma to cope with life. The pain, buried under the typical day-to-day challenges, stay unresolved but still influences thoughts, feelings and behaviors. Buried emotions can be triggered by events in the present, often at inopportune times. Resulting behaviors may not make sense in light of what is at hand. Pain and buried emotions are stored in the limbic system (emotional brain) and must be accessed nonverbally.

David Servan-Schreiber, MD, PhD, is a psychiatrist from the University of Pittsburgh Medical Center. In *The Instinct to Heal* (Servan-Schreiber, 2004) he outlines empirically validated techniques for treating depression, anxiety and stress that activate the mind's innate healing systems. The use of medications or conventional talk therapy are not necessarily required. Servan-Schreiber draws on the work of prominent neuroscientists, Joseph LeDoux and Antonio Damasio, as well as traumatologists Bessel van der Kolk and Judith Hermann. According to Servan-Schreiber, "Emotional disorders result from dysfunctions in the emotional brain. For many people, these dysfunctions originated with painful past experiences that have no relation to the present yet still continue to control their behavior." Further, the "primary task of treatment is to 'reprogram' the emotional brain so that it adapts to the present instead of continuing to react to past experiences." The emotional brain contains natural mechanisms for self-healing which Servan-Schreiber calls an "instinct to heal." This instinct to heal revolves around the "emotional brain's innate abilities to find balance and well-being, comparable to other mechanisms of self-healing in the body, like the scarring of a wound or the elimination of an infection." In order to access the emotional brain, one must use nonverbal techniques rather than language (Servan-Schreiber, 2004, 11).

In opening up deeper levels of healing, Wardle recommends nonverbal techniques such as the use of symbols, art, poetry, or other creative activities to help individuals gain access to unresolved pain. While these "techniques" are not derived from scripture, Roy Gane notes that the Bible, especially the Old Testament, is rich in symbolism. Gane is professor of Hebrew Bible and ancient Near Eastern languages at the Theological Seminary of Andrews University and author of the NIV *Application Commentary for Leviticus and Numbers*. He points out that rituals in the Old Testament, even sanctuary and temple design, speak truth about God to the heart *nonverbally*. Consider the powerful New Testament symbolism in the Last Supper: bread, wine, foot washing. Think of baptism. Christ taught in parables, stories designed to reach the hearts of his hearers. When using Formational Prayer with unresolved pain, Wardle suggests first dealing with dysfunctional or sinful behaviors, then inner lies or negative self-talk, and last, emotional upheaval.-

First: *Behaviors*

Individuals will often engage in dysfunctional behaviors to repress painful memories or numb their pain. Beginning with sinful or dysfunctional behaviors, Wardle recommends finding a symbol for the behavior. Finding a symbol typically opens the person up emotionally, enabling him or her to examine the impact of that behavior. In their imagination they take the symbol of their sin or dysfunction to Jesus. This allows them to repent and experience forgiveness. The story of Abraham's offering Isaac is a powerful symbol of how God wants us to relate to gifts he has given us. Often in the Christian walk, one may be asked to offer up "Isaac" when some gift that God has given is cherished more than the Giver.

Second: *Thoughts*

A traumatic event, large or small, may cause negative feelings to develop about oneself, resulting in low self-esteem. Such beliefs contrast with what scripture teaches us about our worth. Wardle recommends a nonverbal technique to deal with this cognitive distortion. Ask the person to find a stick to represent the false belief or lie. Then invite the Holy Spirit to break the power of the lie and replace it with the truth of God's word, as he or she physically breaks the stick. This exercise speaks to both the left- and right-brain, to the cerebral cortex and the limbic system; negative self-beliefs are replaced by the truth of God's word on emotional and cognitive levels. Compare this "technique" with Jesus' instruction to Peter to go to the lake, throw out his line, and take the first fish he caught. Peter was to open the fish's mouth and find a coin in order to pay his taxes (Mt 17:26). Jesus used this to teach Peter an important spiritual truth about who he is and how he can and will provide for us.

Last: *Emotions*

The next layer contains emotions that come as a result of what has happened. Emotional upheaval after a traumatic experience can defines a person's emotional world. The wound itself is at the very deepest level. To assist individuals to deal honestly and openly with feelings, Wardle recommends several approaches. With one, an individual reads a psalm of lament, which models an open expression of feeling. Then the person writes his or her own lament. Writing one's feelings allows the process of healing to begin.

Frauke and Charlie talked about this in their chapter on spiritual resources, where psalms of lament are listed. Another approach uses art or music to get in touch with feelings. The goal of both is honest acknowledgement and expression of true feelings in a direct way. Once this occurs, the person enters into meditative prayer by "going to their safe place," expressing these feelings to Jesus, and allowing transformation and healing.

Step Five
Revisiting Past Wounds in the Light of the Cross of Jesus

Dealing with behavioral, emotional, and cognitive dysfunctions enables an individual to deal more effectively with the core emotional wounds. With an unresolved emotional wound, Wardle recommends using symbols to get in touch with emotions. These symbols may be bandages, crutches, or art to symbolize a wound or injury. Individuals are to write down wounds from the past, then ask the Holy Spirit for guidance in choosing one to revisit. Both writing, and asking the Holy Spirit, positions a person for healing. Inviting Jesus to enter the memory of a past wound redefines and transforms it in a way that a cognitive function alone cannot. Many individuals encounter a very real Jesus in this process. Just as Jesus extended forgiveness to those who caused him pain, forgiveness is an important part of healing for those who allow transformation. Revisiting emotional wounds and processing them in light of the cross of Jesus enables emotional healing.

Formational Prayer is a psycho-spiritual intervention to treat the wounds of trauma. It not only positions an individual for healing, it addresses the cognitive, emotional, and behavioral aspects of healing. In this way a person is enabled to renounce false beliefs and replace them with the God's truth, process emotional pain in the light of Christ's suffering, and repent of and put aside dysfunctional or sinful behaviors.

C. Healing Prayer in Practice: Examples

Healing prayer techniques may seem contrived to some but most are practices that prayerful, committed Christians often follow as they seek Jesus and transformation into his image. Jesus used symbols and images to explain the intimate relationship he wants to have with us: bride and bridegroom, father and child, a vine and its branches. On a daily basis, ordinary Christians must come to terms with sinful and dysfunctional behaviors, the lies of the enemy, and negative emotions. Powerful symbols from scripture can help free a person of the hold of sin. With the rich young ruler (Lk 18:18), Jesus was more interested in the state of the man's heart than his wealth. Modern Christians have felt called to sell cars, houses, or jewelry; to get rid of their televisions, to stop drinking coffee, or any number of other things that are insignificant in and of themselves but may represent deeper issues in our lives. Do not mistake a symbol for the deeper issue that God is asking us to face.

Unresolved trauma is a hindrance in our relationship with God and others. Scriptural and traditional symbols can draw us closer to Jesus and bring healing, just as bread and wine, baptism, or selling all we have to follow Jesus can. The following examples show how techniques can deepen a relationship with Christ.

Safe Place

When I asked one missionary to imagine a peaceful, safe place where he had been or would like to go and to imagine Jesus in that place, he became uncomfortable. Before starting, I instructed him to persist in the exercise for about 20 minutes, and to notice his feelings as he continued. One must persist even when discomfort tempts us to give up. The man continued, and in his mind Jesus came laughing and having a good time. Then Jesus said, "David, I've got a verse for you," and the tone of voice was as if he wanted to tell a joke. Then Jesus smiled at him and said, "Your father and I are not one." This was a healing moment for this missionary as he laughed with Jesus. Prior to this, David had not recognized how much his relationship with his overbearing and controlling father had impacted his relationship with God. Indeed, God was not like his father! After this, David often experienced this "laughing Jesus" during his quiet times with God and was able to gain meaningful spiritual insights.

Past Trauma

Each year I work with groups of missionaries in training seminars both here and abroad. Missionaries often experience hardships and challenges that impact them profoundly. Many carry early life stress that affects their ability to cope with current life stressors. Recently I traveled overseas to work with a group of missionaries in Africa. One woman, serving with her husband in an unstable country, was in deep depression. As a three-year-old child she and her younger brother were abandoned by their mother and placed in foster care because their father was not able to care for them. Eventually their father stopped visiting them. In addition to this abandonment, her foster parents were emotionally and physically abusive. She became a Christian as a teenager, and at 18 moved to another country where she met her future husband. She believed that God brought him into her life and gave her the home and family that she missed out on as a child. Once their two children were born, she became seriously depressed. When I met with her, she was on medication and felt deeply inadequate and unworthy as a wife and mother. She found it hard to believe that her husband and children could really love her. At times she believed they would be better off without her and thoughts of suicide entered her mind.

As I got her history it was obvious that she was experiencing emotions in the present that reflected the reality of her childhood, not the reality of her current life. She "bought into" her foster father's painful lies and lived as though they were true. He told her that no one would ever love her because not even her own mother or father cared enough to take care of her. The pain of his words was deep, and she felt her unworthiness. As a Christian, she knew the truth of God's word that she is of great value and a daughter of the King of the Universe. Emotionally it was impossible for her to grasp this truth. In prayer, I asked this young mother to invite Jesus into the painful memories of what her foster father told her, and to imagine Jesus holding her as a small child and whispering words of love and affirmation into her heart. She pictured in her mind, with the eyes of her heart, our Savior holding her as she would hold her own daughter, and was able to feel his healing love and power. Together we invited Jesus into other painful memories from her childhood and she felt his healing touch. It was a process of experiencing the love of Jesus in a very personal way. I sat with her, held her hand, and allowed her to grieve the painful memories of her past.

Other painful memories will probably surface once this woman arrives in the country where she and her husband will be serving and encounters the usual things that cause missionaries to feel inadequate and unprepared. The current challenges can become overwhelming if feelings of inadequacy from the past resurface and flood the emotions. When this happens she can seek quiet time with God and connect past events with current feelings. She can ask the Holy Spirit to take her back to the time, invite Jesus into past memories, and ask for healing. This process it is not about intellectual assent to our worth, but a personal experience of God's love and desire to make us whole.

Recent Trauma

This past summer I worked with a young missionary family serving in Asia. The couple had an eight-year-old son and a four-year-old daughter and had been living in Asia for several years. Last April, while the father traveled outside the country, the mother and children stayed. They were a part of an established mission community, so the mother felt comfortable leaving her son with friends at church while she ran home briefly. Putting her four-year-old daughter on the back of her motorbike they headed home. Just after entering a busy road they were hit by a truck and knocked off. The mother was unhurt but her daughter was killed instantly. No one stopped on that busy road to help, so this young mother picked her lifeless little girl up and ran back to the church.

I met with this family three months later. There was no need for the use of imagery or other techniques to get at emotions, because they were readily accessible. The couple needed to tell their story. The young mother needed to express her guilt for not being able to protect her daughter. The family needed a caring and safe place to share their feelings. Healing from this kind of tragedy is a gradual process and much had already been done to help them.. When the woman came back to the church after the accident, supportive missionaries and friends surrounded her. One family took her son and cared for him until her husband arrived a few hours later. Fellow missionaries stayed with them overnight and prayed with and for them. The couple chose to take their daughter's body back to their homeland for burial. They wanted to be surrounded by loving family who grieved with them and supported them in the way that felt most natural. The mission director took care of all the practical aspects of arranging the transfer. Once they returned to Asia, fellow missionaries continued to be with them and support them as they gradually resumed normal responsibilities.

This couple chose to transfer to an African country where they would take on new responsibilities. Both husband and wife felt that a new start would help them move past the loss. Neither of them expressed any anger or disappointment with God. This young couple was from a developing country themselves and, unlike many of us from the West, didn't have the expectation that God would or should protect them from bad things. They were able to sense the presence of Jesus in their loss. The wife was able to sense the presence of Jesus, particularly in retrospect, as she picked her daughter up off that road and ran back to the church. As they shared their story we would often ask God to give us an awareness of his presence in that moment. The sense of his presence brought strength and healing.

This kind of loss is always painful and the process of healing takes time. I met with this couple over a period of a few weeks as they were transferring from Asia to Africa. They had received good support prior to seeing me. At the time I met with them, they appeared to be progressing through the stages of grief in a healthy way. Their move to Africa will bring new challenges that will impact the grieving process, likely in both positive and negative ways.

D. In Summary

Terry Wardle defines Formational Prayer as a "ministry of the Holy Spirit moving through a Christian caregiver, bringing the healing presence of Jesus Christ into the place of pain and brokenness within a wounded person" (Wardle, 2001, 13). Although Formational Prayer and the other forms of healing prayer are designed to deal with unresolved emotional trauma from the past, the principles common to them all are also useful in dealing with current trauma.

1. The first principle is that trauma, past and present, is primarily a limbic system process: experiential, nonverbal, right-brain, and emotional. "Trauma resides in the primitive, instinctual parts of our brains and nervous systems and is not under our conscious control" (Levine, 1997, 17). Healing from trauma must address the emotions.
2. The second principle is that healing of trauma, past or present, occurs experientially. Treatment, whether spiritual or clinical, must address the trauma in the same neurological code in which it is written within the human brain. Imagery is a useful way to access past trauma experientially, bringing about emotional healing as that experience is transformed in light of Christ and his suffering.
3. The third principle concerns the neurobiological reality that trauma

as well as spiritual experience both take place in the same part of the brain, the limbic system. Pain opens our eyes to spiritual realities as little else can.

4. The fourth principle is that God typically uses human beings as channels of his healing power. Just as he doesn't *need* us to take the Gospel to the world, he *chooses* to use us.

This reminds me of a story of a little girl who was afraid to stay in her room alone at night. Her mother told her that she didn't need to be afraid because Jesus and the angels were there. The little girl replied, "Yes, but I need someone with skin." As lay or professional caregivers, we need to remember God's design to use *us* as a channel of blessing and healing to his wounded children. Traumatologists recommend getting a victim into the presence of a loving and caring person as a first line of treatment.

As we bring people first into the presence of Christ and inner safety, we can then move together into the pain of the past. When the traumatized person can connect his or her pain to Jesus Christ, the pain or trauma can be transformed.

SUMMARY OF MAIN POINTS
Frauke and Charlie Schaefer

- Trauma and suffering are part of our human experience.

- A bible based, personal theology of suffering equips Christians with realistic expectations about suffering. It also facilitates understanding of the source of hope in the midst of suffering: God's presence and compassion, growth, the possibility of becoming more like Christ, and hope that pain and suffering will ultimately be overcome when Christ returns.

- It is normal human experience, not a sign of weakness, to be affected by traumatic events. This includes post-traumatic stress, anxiety reactions, and depression.

- Biological, environmental, psychological, and spiritual factors modify the degree of impact of traumatic events. Awareness of these factors should inform preventative and supportive resilience-enhancing strategies at the individual, community, and organizational level.

- Christian communities and organizations need to incorporate resilience-enhancing principles and strategies into their life together. They should also consider training a group of naturally talented, peer trauma-responders who would be available to support others in times of crisis.

- We were created with a need for community to be around us in times of suffering. The presence of Christian community (as Body of Christ) often tangibly represents God's presence after trauma.

- Spiritual struggle is normal after severe traumatic events. Believers often struggle more intensely right after an event because aspects of their faith, the foundation to the purpose and meaning of their lives, may be in question.

- Certain spiritual characteristics and practices support the struggling believer, allowing for faith to be deepened, and resilience and spiritual vitality to grow.

- Prayer for healing helps restore a disrupted relationship with God after trauma.

- The sovereign God is the author and perfector of restoration and growth after trauma, whether through human efforts or without them. God is present and often working in ways that we do not understand.

APPENDICES

APPENDIX A

Toward a Theology of Risk and Suffering Worksheet

Scott E. Shaum (Barnabas International)

TOWARD A THEOLOGY OF RISK

Preliminary Thoughts on Risk:
- Risk is part of life in a fallen world. Each of us take risks every day, but we have gotten used to them. Repeated exposure to a certain type of risk desensitizes us to it. As risks become more familiar, we become more tolerant of them. For example, we ride around in motor vehicles even though there are far more deaths in automobiles than public aircraft.
- The type, degree and frequency of risk people experience is related to the location in which they live. What may be perceived as risky for a believer in the US who has not traveled internationally may seem like minimal or commonplace risks to cross-cultural workers who move in and out of multiple and/or unstable regions.
- Risk thresholds vary among people. Some personalities do well with a higher degree of risk whereas others tend toward conservatism and caution in actions.
- Thus, it is not wise to treat decisions about risk as if they are moral issues. Often a decision to "risk" is not an issue of right or wrong -especially in non-western cultures. Awareness of this personal variability and resisting judging the morality of others based solely on their decisions about risk is a mature perspective.
- As is seen from the passages below, there are times to flee risk and other times to not only stand your ground but willingly head into harm for a greater cause. Jesus and Paul did both.
- Wise organizations allow for these variances in determining policy.

Develop a Biblical theology of risk by listing facts and principles based on the following passages, and identifying guiding themes. Below is a list of examples from Jesus and the Apostles:

Examples from Jesus and the Apostles
- Luke 4:24-30
- Matthew 12:14-15; Mark 3:6-7
- Luke 13:31-33
- John 8:59
- Matthew 24:1-14
- Acts 4:1-31
- Acts 5:17-41
- Acts 8:1-8; 26-30
- Acts 9:20-30
- Acts 14:1-7; 19-28
- Acts 17:1-15
- Acts 18:9-11; 22-24
- Acts 20:22-25; 211-14

TOWARD A THEOLOGY OF SUFFERING

Preliminary Thoughts on Suffering:
- The western culture is one of commitment to comfort. Many have not received much teaching on suffering, let alone on journeying well through suffering.
- All suffer. Further, those in Christ are invited to share in his sufferings.
- Thus, it is crucial to consider carefully and develop a biblically based theology of suffering.

There are many Greek words that are translated suffering, adversity, trials, temptations, training, reproof, etc. You can begin developing a biblical theology of suffering through word studies of the following passages. The following list is not exhaustive.

Passages on How Others Suffered:
- Jesus' personal experiences of suffering: Matthew 4:1; 13:53-58; Luke 4:16-30; John 1:10-11; 12:32
- Paul's experiences and lessons of various hardships: 2 Corinthians

1:3-11; 4:7-18; 6:1-10; 7:2-16; 11:22-28; 12:7-10; Galatians 6:17; Philippians 1:7; 12; 19-20; 4:11-14; Colossians 1:24; 2 Timothy 1:8,12; 2:8-9
- Suffering can be part of a walk of faith: Hebrews 11:36-40
- Remember others who suffer. Hebrews 13:3

NT Passages to Develop a Theology of Suffering
- Jesus' teachings on suffering: Matthew 5:10-12 suffering is our heritage Luke 12:4-12; John 12:23-26; 15:20; 16:1-4, 33;
- Paul's teachings on suffering: Romans 5; 9:2; 12:9-21; Philippians 27-30; 2:17-18; 2:25-30; 3:7-11; 1 Thessalonians 1:6-7; 3:3-4, 2 Timothy 3:12
- Two central passages that are identical in teaching: James 1:2-4 and Romans 5:2-4
- Suffering is gift (grace) just as justification is: Philippians 1:29
- Reward is tied to suffering well Romans 8:17-39 ;
- Peter's teachings on persecution with applications to any suffering: 1 Peter 1:11; 2:19-23;3:14-19; 4:13; 5:1, 9-10
- Suffering can strengthen our faith: 1 Peter 1:3-7
- Suffering can teach us obedience: 1 Peter 4:1-2
- We are blessed as we endure: James 1:12; 5:11
- Teachings on suffering around the second advent of Christ: Revelation 2:10; 6:9; 12:11; 17:6; 18:24; 19:1-5; 21:4

APPENDIX B
Common Reactions to Trauma
ADULTS
Karen Carr

Below you will find some reactions and symptoms that are often experienced by individuals who have been through a trauma. These symptoms reflect your body's way of trying to cope and adjust to what has happened.

Behavioral

Avoidance behaviors
Use of alcohol to numb
Use of drugs (prescription or not) to numb
Abandonment of fun activities
Overly involved in work
Desire to leave field
Less productive
Losing or misplacing things
Easily startled/Hyperalert to environment
Tearful
Slowed down or Hyperactivity
Aimless wandering
Dejection
Hysteria
Sudden lifestyle changes
Sleep disorders

Risky/Self-Destructive Behaviors

Increased smoking
Excessive spending
Accident prone
Sexual immorality

Affective (Emotional)

Numb/Emotionally shut down
Shocked
Anxious/Fearful
Fear of recurrence
Agitated
Irritability
Frustration
Panicked or fearful (specific or general)
Overwhelmed
Anger (at self, others, God)
Resentment/Rage
Mood swings
Troubling dreams
Sad
Depression
Grief
Helpless or inadequate feelings
Sense of guilt
Loss of sense of humor
Less able to cope with new or continued emotional stress

ADULTS Continued

Somatic (Physical)
Pounding heart
Sweating
Flushed
Shortness of Breath/ Hyperventilation
Chest Pains
Nausea/Vomiting
Upset stomach, Cramps, Diarrhea
Loss of appetite or craving junk food
Muscle Tremors
Muffled hearing
Loss of Coordination
Frequent headaches or migraines
Muscle soreness
Rapid uncontrolled speech
Difficulty sitting or relaxing
Dizzy or fainting
Dryness of mouth and throat
Frequent need to urinate
Grinding of teeth
Inability to shake a cold
Weight change (gain or loss)
Insomnia, nightmares
Feeling of exhaustion and fatigue
Change in sexual functioning or desire
Missed menstrual cycle

Interpersonal
Irritability
Easily Frustrated
Insensitivity

Interpersonal continued
Loss of interest in others
Isolating/Distancing (Avoiding fellowship)
Insecurity
Avoidance of intimacy
Suspicious
Clingy
Discord/Arguments
Critical of others
Scapegoating (a focal point for suppressed anger and depression)
Hypersensitivity (feelings easily hurt)
Family problems
Compulsive talking

Cognitive (Thoughts)
Disbelief
Horror
Confusion
Poor concentration
Spaciness
Poor decision making abilities
Trouble prioritizing
Disorientation
Poor memory
Poor attention (not retaining information)
Preoccupied with trauma memories
Preoccupation with health
Time distortion (slows down or speeds up)

ADULTS Continued

Cognitive (Thoughts) continued

Increased rigidity and closed thinking (Inflexibility)
Feeling omnipotent (unrealistic appraisal of situation)
Cynicism or negativism
Absolute thinking (I will never; this always)
Negative/critical judgments against self (I am such a failure)
Hindsight thinking (If only; why didn't)
Flashbacks or other intrusive imagery

Meaning/Ministry

Increasingly busy with task orientation
Loss of sense of purpose/role
Less meaning in ministry
Disappointment with God
Loss of motivation
Questioning former beliefs

CONCLUSIONS:

Each person is unique in how they respond to a trauma, so your response may not be the same as another person who has gone through the same or a similar experience. Remember that it takes time to heal. After you work through these reactions, you will come to a new place in your life that is characterized by deeper understanding, healthy conclusions, resilience, deeper trust, and an expanded world view. You will be one who has suffered and yet thrived. Even after many of the memories are gone and you are feeling much better, there may still be things which "trigger" these symptoms and painful memories. If these symptoms become very intense and persist over a long period of time, or if you are noticing impairment in your ministry or relationships, you may want to consider talking with a counselor who specializes in trauma. This does not mean that you are crazy, only that you need some help. For more information, see www.mmct.org or contact MMCT at carrmmct@gmail.com.

For a printable format of this worksheet, please visit:
http://www.mmct.org/#/resources/debriefings-english

APPENDIX B
Common Reactions to Trauma
CHILDREN
Karen Carr

Behavioral (and Interpersonal)

Pre-school
Bedwetting
Thumb sucking
Repetitive play; reenacting trauma
Anxious attachment, clinging
Aggression/disobedience

Elementary School
Clinging
Resumption of outgrown habits
Competition with siblings
Repetitive talking; reenacting trauma
Disobedience
Drop in school performance

Junior/Senior High
Can't meet responsibilities
Resumes earlier coping styles
Withdraws socially;
  interpersonal problems
Self-deprecation
Exhibits antisocial behavior
Abuses alcohol/drugs
Decline in school performance
Sudden changes in attitudes, styles,
  relationships, personality
Acts "too old, too soon" (dropping
  out, pregnancy, marriage)
Apathy

Affective (Emotional)

Pre-school
Generalized fears
Nervousness, anxieties, and worries
Separation anxiety
Fearful of reminders
Panicked/hysterical
Irritability
Blunted or numb

Elementary School
Fear of recurrence, related stimuli
Wanting to be fed, dressed
School phobia
Avoidance of large groups
Aggression
Overconcern for family safety
Anger, hostility, belligerence
Apathy, withdrawal
Guilt
Sadness/Depression
Blunted or numb

Junior/Senior High
Anger, hostility, belligerence
Guilt
Chronic sadness/depression
Anxiety

CHILDREN Continued

Somatic (Physical)

Pre-School
Loss of appetite
Pale appearance
Overeating
Bowel/bladder problems
Sleep disturbances
Nightmares

Elementary School
Complaints about vision
Complaints about
stomach problems
Headaches
Pale appearance
Itching
Sleep disturbances

Junior/Senior High
Headaches
Vague complaints, pain
Skin rashes
Loss of appetite/overeating

Cognitive (Thoughts)

Pre-School
Shorter attention span
Confusion regarding:
- event
- locations
- sequencing
- death

Elementary School
Confusion regarding:
- event
- sequencing

Inability to concentrate

Junior/Senior High
Problems concentrating
Overconcern re: health
Intellectualization
Rationalization

Taken from Johnson, Kendall.1993. *School crisis management.* Alameda, CA: Hunter House

For a printable format of this worksheet, please visit:
http://www.mmct.org/#/resources/debriefings-english

APPENDIX B
Common Reactions to Trauma
ADOLESCENTS
Karen Carr

Behavioral (and Interpersonal)

Difficulty taking on responsibilities
Going back to old habits
Withdraw socially
Down on yourself
Abuse alcohol/drugs
Decline in school performance
Sudden changes in attitudes, styles, relationships, personality
Act "too old, too soon" (dropping out, pregnancy, marriage)
Apathy – don't care as much about things
Aggressive
Changes in friends, peer groups
Difficulty following rules

Affective (Emotional)

Anger, hostility
Guilt
Chronic sadness/depression
Anxiety
Numbness
Shame
Despair
Panic
Blame
Sense of betrayal
Feel abandoned/alone

Somatic (Physical)

Headaches
Vague complaints, pain
Skin rashes
Loss of appetite/overeating
Sleeping problems
Illness

Cognitive (Thoughts)

Problems concentrating
Concerns about health
Intellectualization/Rationalization – staying in your head and not wanting to talk or think about painful things
Confusion
Fleeting thoughts of suicide*
Disoriented

Spiritual

Questioning long held beliefs
Questioning your faith
Anger at God

*If you have these thoughts please share with a trusted adult

For a printable format of this worksheet, please visit:
http://www.mmct.org/#/resources/debriefings-english

APPENDIX B
Cross-Cultural Worker Stress Inventory
Karen Carr

On the following pages, rate your frequency of feeling stressed by each of these aspects of cross-cultural life using a scale of 1-5. A higher number indicates that you are feeling very stressed in this part of your life. A lower number indicates that this is not an area of stress for you right now or you have found ways of coping that are decreasing your feelings of stress.

For a printable format of this worksheet, please visit:
http://www.mmct.org/#/resources/member-care

1 – Hardly Ever 2 – Seldom 3 – Sometimes 4 – Often 5 – Frequently

Ministry
___ Expectations from others
___ Expectations from myself
___ Ability to set priorities
___ Sense of making a difference
___ Ability to meet my goals
___ Financial support

Total Ministry score: ___

Spiritual
___ Relationship with God
___ Prayer time
___ Time in the Word
___ Accountability
___ Fellowship
___ Spiritual growth

Total Spiritual score: ___

Relational
___ Marriage/Housemate relationships
___ Relationships with family
___ Relationships with friends
___ Relationships with leadership
___ Relationships with co-workers
___ Relationships with host culture

Total Relational Score: ___

Emotional
___ Disappointment and frustrations
___ Hurts and betrayal
___ Angry feelings
___ Fears and anxieties
___ Feeling lack of joy and happiness
___ Loss of sense of humor

Total Emotional Score ___

Environmental
___ Climate
___ Traffic
___ Infrastructure (power/water/email)
___ Dangers/Instability
___ Oppression: socio-political/spiritual
___ Corruption

Total Environmental Score ___

Trauma
___ Human induced violent trauma
___ Threat of harm
___ Accidents
___ Deaths
___ Natural Disasters
___ Loss

Total Trauma Score ___

Cross-Cultural
___Cultural values differences
___Language
___Feeling lonely
___Cross cultural expectations
___Feel judgmental/critical of culture
___Gender differences

Total Cross-Cultural Score ___

Developmental/Transition
___Children: education, adjustment
___Aging process (self or parents)
___Change in role
___Change in location
___Change of support system
___Retirement

Total Developmental/ Transition Score ___

Health
___Physical well-being
___Emotional well-being
___Mental well-being
___Sexual well-being
___Sleep
___Time for rest

Total Health Score ___

SUMMARY OF SCORES AND NEXT STEPS:

1. Write the categories and their total scores in order of the highest score (indicating the most stressful area) to the lowest score (indicating the least stressful area).

  Category   *Total Score for Category*
1.
2.
3.
4.
5.
6.
7.
8.
9.

2. Look back over the inventory and notice those items where you have given a score of 1 or 2– these are areas of low stress and are worth noting!

3. Write all the individual items that you gave scores of 4 or 5 (indicating that these are areas of high stress and you have not been coping well with them).

4. Identify ways that you can use your strengths and coping resources to begin to address your areas of greatest concern. List current supports that can help you with these stressors.

5. Write 3-4 specific action steps you can take in the next couple of weeks.

Note: This inventory is only meant to be used as a tool to stimulate reflection and discussion about sources of cross cultural stress and means of coping. It has not been subjected to validation studies and the scores should not be used as a basis for clinical decision making. For information about an inventory which has been developed after extensive research see www.cernysmith.com.

APPENDIX C
BOOKS, ONLINE RESOURCES, COUNSELING CENTERS, CONFERENCES AND TRAINING
Charlie Schaefer

OVERVIEW
A. Books
Spiritual and Emotional Resources
1. Balance: Spiritual and Emotional
2. Forgiveness and Guilt
3. Grace and Shame
4. Grief and Loss
5. Lament
6. Spiritual Struggle in Adversity

Healing Prayer

Tools for Crisis Care
1. Crisis Management
2. Member Care
3. PTSD Treatment
4. Sleep Hygiene

B. Online Resources, Libraries, and Publishers

C. Counseling Centers

D. Conferences and Training

A. Books
Spiritual and Emotional Resources
1. Balance: Spiritual and Emotional

Buchanan, Mark. 2006. *The Rest of God: Restoring Your Soul by Restoring Sabbath.* Nashville, TN: Thomas Nelson. Sabbath is not just a day focused on God but also an attitude of stillness and listening where God's rest can be found.

Williams, Gaylyn R., and Ken Williams. 2010. *All Stressed Up and Everywhere to Go.* Colorado Springs, CO: Relationship Resources. This workbook contains practical, biblical tools and illustrative stories for attaining spiritual, emotional, physical, and interpersonal balance.

2. Forgiveness and Guilt

Luskin, Fred. 2002. *Forgive for Good: A Proven Prescription for Health and Happiness.* New York, NY: HarperCollins Publishers. Luskin presents the healing power and medical benefits of forgiveness along with a nine-step forgiveness method.

Shores, Steve. 1993. *False Guilt: Breaking the Tyranny of an Overactive Conscience.* Colorado Springs, CO: NavPress Publishing. Shores offers an understanding of the tyranny of performance-based, self-inflicted criticism and a pathway to experiencing the freedom God has provided through his forgiveness.

Smedes, Lewis. 1984. *Forgive and Forget.* New York, NY: Pocket Books. Smedes writes about the practice of forgiveness in a very accessible, down-to-earth style discussing not only forgiveness of others who have hurt us but also forgiveness of ourselves, God, and others who have already died.

3. Grace and Shame

Smedes, Lewis. 1993. *Shame and Grace.* New York, NY: HarperCollins Publishers. Smedes presents a step-by-step spiritual plan for healing from the heaviness of shame.

4. Grief and Loss

Greeson, Charlotte, Mary Hollingsworth, and Michael Washburn. 1990. *The Grief Adjustment Guide.* Sisters, OR: Questar Publishers. This book provides helpful, practical suggestions for dealing with grief.

Lewis, C.S. 1961. *A Grief Observed.* New York, NY: HarperCollins Publishers. C.S. Lewis reflects honestly on the fundamental issues of life, death, and faith in the midst of loss based on his own experience following his wife's tragic death.

Mason, Mike. 1994. *The Gospel According to Job: An Honest Look at pain and Doubt from the Life of One Who Lost Everything.* Wheaton, IL: Crossway Books. A devotional commentary on the book of Job that addresses issues of human doubt, suffering, and faith.

Means, James. 2006. *Tearful Celebration: Finding God in the Midst of Loss.* Sisters, OR: Multnomah Publishers. The author shares his desperation after cancer took his wife, describing his struggle to understand God's ways in the face of tragic loss.

Sittser, Gerald. 1995. *A Grace Disguised.* Grand Rapids, MI: Zondervan Publishing. Sittser shares the raw story of his tragic loss of three family members in an automobile accident, his journey through deep grief, and how others related to him during that grief.

Wangerin, Walt. 1992. *Mourning into Dancing.* Grand Rapids, MI: Zondervan Publishing. The author describes a Christian experience of death, grief, and mourning through a focus on the small deaths occurring in daily life.

Westberg, Granger E. 2004. *Good Grief: Turning the Showers of Disappointment and Pain into Sunshine.* Minneapolis, MN: Augsburg Fortress. Westberg describes the process of loss and grieving in light of Christian faith and human nature.

5. Lament

Brueggemann, Walter. 1984. *The Message of the Psalms – A Theological Commentary.* Little Falls, MN: Augsburg Publishing. Brueggemann describes lament and praise as expressed in the Psalms.

"Grief Journaling with the Psalms of Lament" at http://www.journey-through-grief.com/grief-journaling-with-laments.html. This on-line resource provides a guide for journaling about grief following the structure of the Psalms of Lament.

Wolterstorff, Nicholas. 1987. *Lament for a Son.* Grand Rapids, MI: William B. Eerdmans Publishing. The author writes about grief for his son's tragic death in a manner that will help others lament the loss of their children or loved ones.

6. Spiritual Struggle in Adversity

Green, Thomas H. 1991. *Drinking from a Dry Well: Prayers Beyond the Beginning.* Notre Dame, IN: Ave Maria Press. Green is a Catholic priest who spent most of his years in the Philippines. He guides the reader through a personal "dark night of the soul," helping to understand what God might be up to and how to respond.

Jervis, L. Ann. 2007. *At the Heart of the Gospel: Suffering in the Earliest Christian*

Message. Grand Rapids, MI: Eerdmans Publishing. This is one of the best theological books on suffering. Jervis takes an in-depth look at the development of Paul's understanding of suffering in his own journey through writings in 1 Thessalonians, Philippians, and Romans, in the order the letters were written.

May, Gerald. 2004. *The Dark Night of the Soul: A Psychiatrist Explores the Connection between Darkness and Spiritual Formation*. New York, NY: HarperCollins Publishers Inc. May helps us grasp St. John of the Cross' and Teresa of Avila's writings on the dark night of the soul. As a psychiatrist, May also talks about the connection between the spiritual dark night and clinical depression.

Mother Teresa. 2007. *Come Be My Light: The Private Writings of the "Saint of Calcutta."* New York, NY: Doubleday. Mother Teresa lived about 40 years of her life in what she called an absence of knowing God's presence in her life, a "dark night of the soul." Through it all she cared for those who were deeply suffering. This book contains very deep waters, but is full of lessons on God's work in darkness and struggles.

Sproul, R. C. 2009. *Surprised by Suffering: The Role of Pain and Death in the Christian Life*. Lake Mary, FL: Reformation Trust. Sproul explores the problems posed by suffering in the Christian life. He provides biblical answers on suffering's place in the realm of God's providence and good purposes.

Yancey, Philip. 1988. *Disappointment with God*. Grand Rapids, MI: Zondervan Publishing. Yancey addresses the deepening of faith in the midst of struggles with the seeming silence, invisibility, and unfairness of God.

Yancey, Philip. 2010. *What Good is God? In Search of a Faith that Matters*. New York, NY: FaithWords Hachette Book Group. Yancey explores the relevance and value of faith in God when severely tested by trauma and tragedies.

Healing Prayer

Boyd, Gregory. 2004. *Seeing is Believing*. Grand Rapids, MI: Baker Books. Boyd writes about the role of Spirit-inspired imagination in prayer to better know the transformative reality of meeting Jesus face-to-face.

Lawrence, Roy. 2003. *How to Pray When Life Hurts: Experiencing the Power of Healing Prayer*. England: Scripture Union. Lawrence offers practical guidance for ways to pray with people in the midst of pain and crisis.

Miller, Calvin. 2000. *Into the Depths of God: Where Eyes See the Invisible, Ears Hear the Inaudible, and Minds Conceive the Inconceivable.* Minneapolis, MN: Bethany House. Miller encourages Christian awareness of the depth of God through unhurried, quality time away from pressures, to prayerfully listen to God.

Sanford, Agnes. 1983. *The Healing Light.* New York, NY: Ballantine Books. Sanford is considered the founder of the inner healing prayer movement and was both a missionary kid and a missionary herself. In this book she outlined what she learned about the healing power of God's presence and love.

Seamands, David A. 1973. *Healing of Memories.* Wheaton, IL: Victor Books. Seamands writes about power of the Holy Spirit to heal traumatic memories that can be present in Christian counseling with prayer.

Wardle, Terry. 2001. *Healing Care, Healing Prayer.* Orange, CA: New Leaf Books. Wardle develops and explains the inner healing prayer methodology called Formational Prayer.

Tools for Crisis Care
1. Crisis Management

Slaikeu, Karl. 1990. *Crisis Intervention: A Handbook for Practice and Research.* Boston, MA: Allyn and Bacon. Slaikeu presents a crisis intervention model and illustrates its application by clergy, nurses, counselors and other professionals.

Slaikeu, Karl and Steve Lawhead. 1984. *Up from the Ashes.* Grand Rapids, MI: Zondervan Publishing. Slaikeu and Lawhead provide a guide to personal crisis management.

2. Member Care

Hay, Rob, et al. 2007. *Worth Keeping: Global Perspectives on Best Practice in Missionary Retention,* eds. Hay, Rob, Valerie Lim, Detlef Blocher, Jaap Ketelaar, and Sarah Hay. Pasadena, CA: William Carey Library. A well-researched study by the WEA Mission Commission that provides practical principles for the support and empowerment of global mission workers: team and staff selection and development, spiritual life, work-life balance, team building, leadership, conflict resolution, and communication.

Powell, John R., and Joyce M. Bowers. 2002. *Enhancing Missionary Vitality.* Palmer Lake, CO: Mission Training International. A compendium of articles that include research, insights, models, and case studies regarding missionary life with topics such as team selection and building, preventative services, crisis intervention and debriefing, and facilitating forgiveness and reconciliation.

3. PTSD Treatment

Dolan, Yvonne. 1998. *One Small Step: Moving Beyond Trauma and Therapy to a Life of Joy*. Watsonville, CA: Papier-Mache Press. The author presents exercises to aid movement beyond surviving trauma to embracing life again.

Najavits, Lisa M. 2002. *Seeking Safety: A Treatment Manual for PTSD and Substance Abuse*. New York, NY: Guilford Press. This book is written for a mental health clinician; however, it is filled with practical tools and handouts helpful for caregivers and those in crisis, such as a description of various types of grounding skills for times when emotions are overwhelming.

Williams, Mary Beth, and Sili Poijula. 2002. *The PTSD Workbook: Simple, Effective Techniques for Overcoming Traumatic Stress Symptoms*. Oakland, CA: New Harbinger Publications. A self-help workbook that describes emotional and physiological effects of trauma and methods for dealing with those effects.

4. Sleep Hygiene

Edinger, Jack D. 2008. *Overcoming Insomnia: A Cognitive-Behavioral Approach Workbook (Treatments that Work)*. New York, NY: Oxford University Press. Cognitive-Behavioral techniques have been proven helpful for treating insomnia. This workbook presents both an understanding of sleep-related problems and skills and tools to improve sleeping quality.

Stewardship of Self for Cross-Cultural Workers: Sleep – article by Ronald Koteskey and Marty Seitz at www.crossculturalworkers.com/ss_sleep.htm

4a. Online Resources for Sleep Hygiene

www.webmd.com/sleep-disorders/guide/sleep-hygiene

www.cdc.gov/sleep/hygiene.htm

www.umm.edu/sleep/sleep_hyg.htm#b

B. Online Resources, Libraries, and Publishers

Barnabas International - a list of resources for a variety of member care situations www.barnabas.org/resources.php

CaringBridge – personalized websites for those who are in medical need that are useful in providing news updates to others who will support them www.caringbridge.org

Crisis Consulting International - provides security and crisis management support and services for Christian missionaries www.cricon.org

FEMA for Kids – Federal Emergency Management Agency: provides resources, recommends books, games, activities for helping children through emergencies www.ready.gov/kids

Headington Institute – provides care for caregivers and global aid workers worldwide through a variety of online resources, training workshops, education materials, counseling and consulting services www.headington-institute.org

Mental Health Resources for Cross Cultural Workers – articles for cross-cultural workers by Ron and Bonnie Koteskey www.crossculturalworkers.com/about.htm

Mobile Member Care Teams Resources - includes a periodic digest of mental health resource materials (MMCT Communiqué) and articles on crisis and trauma response and resilience www.mmct.org/#/resources

People In Aid – focuses on improving the effectiveness of global aid organizations through providing workshops, coaching, publications, examples of good practices, and other resources www.peopleinaid.org

World Federation for Mental Health – international resources on mental health topics www.wfmh.org/01Links.htm

C. Counseling Centers for Missionaries and Others in Ministry

Alongside – specialty retreats for ministry personnel, counseling services, church consultations, missions candidate assessments, and workshops (Michigan, U.S.A.) www.alongsidecares.net

Barnabas Zentrum – counseling, consulting, retreats, training and encouragement to missionaries and Christian workers in Europe, Africa, Asia, and the Middle East (Colorado, US, and Austria) www.barnabaszentrum.com

Cornerstone Counseling Foundation – professional counseling, consultation, and training from a Christian perspective for Christian workers throughout Asia as well as the people of Thailand (Chiang Mai, Thailand) www.cornerstonecounseling.in.th

Global Map of Counseling Centers Worldwide – a map of Member Care providers and services located around the world maintained by the Global Member Care Network http://www.globalmembercare.com/index.php?id=41

International Health Management – prevention and treatment (medical and psychological) in the care of expatriates, leadership of nonprofit charitable agencies, and NGOs through travel health services, pre-departure health management, overseas health management, and reentry health management (Ontario, Canada) www.ihm.ca

Le Rucher Ministries – brief counseling, debriefing and crisis debriefing, and training courses by pastoral care workers from a Christian perspective (France) www.lerucher.org

Link Care Center – Christian mental health professionals and pastoral counselors caring for missionaries, pastors, Christian workers and their families; on-campus housing is available (California, U.S.A.) www.linkcare.org

Mobile Member Care Teams - offers counseling services but is not a counseling center, (Africa) www.mmct.org

The Well – Christian member-care center providing counseling, debriefing, pastoral care, leadership and organizational consultation, conflict resolution, and team building for Christian workers and organizations serving in Asia (Chiang Mai, Thailand) www.thewellcm.com

Tumaini Counseling Centre – preventative and restorative mental health services and pastoral care to enhance missionary resilience and fruitfulness (Nairobi, Kenya) tumainicounselling.net

D. Conferences and Training

Global Member Care Conference   http://www.globalmembercare.org/

Le Rucher Ministries – debriefings and training courses http://www.lerucher.org/index.html

Mental Health and Missions Conference   http://www.mti.org/mhm.htm

Mobile Member Care Teams   http://www.mmct.org/#/workshops

Pastors to Missionaries Conference (PTM), Barnabas International http://www.barnabas.org/ptm.php

BIBLIOGRAPHY

PREFACE

Schaefer, Frauke C., Dan G. Blazer, Karen F. Carr, Kathryn M. Connor, Bruce Burchett, Charles A. Schaefer, and Jonathan R.T. Davidson. 2007. "Traumatic Events and Posttraumatic Stress in Cross-Cultural Mission Assignments." *Journal of Traumatic Stress* 20: 529–539.

_____, Dan G. Blazer, and Harold G. Koenig. 2008. "Religious and Spiritual Factors and the Consequences of Trauma: A Review and Model of the Interrelationship." *International Journal of Psychiatry in Medicine* 38: 507–524.

CHAPTER I - REFLECTIONS ON A THEOLOGY OF SUFFERING
Scott E. Shaum

Sittser, Gerald. 1995. *A Grace Disguised*. Grand Rapids, MI: Zondervan Publishing.

Hodges, Zane C. 1994. *The Epistle of James: Proven Character Through Testing*. Irving, TX: Grace Evangelical Society.

Russell, Pat. 2011. "The Beauty of the Cracked Vessel." *Conversations Journal* 9.2: 29.

CHAPTER III - RESOURCES FOR EFFECTIVE SUPPORT SECTIONS 1-3
Normal Reactions After Trauma and Effective Community Support and Personal Resilience
Karen Carr

American Psychiatric Association. 2000. Diagnostic and statistical manual of mental disorders (4th ed., text rev.). Washington, DC: Author.

Berry, Wendell. 1996. A World Lost. Washington, DC: Counterpoint.

_____. 2009. Whitefoot: A Story from the Center of the World. Berkeley, CA: Counterpoint.

Brown, Ron. 2007. "Case Study" in Worth Keeping: Global Perspectives on Best Practice in Missionary Retention, ed. Hay, Rob, Valerie Lim, Detlef Blöcher, Jaap Ketelaar, and Sarah Hay. Pasadena, CA: William Carey Library.

Bunyan, John. 1968. The Pilgrim's Progress. New York: Dodd, Mead, & Company.

Collier, Winn. 2007. Let God: The Transforming Wisdom of Fenelon. Brewster, Massachusetts: Paraclete Press.

Dolan, Yvonne. 1998. One Small Step: Moving Beyond Trauma and Therapy to a Life of Joy. Watsonville, CA: Papier-Mache Press.

Dyregrov, A. 1997. "The process in psychological debriefings." Journal of Traumatic Stress 10: 589-605.

Fawcett, J. 2002. "Preventing broken hearts, healing broken minds" in Danieli, Y. (Ed.). Sharing the front line and the back hills. Amityville, New York: Baywood Publishing Company, Inc.

Forbes, A. and D. Roger. 1999. "Stress, social support and fear of disclosure." British Journal of Health Psychology 4: 165-179.

Greeson, Charlotte, Mary Hollingsworth, and Michael Washburn. 1990. The Grief Adjustment Guide. Sisters, OR: Questar Publishers, Inc.

Hart, Archibald. 2001. Unmasking Male Depression. Nashville, TN: Word Publishing.

Kessler, Ronald C., Amanda Sonnega, Evelyn Bromet, Michael Hughes, and Christopher B. Nelson. 1995. "Posttraumatic stress disorder in the National Comorbidity Survey." Archives of General Psychiatry 52, no. 12 : 1048.

Keane, T.M., W. O. Scott, G. A. Cavoya, D. M. Lamparski, and J. A. Fairbank. 1985. "Social support in Vietnam veterans with Posttraumatic Stress Disorder: A comparative analysis." Journal of Consulting and Clinical Psychology 53: 95-102.

Lake, Frank. 1966. "The Dynamic Cycle." Clinical Theology: A Clinical and Psychiatric Basis to Clinical Pastoral Care, Vol 1. Great Britain: Darton, Longman and Todd.

Mason, Mike. 1994. The Gospel According to Job. Illinois: Crossway Books.

Means, James. 2006. Tearful Celebration: Finding God in the Midst of Loss, Oregon: Multnomah Publishers, Inc.

Mitchell, J. 1983. "When disaster strikes: The critical incident debriefing process." Journal of the Emergency Medical Services 8: 36-39.

National Child Traumatic Stress Network and National Center for PTSD. 2006. Psychological First Aid: Field Operations Guide, 2nd Edition.

Nouwen, Henri. 1990. The Road to Daybreak. New York: Doubleday.

Schaefer, Frauke C., Dan G. Blazer, Karen F. Carr, Kathryn M. Connor, Bruce Burchett, Charles A. Schaefer, and Jonathan RT Davidson. 2007. "Traumatic events and posttraumatic stress in cross-cultural mission assignments." Journal of Traumatic Stress 20, no. 4: 529-539.

Schiraldi, Glenn R. 2000. The post-traumatic stress disorder sourcebook. Los Angeles, CA: Lowell House.

Slaikeu, Karl. 1990. Crisis Intervention: A Handbook for Practice and Research. Boston, MA: Allyn and Bacon.

_____, and Steve Lawhead. 1984. Up from the Ashes. Grand Rapids, MI: Zondervan Publishing House.

Snelgrove, Toby. 1999. Critical incident stress: Sources, symptoms, and solutions. New Westminster, B.C.: Justice Institute of British Columbia.

Vanier, Jean. 1989. Community and Growth. Paramus, NJ: Paulist Press.

Wangerin, Walter. 1992. Mourning into Dancing. Grand Rapids, MI: Zondervan Publishing House.

SECTIONS 4 -5
Healthy Stress Management and Managing Severe Traumatic Stress
Frauke Schaefer

Bannano, George A. 2004. "Loss, Trauma, and Human Resilience: Have We Underestimated the Human Capacity to Thrive After Extremely Aversive Events?" *American Psychologist* 59: 20–28.

Coppen, Alec and John Bailey. 2000. "Enhancement of the Antidepressant Action of Fluoxetine by Folic Acid: A Randomized, Placebo Controlled Trial." *Journal of Affective Disorders* 60: 121-130.

_____, C. Bolander-Gouaille. 2005. "Treatment of Depression: Time to consider Folic Acid and Vitamin B12." *Journal of Psychopharmacology* 19: 59-65.

Davidson, J. R., V. M. Payne, K. M. Connor, E. B. Foa, et al. 2005. "Trauma, Resilience, and Saliostasis: Effects of Treatment in Post-traumatic Stress Disorder." *International*

Clinical Psychopharmacology 20: 43-48.

Frewen, Paul A., and Ruth A. Lanius. 2006. "Neurobiology of Dissociation: Unity and Disunity in Mind–Body–Brain." *Psychiatric Clinics of North America* 29: 113–128.

Jacobson, E. 1938. *Progressive Muscle Relaxation*. Oxford, England: University Chicago Press.

Leproult, Rachel, Georges Copinschi, Orfeu Buxton, and Eve Van Cauter. 1997. "Sleep Loss Results in an Elevation of Cortisol Levels the Next Evening." *Journal of Sleep Research and Sleep Medicine* 20: 865-870.

Mills, David E., and Ron P. Ward. 1986. "Attenuation of Stress-induced Hypertension by Exercise Independent of Training Effects: An Animal Model." *Journal of Behavioral Medicine* 9: 599-605.

Krakow, B., M. Hollifield, L. Johnston, M. Koss, R. Schrader, et al. 2001. "Imagery Rehearsal Therapy for Chronic Nightmares in Sexual Assault Survivors With Posttraumatic Stress Disorder—A Randomized Controlled Trial." *JAMA* 286:537–45.

Nilsson, Ulrica. 2009. "The Effect of Music Intervention in Stress Response to Cardiac Surgery in a Randomized Clinical Trial." *Heart & Lung: The Journal of Acute and Critical Care* 38: 201–207.

———, M. Unosson, and N. Rawal. 2005. "Stress Reduction and Analgesia in Patients Exposed to Calming Music Postoperatively: A Randomized Controlled Trial." *European Journal of Anaesthesiology* 22: 96–102.

Ozer, E. J., Best, S. R., Lipsey,T. L., and D. S. Weiss. 2003. "Predictors of Posttraumatic Stress Disorder and Symptoms in Adults: A Metaanalysis" *Psychological Bulletin* 129: 52–73. Bottom of Form

Patel, Vikram. 2003. *Where There Is No Psychiatrist: A Mental Health Care Manual*. Glasgow, UK: Bell & Baine.

Richardson, G. E. 2002. "The Metatheory of Resilience and Resiliency." *Journal of Clinical Psychology* 58: 307-321.

Rimm, D. C. and J. C. Masters. 1979. *Behavior Therapy: Techniques and Empirical Findings*. New York: Academic Press.

Salmon, Peter. 2001. "Effects of Physical Exercise on Anxiety, Depression, and Sensitivity to Stress: A Unifying Theory." *Clinical Psychology Review* 21: 33-61.

Sanchez-Villegas, A., M. Delgado-Rodriguez, A. Alonso, J. Schlatter, et. al. 2009. "Association of the Mediterranean Dietary Pattern With the Incidence of Depression." *Archives of General Psychiatry* 66: 1090-1098.

Schaefer, Frauke C., Dan G. Blazer, Karen F. Carr, B. Burchett, Charles A. Schaefer, and Jonathan R. T. Davidson. 2007. "Traumatic Events and Posttraumatic Stress in Cross-Cultural Mission Assignments" *Journal of Traumatic Stress* 20: 529–539.

Shapiro, Francine. 2012. *Getting Past your Past: Take Control of Your Life with Self-help Techniques from EMDR Therapy.* New York: Rodale.

Sittser, Jerry. 2004. *A Grace Disguised: How the Soul Grows Through Loss.* Grand Rapids, MI: Zondervan.

Solomon, Z., R. Shklar, and M. Mikulincer. 2005. "Frontline Treatment of Combat Stress Reaction: A 20-Year Longitudinal Evaluation Study." *American Journal of Psychiatry* 162: 2309-2314.

Starzec, J., D. F. Berger, and R. Hesse. 1983. "Effects of Stress and Exercise on Plasma Corticosterone, Plasma Cholesterol, and Aortic Cholesterol Levels in Rats." *Psychosomatic Medicine* 45: 219-226.

Van der Kolk, Bessel A. "The Body Keeps the Score: Approaches to the Psychobiology of Posttraumatic Stress Disorder." In *Traumatic Stress: The Effects of Overwhelming Experience on Mind, Body, and Society*, ed. Bessel van der Kolk, Alexander C. McFarlane, and Lars Weisaeth. 2007. 303–327. New York: Guildford Press.

_____, O. Van der Hart, and C. R. Marmar. "Dissociation and Information Processing in Posttraumatic Stress Disorder." In *Traumatic Stress: The Effects of Overwhelming Experience on Mind, Body, and Society*, ed. Bessel van der Kolk, Alexander C. McFarlane, and Lars Weisaeth. 2007. 303–327. New York: Guildford Press.

Werner, David, Carol Thuman, and Jane Maxwell. 1992. *Where There Is No Doctor: A Village Health Care Handbook,* revised edition. Berkeley, CA: Hesperidan Foundation.

SECTION 6
Spiritual Resources in Dealing With Trauma
Charlie and Frauke Schaefer

Brueggemann, Walter. 1984. *The Message of the Psalms – A Theological Commentary.* Minneapolis, MN: Augsburg Publishing House.

_____. 1992. "The Rhetoric of Hurt and Hope: Ethics, Odd and Critical." In *Old Testament Theology* by Walter Brueggemann, 45–66. Minneapolis, MN: Fortress Press.

Calhoun, Lawrence G., and Richard G. Tedeschi. 1999. *A Clinician's Guide Facilitating Posttraumatic Growth*. Mahwah, NJ: Lawrence Erlbaum Associates.

_____. 2006. *Handbook of Posttraumatic Growth – Research and Practice*. Mahwah, NJ: Lawrence Erlbaum Associates.

De Saint Exupéry, Antoine. 2000. *The Little Prince*. Mariner Books.

Donahue, Michael J. 1986. "Intrinsic and Extrinsic religiousness: Review and meta-analysis." *Journal of Personality and Social Psychology* 48:400-419.

Fontana, Alan, and Robert Rosenheck. 2004. "Trauma, Change of Religious Faith, and Mental Health Service Use among Veterans Treated for PTSD." *The Journal of Nervous and Mental Disease* 192: 579-584.

Fuller Youth Institute. 2008. "Leadership Team Training Resource–Trauma and Lament." Posted August 21, 2008. Accessed July 6, 2012. http://www.fulleryouthinstitute.org/pdfs/Trauma-Lament_Leader_Resource.pdf

Hackney, Charles H., and Glenn S. Sanders. 2003. "Religiosity and Mental Health: A Meta-analysis of Recent Studies." *Journal for the Scientific Study of Religion* 42(1):43-65.

Hillenbrand, Laura. 2010. *Unbroken: A World War II Story of Survival, Resilience, and Redemption*. New York: Random House.

Journey-Through-Grief.com. "Grief Journaling with the Psalms of Lament". Last accessed July 7, 2012. http://www.journey-through-grief.com/grief-journaling-with-laments.html

Kelsey, David H. 2005. *Imagining Redemption*. Louisville, KY: Westminster John Knox Press.

Luskin, Fred. 2002. *Forgive for Good: A Proven Prescription for Health and Happiness*. New York: HarperCollins Publishers.

Meador, Keith G., Harold G. Koenig; Dana C. Hughes, Dan G. Blazer, et al. 1992. "Religious Affiliation and Major Depression." *Hospital & Community Psychiatry* 43: 1204–1208.

Orth, Ulrich; and Elias Wieland. 2006. "Anger, Hostility, and Posttraumatic Stress Disorder in Trauma-exposed Adults: A Meta-analysis." *Journal of Consulting and Clinical*

Psychology 74(4): 698–706.

Osbeck, Kenneth W. 1990. *Amazing Grace*. Grand Rapids, MI: Kregel Publications.

Pargament, Kenneth I., Bruce W. Smith, Harold G. Koenig, and Lisa Perez. 1998. "Patterns of Positive and Negative Religious Coping with Major Life Stressors." *Journal for the Scientific Study of Religion* 37: 710–724.

_____, and P. J. Sweeney. 2011. "Building Spiritual Fitness in the Army: An Innovative Approach to a Vital Aspect of Human Development." *American Psychologist* 66(1):58–64.

Park, Crystal L. 2005. "Religion as a Meaning-Making Framework in Coping with Life Stress." *Journal of Social Issues* 61:707–729.

Schaefer, Frauke C., Dan G. Blazer, and Harold G. Koenig. 2008. "Religious and Spiritual Factors and the Consequences of Trauma: A Review and Model of the Interrelationship." *The International Journal of Psychiatry in Medicine* 38(4): 507–524.

Sittser, Jerry. 2004. *A Grace Disguised: How the Soul Grows Through Loss*. Expanded Edition. Grand Rapids, MI: Zondervan Publishing House.

Smedes, Lewis. 1984. *Forgive and Forget*. New York: Pocket Books.

Smith, Timothy B., Michael E. McCullough, and Justin Poll. 2003. "Religiousness and Depression: Evidence for a Main Effect and the Moderating Influence of Stressful Life Events." *Psychological Bulletin* 129(4): 614–636.

Wolterstorff, Nicholas. 1987. *Lament for a Son*. Grand Rapids, MI: William B. Eerdmans Publishing Company.

Yancey, Philip. 2010. *What Good is God? In Search of a Faith that Matters*. New York: FaithWords Hachette Book Group.

SECTION 7
Prayer That Heals
Ann Hamel

Boyd, Gregory. 2004. *Seeing Is Believing*. Grand Rapids, MI: Baker Books.

Keating, Thomas. 1999. *The Human Condition: Contemplation and Transformation*. New York: Paulist Press.

Jung, C.G. 1973. *Letters*. Vol. 1. Translated by R. F. C. Hull. Princeton, NJ: Princeton University Press.

Levine, Peter A., and Ann Fredrick. 1997. *Waking the Tiger: Healing Trauma: The Innate Capacity to Transform Overwhelming Experiences*. Berkeley, CA: North Atlantic Books.

Miller, Calvin, 2000. *Into the Depths of God: Where Eyes See the Invisible, Ears Hear the Inaudible, and Minds Conceive the Inconceivable*. Minneapolis, MN: Bethany House.

Poloma, Margaret M., and George H. Gallup, Jr. 1991. *Varieties of Prayer: A Survey Report*. Philadelphia, PA: Trinity Press International.

Sanford, Agnes. 1983. *The Healing Light*. New York: Ballantine Books.

Seamands, David A. 1973. *Healing of Memories*. Wheaton, IL: Victor Books.

_____. 1981. *Healing for Damaged Emotions*. Wheaton, IL: Victor Books.

Servan-Schreiber, David M.D., Ph.D. 2004. *The Instinct to Heal, Curing Depression, Anxiety, and Stress Without Drugs and Without Talk Therapy*. Paris: Editions Robert Laffont, S.A.

Tozer, A.W. 1992. *The Pursuit of God: The Human Thirst for the Divine*. Camp Hill, PA: Christian Publications, Inc.

Wardle, Terry. 1994. *Wounded: How to Find Wholeness and Inner Healing in Christ*. Ashland, OH: Cornerstone Formation Ministries, Inc.

_____. 2001. *Healing Care, Healing Prayer*. Orange, CA: New Leaf Books

White, Ellen G. 2001. *The Desire of Ages*. Coldwater, MI: Remnant Publications.

ABOUT THE AUTHORS

Karen F. Carr, Ph.D., a member of Barnabas International, is a missionary and clinical psychologist working as Clinical Director of Mobile Member Care Team (MMCT). She received her Ph.D. in Clinical Psychology from Virginia Commonwealth University in 1989 and completed a Postdoctorate in Forensic Psychology at the University of Virginia in 1990. For eight years she worked at a community mental health center in Virginia, first as a Clinical Supervisor and then as Program Manager of Emergency Services. She has lived in West Africa since 2000, first in Côte d'Ivoire and now in Ghana. Karen serves the MMCT-West Africa team by providing crisis training, assessments, counseling, clinical supervision, and consultations. She serves the MMCT-International team by providing clinical supervision and recruitment of clinical staff.
Further information about MMCT: www.mmct.org

L. Ann Hamel, Ph.D., D.Min. is a clinical psychologist at the University Medical Center in Berrien Springs, Michigan. Before coming to Berrien Springs in 1990, Ann served as a missionary in central Africa for eleven years. In 1990 Ann, her husband, and her three young sons were involved in a car accident in Rwanda in which Ann was left a widow and she and her youngest son were seriously injured. Just months after their accident and return to the United States Ann began working toward a Ph.D. in counseling psychology from Andrews University in Berrien Springs, with the goal of serving missionaries and others who have experienced life altering events. During this time she met Dr. Loren Hamel, a physician and single parent of four children. In 1995 they blended their seven children into a family of nine. Ann did her doctoral internship at Pine Rest, a Christian Psychiatric Hospital in Grand Rapids, Michigan. In 2007 she completed a Doctor of Ministry degree in Formational Counseling at Ashland Theological Seminary. Ann works extensively with missionaries, both at home and abroad. Her specialty is the integration of religion and psychology as it relates to the treatment of trauma.

Scott E. Shaum, M.A. presently serves with Barnabas International as Director of Staff Development and provides coaching, spiritual direction, and training of mission leaders globally, taking him to many nations every year. Scott's life calling is to be a shepherd, and he strives to manifest that in every context by guiding people to the Living Christ. Formerly he served as a church planter in Hong Kong. He holds a Master of Arts in Biblical Studies from Dallas Theological Seminary and is trained in spiritual direction and pastoral counseling amongst other areas. Scott is married to Beth with whom he has three adult sons.
Further information about Barnabas International: www.barnabas.org

Charles A. Schaefer, Ph.D. is a clinical psychologist in Chapel Hill, NC. His original training was in physics and electrical engineering before serving with Wycliffe Bible Translators in Togo and Benin, West Africa. His interest in supporting those involved in full-time Christian ministry led him to pursue further training. He received his Master of Arts in Theology and his Ph.D. in Clinical Psychology at Fuller Theological Seminary. He has been in private practice for over twenty years. Charlie has worked in community mental health, church, and mission settings. He and his wife, Frauke Schaefer, share a continued focus on supporting Christian churches and missions through consulting with pastors and mission organizations, traveling internationally to lead and teach at workshops and retreats, and working clinically with those in full-time ministry. In addition, Charlie serves as one of the coordinators of the annual Mental Health and Missions Conference. He has a particular interest in the Christian spiritual resources to foster resilience in times of trauma, grief, conflict, shame, and guilt.
Website: www.CharlieSchaefer.com

Frauke C. Schaefer, M.D., a German family physician, served with International Nepal Fellowship as Superintendent of Green Pastures Hospital in Pokhara, Nepal, from 1990-1997. Interest in mental health in missions prompted her training in psychotherapy at a Christian psychiatric hospital (Klink Hohe Mark) in Germany. During this time she met and married her husband Charlie Schaefer, an American Christian psychologist with similar interests, and moved to North Carolina, U.S.A. in 2000. Her residency in psychiatry at Duke University allowed her to conduct research about trauma and resilience in missionaries. During a research fellowship in Religion and Health (Duke Center for Spirituality, Theology, and Health) she reviewed how spiritual factors affect consequences of trauma. She remains consulting faculty at Duke while working in private practice in Chapel Hill, NC since 2006, serving many people in ministry, both in the local church and in cross-cultural missions. She provides consultation, assessments, training, and clinical support.

Website: www.FraukeSchaeferMD.com

www.ingramcontent.com/pod-product-compliance
Lightning Source LLC
Chambersburg PA
CBHW071904290426
44110CB00013B/1277